STUDIES IN BAPTIST HISTORY AND THOUGHT

Journeying to Justice

Contributions to the Baptist Tradition across the Black Atlantic

STUDIES IN BAPTIST HISTORY AND THOUGHT

Journeying to Justice

Contributions to the Baptist Tradition across the Black Atlantic

Edited by
Anthony G. Reddie

with
Wale Hudson-Roberts and Gale Richards

Copyright © Paternoster 2017

First published 2017 by Paternoster

Paternoster is an imprint of Authentic Media Limited
PO Box 6326, Bletchley, Milton Keynes MK1 9GG

authenticmedia.co.uk

The right of Anthony G. Reddie to be identified as the Editor of this Work has been asserted by him in accordance with the Copyright, Designs and Patents Act 1988.

All rights reserved. No part of this publication may be reproduced, stored in a retrieval system, or transmitted, in any form or by any means, electronic, mechanical, photocopying, recording or otherwise, without the prior permission of the publisher or a license permitting restricted copying. In the UK such licenses are issued by the Copyright Licensing Agency, Barnard's Inn, 86 Fetter Lane, London EC4A 1EN

British Library Cataloguing in Publication Data
A catalogue record for this book is available from the British Library

ISBN 978-1-84227-983-0
978-1-84227-401-4 (e-book)

Printed and bound by Lightning Source

STUDIES IN BAPTIST HISTORY AND THOUGHT

Series Preface

Baptists form one of the largest Christian communities in the world, and while they hold the historic faith in common with other mainstream Christian traditions, they nevertheless have important insights which they can offer to the worldwide church. *Studies in Baptist History and Thought* will be one means towards that end. It is an international series of academic studies which includes original monographs, revised dissertations, collections of essays and conference papers, and aims to cover any aspect of Baptist history and thought. While not all authors are themselves Baptists, they nevertheless share an interest in relating Baptist history and thought to other branches of the Christian church and to the wider life of the world.

The series includes studies in various aspects of Baptist history from the seventeenth century down to the present day, including biographical works, and Baptist thought is understood as covering the subject-matter of theology (including interdisciplinary studies embracing biblical studies, philosophy, sociology, practical theology, liturgy and women's studies). The diverse streams of Baptist life throughout the world are all within the scope of these volumes.

The series editors and consultants believe that the academic disciplines of history and theology are of vital importance to the spiritual vitality of the churches of the Baptist faith and order. The series sets out to discuss, examine and explore the many dimensions of their tradition and so to contribute to their on-going intellectual vigour.

Series Editors

Curtis W. Freeman, Research Professor of Theology and Director of the Baptist House of Studies, Duke University, North Carolina, USA

Stephen R. Holmes, Senior Lecturer in Theology, University of St Andrews, Scotland, UK

Elizabeth Newman, Professor of Theology and Ethics, Baptist Theological Seminary, Richmond, Virginia, USA

Philip E. Thompson, Assistant Professor of Systematic Theology and Christian Heritage, North American Baptist Seminary, Sioux Falls, South Dakota, USA

Series Consultant Editors

David Bebbington, Professor of History, University of Stirling, Scotland, UK

Paul S. Fiddes, Professor of Systematic Theology, Oxford University; former Principal of Regent's Park College, Oxford; Professor of Systematic Theology, University of Oxford, UK

Stanley E. Porter, President and Professor of New Testament, McMaster Divinity College, Hamilton, Ontario, Canada

Contents

Foreword		*Revd Neville Callam*	ix
Contributors			xii
Introduction		*Anthony G. Reddie*	1

Part One - Pre-Apology

1.	Noel Leo Erskine	*Baptists and Emancipation in Jamaica*	11
2.	Paul Walker	*Black British History: A Critical Reappraisal*	26
3.	Dave Ellis	*Reflections on the Atlanta trip and its legacy*	38
4.	Johnathan Hemmings	*25th Anniversary Ordination*	45

Part Two – The Apology

5.	Karl E. Henlin	*In Search of Freedom*	49
6.	David Shosanya	*Legacies of the Transatlantic Slave Trade*	56
7.	Wale Hudson-Roberts	*The Apology: A Journey towards Justice*	70
8.	Steve Latham	*A White Guy Talks 'Race'*	83

Part Three – Post-Apology

9.	Graham Sparkes	*The Journey: The Research Process*	94
10.	Gale Richards	*Reflections on the Implementation of the Journey*	102
11.	Sivakumar Rajagopalan	*Standpoint Theory as a Tool to Understand Baptist Resistance to Owning the Apology and as a Tool to Own and En-flesh the Apology*	110
12.	Michele Mahon	*Sisters with Voices: A study of the experiences and challenges faced by Black women in*	124

13.	R. David Muir	*London Baptist Association Church Ministry Settings Abolition, Diasporan Memory and the Curious Invisibility of Sam Sharpe from the Baptist Centenary Historiography*	139
14.	Doreen Morrison	*Reparations: A call to fulfil the promise of education made by Baptists to the enslaved and their descendants through the 1835 Negro Education Grant*	149

Part Four – The Future

15.	Dwight N. Hopkins	*Martin Luther King, Jr.*	167
16.	Richard L. Kidd	*An Ongoing Apology*	177
17.	Malcolm Patten	*Developing Multi-Ethnically minded leaders*	182
18.	Rhea Russell Cartwright	*The Passion of the New Generations: Where Next in the Struggle for Justice*	191
19.	Tim Judson	*Mrs Ferguson*	200
20.	Lynn Green	*Leadership Perspectives within Baptists Together*	203
21.	Karl B. Johnson and Merlyn Hyde-Riley	*Reflections on the Bicentenary of the Relationship between BUGB, BMS and the JBU and on the reaction to the delivery of 'the Apology' to the JBU from a Jamaican Perspective*	212

Appendices   223

Foreword

History, it has been said, is both the 'teacher of life' and the 'life of our memories'. People need to engage in thoughtful reflection on their past and that of their forbears. One reason for this is that our own evaluation of our history will allow us to assess the conclusions drawn by others who do not share our experience. It will also contribute to an increase in our understanding of the impulses that impact interpretations of the same history that are contrary to our own. The narration we develop of our history will enable our heirs to erect the edifice of a greater future for themselves and the neighbours who share our tradition.

Memories are the stuff from which people carve out their identity. A people without a properly informed collective memory are a people destined to fall prey to caricatures of their history and perverted interpretations of their identity.

One person who understood the importance of memory in the formation of a people's identity is Aimé Césaire who, together with others, immortalized his deep insights in the concept of Negritude. Born on the Caribbean island of Martinique, Césaire longed for the day when formerly enslaved Africans in the Diaspora would escape their estrangement from their African roots and vigorously continue the struggle to overcome their dehumanization. One way to achieve this liberation, Césaire urged, was through the acknowledgement of a memory featuring 'lagoons ... covered by the skulls of the dead', 'wrapped in blood', and having 'its belt of corpses'. Cruel images of the past will not prevent a people from rising up to create an authentic and compelling peoplehood that is strong enough to meet the demands of contemporary life with its contemptuous assumptions about otherness.

Yet, of what value are our memories if they are not shared with the wider community? By committing our memories to writing, we potentially contribute to the emancipation of those who are not yet able to see controversial issues from the perspective of others.

Written accounts of our memories afford others the benefit of our own construction of what we or our forbears saw, felt and experienced. From what we write, discerning readers will be able to discover our particular understanding of what happened to us and our forbears. They will not only have the interpretations that are preserved by others but also those we ourselves espouse. Meanwhile, we will be able to subject the thoughts we have expressed to fresh analysis and evaluation from time to time.

If we do not tell our stories, others may do so for us even though they may not first consult us concerning our account or understanding of what really happened. The narrative others create cannot help but be filtered through the lenses of their own experience and their own understanding. In some instances, self-serving motives, sometimes subconsciously applied, lead to distortions that may mislead an unsuspecting reader. When we tell the story of our own and our forbears' unforgettable experiences, we open for others a new window on our existence and experience as a people.

This book aims to fill a gap that has existed for far too long. It appears after the long night of disappointment preceding the dawn of the day when many British Baptists were ready to accept some responsibility for slavery and the slave trade. They were also able to acknowledge the fact that they are beneficiaries of that horrific African holocaust.

On the 4th July 2007, Baptists from around the world journeyed to Accra, Ghana, for their Annual Gathering. A highlight of the week's programme was a *Service of Memory and Reconciliation* that took place near the 'Door of No Return' at the Slave Castle in Cape Coast, Ghana. The service included this prayer:

> Despite the pain whose memory still causes the soul to ache,
> we have learnt from you, gracious God, to forgive one another
> and to receive each other as sisters and brothers.
> You made us, O God, and you have constituted us to be a community
> of persons pledged in loyal service to you and in love toward each other.
> Reconcile our memories; cleanse our minds,
> and teach us to walk in your way.

Having been a principal collaborator with Denton Lotz, then General Secretary of the Baptist World Alliance, in the preparation of the liturgy for the service, I was among those who were deeply disappointed that the Baptist Union of Great Britain did not find it possible to join with other Baptists who were eager to confess the complicity of their forbears in the sin of slavery and the slave trade and to ask for forgiveness. The concluding affirmation in that service confidently asserted the hope that what happened at Cape Coast would inspire Baptists to share in a process of reflection that would contribute to the breaking down of barriers between human communities. It included the words:

> 'The God of tomorrow will perform great wonders for us:
> Thanks be to God!'

Words that adequately express the relief I felt when finally the British Baptists managed to find the courage to do the right thing are hard to find. The 'Apology' by British Baptists has unleashed a font of goodwill out of which genuine sharing can now take place about the Black experience in the United Kingdom and across the Atlantic.

This book makes a rich contribution to the reconciliation of memories that communities need if they are to live harmoniously. Not content merely to look back on the distant past, the essays in this book reveal that progress is being made on all sides in dealing with a wound that was left to fester for far too

Foreword

long. Not surprisingly, honest engagement with, and exchange over, the contemporary experience of being a minority ethnic community in a majority White community has become possible.

We owe a debt of gratitude to the team that has produced this book. Their contribution to a welcome consciousness-raising enterprise is invaluable. The worldwide Baptist family will be among the many people who benefit from careful reflection on the insights provided in this illuminating book.

Neville Callam
General Secretary
Baptist World Alliance

Contributors

Dave Ellis is a Regional Minister with the 'Heart of England Baptist Association'. He was born in Wolverhampton. His parents are Jamaicans who came to England and are his heroes. He is proud of his Jamaican heritage and is equally proud to be a Wulfrunian. He has been married to Vivienne for over 30 years and they have three beautiful children. Prior to becoming a Regional Minister he had been a Pastor for 24 years in two amazing churches with amazing congregations, Totterdown in Bristol and Small Heath Baptist Church in a Muslim majority part of East Birmingham. In the pastorate he has seen many miracles great and small. Whilst in Bristol, he was the chairperson of Keyboard Racial Justice Project in Bristol for six years. He has also been the chairperson, secretary and treasurer of a number of local Birmingham community forums and director of a variety of different charities.

Noel Leo Erskine is Professor of Theology & Ethics at Candler School of Theology and the Laney Graduate School of Arts and Sciences at Emory University. He has authored and edited eleven books. Among them are *Decolonizing Theology: A Caribbean Perspective (1981, 1998), King Among the Theologians (1994), From Garvey to Marley: Rastafari Theology (2005), Black Theology and Pedagogy (2008), and Plantation Church: How African American Religion was born in Caribbean Slavery (2014)*. His research interests include Caribbean and Black theologies, the history and development of Plantation and Black churches, and theological method in the work of James Cone, Karl Barth, Paul Tillich and Dietrich Bonhoeffer.

Lynn Green is currently the General Secretary of BUGB having served previously in local and regional ministry roles. Prior to church based ministry she was Corporate Identity Manager for Royal Mail. She believes that Baptists have a significant contribution to make to the wider church and society and is passionate about inspiring our Union to have a deeper longing for God, a deeper longing for mission and a deeper longing for forging authentic relationships. As part of her network of callings Lynn is also a wife and mother; she has been married to Stuart for 30 years and they have four children aged from 7 to 19 years old!

Johnathan Hemmings is minister in charge of the Ocho Rios circuit of Baptist churches in Jamaica which is comprised of four congregations. He served as President of the Jamaica Baptist Union (JBU) and is currently one of its Vice presidents. He currently chairs the superintendent's council of the JBU. He is presently doing some work on Peace Making and hopes to publish something on this in the not too distant future.

Contributors

Karl E. Henlin is an ordained minister of the Jamaica Baptist Union (JBU) and serves as pastor of the Gregory Park Baptist Church. He has served as President of the JBU and also as the Acting General Secretary. He earned the Master of Philosophy (MPhil) and the Bachelor of Arts from the University of the West Indies and currently serves as an Adjunct Lecturer in New Testament Studies at the United Theological College of the West Indies. He has made contributions to the following publications: *Baptist Preaching – a Global Anthology* published by Baptist World Alliance, *Baptist Preaching in Jamaica: Celebrating Christ for Today 1964-2014*, published by the Jamaica Baptist Union and *Environment Stewardship Series* published by Caribbean Christian Publications. He has a passion for congregational worship and has read widely on the subject. He sometimes dabbles in a game of lawn tennis and can often be found at Sabina Park watching the 'exploits' of West Indian cricketers. He is married to Lisa and together they have two young adult sons, David and Philip.

Dwight N. Hopkins is Professor of Theology at Chicago University Divinity School. He holds a BA from Harvard University, an MDiv, MPhil and PhD degrees from Union Theological Seminary, New York City. He also holds a PhD from the University of Cape Town, South Africa. He has authored *Shoes that Fit Our Feet: Sources for a Constructive Black Theology* and *Being Human: race, culture, and religion*, amongst his many publications.

Wale Hudson-Roberts is the Justice Enabler for the Baptist Union. He was a pastor of Stroud Green Baptist Church, is married to Christine and has a son – Joshua. Both are foster carers and have many god children.

Merlyn Hyde-Riley has been a minister of the Jamaica Baptist Union since 1999. She served in pastoral ministry for several years and is currently an Associate General Secretary. She holds diplomas in Ecumenical Studies (University of Geneva & the Ecumenical Institute of Bossey) and in Ministerial Studies (United Theological College of the West Indies) and degrees in Theology and History (University of the West Indies, Mona). She is currently engaged in postgraduate work in Gender and Development at the University of the West Indies, Mona. Merlyn is married and has two sons.

Karl B. Johnson is an ordained minister of the Jamaica Baptist Union. He has served the denomination as pastor and now as General Secretary. A committed ecumenist, Karl is married to Yvette and together they have three children, Nicholas, Joel and Nathan.

Tim Judson finished studying at Bristol Baptist College in 2016 and is a pioneer minister based in Bristol. He is discipled mostly by his wife, Becca, who teaches in a local primary school. Tim is currently reading for a PhD, exploring the prophetic role of lament through song and is particularly interested in finding ways to empower voices from the margins to offer their critique of the Christian faith and society as a whole. He has recorded a number of albums and enjoys gigging in a range of places, advocating justice and an honest perspective on life, relationships and the Kingdom of God.

Richard Kidd retired in 2012 after nearly 40 years as a Baptist Minister and 25 years as a Theological Educator, latterly Principal and then Co-Principal of the Baptist College in Manchester. Richard has always been interested in apologetic engagement, along the many boundaries where Christian believing meets the modern world. He has taught and written widely around themes of 'theology and ...' - theology and disability, theology and justice, theology and education, theology and science, theology and the arts, etc. Today he is largely occupied as painter and poet, selling his work to raise money for 'Freeset' in Kolkata, India, an inspiring Christian venture now offering the choice of quality employment to hundreds of women previously caught in the snare of India's brutally unjust sex-trade. A recent anthology of Richard's paintings, poems and writings is entitled *Painting for Freedom,* and is available on his website with that name.

Steve Latham is Pastor of Kings Cross Baptist Church in central London, and an Associate Tutor at Spurgeon's College. He is committed to urban mission, and has been involved in several racial justice initiatives. He has edited the book *Urban Church: A Practitioner's Handbook*, with Michael Eastman. He blogs at urban-shepherd.co.uk. He is married to Sue, and has two adult children.

Michele Mahon has an MA in Pastoral Ministry and a BA in Youth Work and Ministry. Her research interests focus on the experience and role of women, especially Black women, in Christian ministry. She serves as Youth Pastor at Brockley Baptist church, is also a part of the editorial team for the Baptists Together magazine, and is a member of Spurgeon's College Council and the Baptist Union Council. She is also a Chaplain at Lewisham College and a Trustee for South Central Youth, a charity based in Brixton, South London, enabling young people of that locality to exit gangs and fulfil their potential.

Doreen Morrison is an ordained minister, independent researcher and the managing director of Liberty Trails, a Baptist history tour company in Jamaica. A member of Churches in Communities International, she has a Ph.D. from the University of Birmingham, England, and a Master of Divinity from Northern Baptist Theological Seminary, Illinois. She is a member of the Baptist World Alliance 'Heritage and Identity Commission' (2015 - 2020), and a CPE supervisor-in-training. Recent publications include: her book, *Slavery's Heroes: George Liele and the Ethiopian Baptists in Jamaica 1783 - 1865,* and an article in the American Baptist Quarterly, 'Silent Witnesses: Jamaica's People and Chapels, Testimony to the Ethiopian Baptist Society, "Spiritual Home" of Sam Sharpe' (Vol. 34, Number 1).

Contributors

R. David Muir is a lecturer in Ministerial Theology at Roehampton University. He has an MA in Political Education and Public Policy from London University and a Ph.D in Theology (Political Theology of James Cone & Pentecostalism in Britain and America) from King's College, London. David lectured in historical and theological studies at the Simon of Cyrene Institute and political theology and Pentecostalism at the Centre for Black & White Christian Partnership in Birmingham. More recently he taught history and politics at London University, African American culture and history at the University of East London, and Caribbean and Black British political history at London Metropolitan University. He was also Public Policy Executive Director, responsible for Public Theology and Public Affairs, for the Evangelical Alliance.

Malcolm Patten MA, D.Min. is Senior Minister at Blackhorse Road Baptist Church in East London and is an Online Tutor at Spurgeon's College. He has a passion for developing healthy multicultural churches and has been involved in training students and developing resources for churches in this area of ministry. His article 'Multicultural Dimensions of the Bible' appeared in the Evangelical Quarterly journal and he is author of the book *Leading a Multicultural Church*.

Sivakumar Rajagopalan has been the London Baptist Association Regional Minister for Racial Justice since 2003. He is also now responsible for Inter-Faith issues and is an advocate of contextually appropriate cross-cultural mission to South Asians. He is also committed to justice for Dalits within the Indian church and wider society. He is married to Georgina, from Northern Ireland, and lives in North London. He is the author of 'What is the Defining Divide? False Post-Racial Dogmas and the Biblical Affirmation of "Race"'. *Black Theology: An International Journal*, Vol.13, No.2, 2015, pp.166-188

Gale Richards is a Baptist minister, and coordinator of the Baptist Union of Great Britain (BUGB) Black and Minority Ethnic Women Ministers' Network. She formerly held the role of Moderator of the BUGB Racial Justice Group, and is author of: *'Text and Story – Prophets for their time and ours' Bible studies* (2014).

Anthony G. Reddie is an Extraordinary Professor of Theological Ethics at the University of South Africa. He has a BA in History and a Ph.D. in Education (with Theology), both degrees conferred by the University of Birmingham. He has written over 70 essays and articles on Christian Education and Black Theology. He is the author and editor of 17 books. His more recent titles include *Is God Colour Blind?: Insights from Black Theology for Christian Ministry* (SPCK, 2009), *Black Theology, Slavery, and Contemporary Christianity* (Edited - Ashgate, 2010), *The SCM Core Text: Black Theology,*

(SCM, 2012) and *Contesting Post-Racialism* (2015) (co-edited with R. Drew Smith, William Ackah and Rothney S. Tshaka. He is editor of *Black Theology: An International Journal*, the only academic periodical of its kind in the world.

Rhea Russell Cartwright is a Theology graduate of the University of Birmingham with a strong interest in race and the development sector, race in the criminal justice system and the rising wave of inequality across borders, class and regions of recent times - all a reflection of social and economic justice issues. She has presented at the Baptist Assembly of Great Britain and has presented to an audience of over 1000 people on her reflections from a trip she took to the refugee camp in Calais, France. She has also sat on a panel with Anthony Reddie on the matter of the MLK legacy, all of which have provided her with the opportunity to learn and engage firsthand in issues of great importance to her and her generation. She is presently undertaking preparations for a masters law degree in Human Rights at the University of Nottingham in September 2016. Her other interests include martial arts – she is a first degree black belt in ITF Taekwon-do. She is also a member of an amateur youth theatre company with whom she has performed in Europe in locations such as Grenoble and Bonn. It was in these contexts that her first inclination towards development grew, as the group's dramatic pieces were based on and held underlying messages of justice within them.

David Shosanya serves as a Regional Minister for The London Baptist Association. He writes a monthly column for *Keep the Faith* magazine, contributes to topical discussions on various radio stations and speaks extensively across the UK to a broad range of audiences within and outside of the church. He is particularly interested in concepts of masculinity in African and Caribbean communities, the impact and legacy of the MAAFA (Transatlantic Slave Trade) on black communities and exploring ways in which they can creatively embody and express a resistance culture dedicated to emancipatory practices personally and collectively. He is the founder of The State of Black Britain Symposium, The Black History Month National Civic Service of Celebration and Co-Founder of the nationally acclaimed Street Pastors Initiative. David also founded and facilitates The Ministers Appreciation Ball.

Graham Sparkes is a Baptist minister. Having served two pastorates in Bristol and Kings Langley, he went on to lead the work of the 'Faith and Unity Department' at Baptist House, which included ecumenical engagement and work on justice issues. In 2011 he became President of Luther King House in Manchester, an ecumenical partnership for theological education, where he teaches Christian Spirituality as well as offering leadership to the partnership. For a number of years he served as a Trustee of Christian Aid, and more recently he has become one of the Patrons of the Retreat Association. Graham has developed a particular interest in the relationship between art and faith, and has co-authored *God and the Art of Seeing: visual resources for a journey of faith.*

Paul Walker is the minister of Highgate Baptist Church, Birmingham, UK, where African American ex-slave Revd Peter T. Stanford, Birmingham's first Black pastor, was minister (1889–1895). He supervises working pastors in their research degrees through the Urban Theology Unit, Sheffield, UK, and is a recognized supervisor in the Department of Philosophy, Theology and Religion at the University of Birmingham, UK. His research into Stanford led to the re-discovery of many other Black activists who were in Britain from the late eighteenth to the early twentieth century. He is the author of 'Captain Paul Cuffe (1759–1817): Nineteenth century African American Seafarer and Entrepreneur'. *Black Theology: An International Journal*, Vol.13, No.3, 2015, pp. 219-229

Introduction

All stories have a beginning. The 'official'[1] version of this story; one that charts the ongoing relationship between British and Jamaican Baptists, begins in 1814 with John Rowe, a White English missionary travelling from Bristol to Jamaica. 2014 marked the bicentenary of the relationship between Jamaican Baptists, British Baptists and the Baptist Missionary Society. This enduring relationship has been forged through the epochs of slavery, colonialism and the Caribbean 'Windrush' to the UK.

I was born into and brought up within British Methodism. Baptistic traditions were not ones that came naturally to me when I look back with thanks on the years I spent within the Baptist Union of Great Britain, which at the time served as my spiritual home. My sojourn within the Baptist tradition led me to work for a year at Bristol Baptist College. It was while working in Bristol that I became aware of the historic relationship between British and Jamaican Baptists. I had not been long in Bristol when I was told with pride of the key role the college had played in the foundation of the Baptist work in Jamaica. John Rowe, who travelled to Jamaica in 1814, was a 'graduate' of the then Bristol Academy, a forerunner of the present day college.

Given that I am a child of Jamaican parents I was intrigued by the association between Jamaican Baptists and their British counterparts. This link was all the more significant given that my Mother had grown up in the Baptist church in East Portland – Belle Castle Baptist; a church to which she rejoined and served as a Deacon upon her return to the island in 1991 after thirty-four years in England. My Mother, who died in February 2014, in many ways represents the embodiment of this relationship. I will say a little more about this shortly. So, influenced by my Baptist reared Mother, my year in Bristol got me thinking about this relationship between Jamaica and Britain, between two Baptist traditions; one in which slavery, colonialism and racism looms large.

The intrigue in my thinking was increased the more I heard about John Rowe and later William Knibb and the crucial role the latter played in the ending of slavery in Jamaica, partially in 1834, and finally, in 1838. The fascination grew when I supervised a final year dissertation of an

---

[1] I say 'official' as there is a contested alternative narrative start to this story, one that begins with enslaved Africans establishing their own spiritual and social movement of African influenced conceptions of Christianity and church that begins in the latter part of the eighteenth century. Aspects of this alternative can be found in this text in the chapters written by Noel Erskine and Doreen Morrison. A more definitive rendering can be found in Noel L. Erskine *Plantation Church: How African American Religion Was Born in Caribbean Slavery* (New York and Oxford: Oxford University Press, 2014)

undergraduate student who focussed his research on William Knibb. The work of William Knibb, Thomas Burchell and James Phillippo, all featured prominently in the relationship between British and Jamaican Baptists. These three White Baptist missionaries from Britain all played important roles in the abolition movement in Jamaica.

If these three White Baptist missionaries represent the visible 'heads' side of the coin, then there is the flip side of the coin, the 'tails,' which represents Black subjectivity. The theology of Black subjectivity and identity that speaks to Black suffering is Black liberation theology.

Black liberation theology seeks to affirm Black self determination and the agency of Black people battling against the backdrop of chattel slavery, colonialism and the ongoing presence of racism. My own introduction to Black theology[2] came via the iconoclastic work of James H. Cone, but the specific Jamaican Baptist contribution to Black liberation theology that brought the discipline alive for me, was Noel Erskine's *Decolonizing Theology*.[3] Erskine's focus on Black theology, via the anti-slavery struggle in Jamaica through the lens of the Black activism of George Liele, Moses Baker and later Sam Sharpe captured my imagination. Erskine's work laid bare the often concealed world of Black Christian activism in Jamaica that offered a liberative, anti-racist model of Christianity. I am extraordinarily proud that Noel Erskine is one of our contributors to this book, given his pivotal role in my own conscientization, via his Caribbean orientated approach to Black liberation theology.

Erskine's groundbreaking book put centre stage the agency of enslaved Africans in their fight for emancipation. Remembering these pivotal figures in Erskine's creative, counter narrative of abolition and Black liberation in Jamaica, I began to reflect on the normative perspective I was hearing while in Bristol.

I am not arguing that the likes of Knibb, Burchell or Phillippo are not deserving of respect or our admiration, but going back to my Mother for a moment, one of her often used phrases was 'who feels it knows it!' The primary, visceral experience of suffering of enslaved Africans is what inspired them and drove the anti-slavery movement in Jamaica and also in the UK. The likes of Knibb et.al., made hugely important contributions to the thrust for

---

[2] Black theology is for me the short hand nomenclature for Black Liberation theology. Black theology was conceived of and indeed is a theology of liberation and forms an important part of the wider family that is 'Theologies of Liberation'. The latter term describes a number of contextual, socially related theologies that emerge from human experience and which seek to reflect on God in light of human suffering and marginalisation, for the purposes of personal and wider structural and systemic transformation. For further details see Marcella Althaus-Reid, Ivan Petrella and Carlos Luis Susin (eds.) *Another Possible World: Reclaiming Liberation Theology* (London: SCM press, 2007).
[3] See Noel L. Erskine *Decolonizing Theology: A Caribbean Perspective* (Maryknoll, New York: Orbis, 1983)

Introduction

freedom, but they did so out of moral choice; enslaved Africans, however, fought for freedom because it was part of their existential DNA. Namely, they had no choice but to protest and fight for their freedom.

No one epitomises this struggle more so than the great Sam Sharpe. Sharpe's pivotal contribution to freedom is detailed in this book by Noel Erskine, R. David Muir and others, and is also explored in much greater detail by Delroy Reid Salmon.[4] Sam Sharpe was able to create a prophetic Christianity by rooting his faith within the existential crisis of his social location as an enslaved human being, endowed with the gift of human subjectivity that belied his socio-political context.

This text is very much built upon the selfless, sacrificial model of Christian discipleship that is exemplified in the life and death of Sam Sharpe. Sharpe has been an inspiration to millions for the selfless way in which he lived out his faith, carrying his cross to the gallows, witnessing to the truth as Jesus himself asserted in Matthew 16:24. Sharpe is perhaps the single most persuasive embodiment for what constitutes the partnership between Jamaican and British Baptists. His life exemplifies the sort of agency and aspirant self determination that underpins the desires of Black people, whether in Jamaica or amongst the Diaspora in Britain.

The present partnership between Jamaican and British Baptists is one that is seeking to rectify the power imbalances that characterised the past, where privilege and superiority were juxtaposed with exploitation and inferiority. Sam Sharpe sought to redress that imbalance. The fight for dignity, mutuality and genuine partnership continues.

Alongside the iconic figure of Sam Sharpe are the invisible, ordinary heroes of faith whose lives exemplify this partnership every bit as much as those who are heralded in print. The Caribbean stalwarts of the 'Windrush'[5] have undertaken the same fight for dignity, agency and self determination as Sam Sharpe, albeit in much less dramatic ways and with less emphatic conclusions.

I would argue that my Mother, Lucille Jestina (Walker) Reddie, a devout Jamaican Baptist woman from Belle Castle Baptist church in East Portland and resident in the UK from 1957-1991, lived out her life in the spirit

---

[4] Delroy A. Reid-Salmon *Burning for Freedom: A Theology of the Black Atlantic Struggle for Liberation* (Kingston: Ian Randle, 2012). See also the 'Sam Sharpe Project' through which BUGB, in partnership with Regents Park College and others, seeks to look at Sharpe's legacy in terms of Black empowerment and conscientization of people of faith in our present epoch. See the following link for further details. http://www.samsharpeproject.org/

[5] This term emanates from a pivotal event on the 22nd June 1948, when 492 people from the Caribbean arrived at Tilbury docks on the *SS. Empire Windrush*. These post war pioneers ushered in a wave of Black migration to Britain from the Caribbean, which (for the most part) forms the basis for Black African and Caribbean communities in Britain. For further information see Mike Phillips and Trevor Phillips *Windrush: the irresistible rise of multi-racial Britain* (London: Harpercollins, 1999).

of Sam Sharpe. Her quiet dignity and determination to carry her cross unselfishly for others was an inspiration. Her life was one of proving to others that she was more than her lowly social location in British society. She, I believe, was representative of this newly emerging partnership between Jamaica and Britain, a redressing of the balance between privilege and alleged superiority, juxtaposed with exploitation and assumed inferiority.   It is invidious to mention specific names, but it would be remiss of us not to express our thanks for a number of individuals. So the less dramatic story of racial justice within BUGB is underpinned by the sacrificial lives of such silent heroes as Desmond Gordon, Fred George, Pat White, Rosemarie Davidson-Gotobed, Kate Coleman, Cham Kaur-Mann, Raj Patel, Rupert Lazar, Jay Chauhan, Ram Gidoomal and Philip Mohabir. We also need to acknowledge the work of a number of key networks, which include the BME Women Minister's Network, the Black and Asian Minister's Forum, the South West London Asian Fellowship, Reach In Reach Out and Progress Within. We apologise if we have overlooked other key people or networks.

This text arrives at an inauspicious moment in the life of this nation. The Brexit[6] vote to leave the European Union in June 2016 was one that was punctuated by myriad concerns related to the loss of sovereignty and fears of immigration. The rise in racist incidents since the vote to leave has brought into sharp relief the importance of this book and its contents therein. Whatever the myriad reasons that people had for voting Brexit there is no doubt in my mind that a good deal of that was to do with British (really English) notions of exceptionalism (we are not like or indeed are better than the rest) and a melancholy for the loss of Empire and the grandeur of imperialism.

Ironic that those who wanted to wrest control back from unelected officials governing them without any mandate to do so, often hark back to a time when Britain did that to 23% of the world - the bits marked in pink on the globe. In the grand scheme of things, this text will not change the world in respect to Brexit, but it is nonetheless, a modest attempt to lay bare the crushing levels of hypocrisy that lie beneath the Brexit construct. Many good people voted for Brexit. Speaking as a Black liberation theologian, however, I will never be convinced that in the final analysis Brexit was not simply fuelled by a deep-seated, residual nostalgia for the time when Britain stood alone, effortlessly condescending to the rest of the world. This neo-imperialistic world view has always been underpinned by a racist subtext that views the other as distinctly less than, particularly, people of African descent.

So this text is, in many respects, a riposte to the post-imperial fuelled restorative push of Brexit and the attempt to turn back the clock to an era when Britain was great. This work seeks to reveal the sordid underbelly of empire and the grave impact British Imperialism exerted on all people, Black and White, enslaved and slave holder, those shackled as chattel and those who

---

[6] See the following link for an outline of the issues contributing to Britain's referendum vote to leave the European Union. http://www.bbc.co.uk/news/uk-politics-32810887

Introduction

considered themselves to be free. 'Brexit' revealed one particular narrative thread for interpreting the meaning and the nature of the British nation and being British – *Journeying to Justice* provides an alternative, anti-imperialistic, anti-racist reading.

While this book has a great deal of resonance with the wider socio-political context of empire, neo-colonialism and post-imperialism, in the final analysis, however, it is primarily about a specific ecclesial relationship between two churches and two peoples. The book seeks to reflect on the historic, enduring relationship between BUGB and the JBU. One of the enduring challenges that has confronted BUGB and the JBU is that of developing models of fellowship and mutuality that echo to the necessity of justice making and truth telling. All too often the former is evoked at the expense of the latter. While not pretending that the historic relationship between BUGB, BMSWM and the JBU has not been fraught with difficulties and misunderstanding, the Apology in 2007, the subsequent 'Journey' and the wider struggle for racial justice, all speak to a commitment to effect the very kind of model of mutuality and justice making that is so often absent in historic and contemporary church practice.

The Jamaican and British Baptists have been involved in active Kingdom work for over two hundred years, beginning with the great George Liele, the first 'unofficial' missionary to Jamaica, and culminating in the 2007 Apology issued by the Baptist Union of Great Britain (BUGB). This two hundred year narrative deserves retelling in print. British and Jamaican Baptists have much to discuss.

This text marks an important watershed in the appreciation of the commitment and the contribution of Black people to the Baptist church. This contribution is reflected upon through the prism of the relationship between the Baptist Union of Great Britain (BUGB), BMS World Mission and the Jamaica Baptist Union (JBU). This text seeks to provide authoritative first-hand accounts of the landmark events and the people that have helped to shape this ongoing narrative of Black engagement in and commitment to the Baptist church across the past two centuries.

As this work is about the broader thematic thrust for racial justice, we are pleased to introduce the contributions of radical White scholars and activists who accept the challenge of addressing issues pertaining to 'White privilege' – the flipside to Black empowerment. The construction of this work is one that works through the lens of the 'Black Atlantic'. The 'Black Atlantic' is a phrase reputedly coined by the great Black British academic, Paul Gilroy[7], to speak of the historic link between Britain and the so called 'New World' of the Americas and the Caribbean that emerged from the transatlantic slave trade. The term is a conceptual one referring to the millions of Black bodies that died and were thrown overboard during the transportation of enslaved Africans from Africa to the so called 'New World', across four centuries. It

---

[7] See Paul Gilroy *The Black Atlantic: Modernity and Double Consciousness* (Harvard: Harvard University Press, 1993)

also refers to the exchange of ideas and theories pertaining to Black existence and experience from Africa to the Americas and Europe.

This text seeks to reflect on this Black Atlantic dynamic through the prism of the ongoing relationship between British and Jamaican Baptists, plus influential guests living in the US. This relationship is one that began in the tumultuous epoch of slavery and the contested nature of Christian faith and its relationship to Black bodies. Freedom in Christ is at the very heart of Christianity and it was this claim to freedom on which many enslaved Africans clung tenaciously. Yet, the slave owning, planter class saw Black bodies and freedom as an oxymoron, and for many in the missionary societies that sought to 'Christianise' enslaved Africans, freedom was seen as a spiritual entity only and not also as a physical or material one. One might have wondered as to the efficacy of enslaved people embracing the faith of their slave masters and yet the wonders of grace, found in the risen Christ, propelled many to see Christianity as their means of transformation. This transformation was to have spiritual *and* physical consequences.

This text was conceived during the 2014 bicentenary of the relationship between Jamaican and British Baptists. The roots of this text, however, lie in the 'Apology' made by BUGB for their collusion with transatlantic slavery. The 'Apology' was issued in 2007. The 'Apology' serves as the transformative catalyst that provides the backdrop to this historic text. The prophetic declaration issued by BUGB (something the British State has yet to accomplish) in 2007 provides the 'Ground Zero' against which this book is shaped.

The eclectic nature of this collection underscores not only the diversity and breadth within this historic narrative, it speaks also to the broader questions of Black involvement in faith-based approaches to social justice and empowerment, particularly of those on the margins of church and society.

I am mindful that all texts of this kind are imperfect entities, replete with wishful thinking and unrealised, best intentions. I am particularly aware that this text suffers from a comparative dearth of Black women's voices. At the outset we had proposed to have parity between male and female voices. Sadly, the pressures of life that invariably impinge on Black women to a greater extent than they do on Black men meant that a number of Black women we had asked to write were unable to do so. Our book is the weaker for their absence and we miss their presence.

This book charts the development of the relationship between Jamaica and Britain, between the metropolitan centre and colonial margins. It is a relationship that was forged in the 17th to the early part of the 21st century. This period marks the 'Pre-Apology' period and encapsulates the first part of the book. The essays in Part 1 are largely historical in nature and illustrate the socio-political, economic and religious climate that foreshadows the 'Apology'. Four essays comprise the first part of the book. The first essay is by Noel Erskine, which charts the often 'untold' story of the foundation of the Baptist church in Jamaica. Paul Walker's essay provides a potted history of the Black presence in Britain, detailing how Black people have contributed to the development of this nation across several centuries. Dave Ellis' essay details his experiences travelling to a landmark Baptist World Alliance sponsored conference addressing racism in Atlanta, Georgia, in 1999. His personal account explores the commitment to challenging racism in the years prior to the 'Apology'. The final piece in this section is a sermon by Johnathan Hemmings, a JBU minister. The sermon was preached during the bicentenary year of 2014 to mark the 25th anniversary of his own ordination to the ordained Baptist ministry. His words give expression to the historic partnership between Jamaican and British Baptists.

Part 2 of the book is the 'Apology' and the essays in this part of this text examine the events leading up to and encapsulating the landmark 'Apology' arising from the historic Baptist Council meeting in 2007. The first piece in this section is another sermon from a senior member of the ordained ranks of the JBU. Karl Henlin's sermon is an appropriate starter for this section as his address at the Joint Baptist Assembly[8], in the bicentenary year of 2007, helped kick-start the process leading to the 'Apology'. David Shosanya's essay analyses his key contribution to the debate at the Baptist Council that discussed the efficacy of BUGB offering an apology for her collusive role in transatlantic slavery. Wale Hudson-Roberts' essay outlines the relationship between the 'Apology' and the post-Apology period that moves into the 'Journey' and the desire to create multicultural churches committed to racial justice. The final essay in this section of the book is by Steve Latham. Latham's essay undertakes a brave and rarely seen work in the UK, namely, an unapologetic repudiation of White privilege and an embrace of the Black Christ as a means of effecting racial justice within BUGB and beyond.

BUGB is to be commended for not resting on its laurels having issued the 'Apology' in 2007. In the years following the 'Apology', BUGB has embarked on the process entitled the 'Journey', in which the Union has committed itself to becoming a truly multicultural and inclusive church. Part 3 of the book marks the 'Post-Apology' period and includes essays that explore the ongoing challenge of living out the values of the 'Journey'. The first essay in this section of the book is by Graham Sparkes, who details the research process that gave rise to the 'Journey', in the post-Apology years within BUGB. This essay is followed by Gale Richards' piece, which reflects on the implementation process that gave rise to the 'Journey'. Taken together, these two pieces show that the 'Journey' was no accidental or unreflective process. Sivakumar Rajagopalan's essay in turn builds on Sparkes' and Richards' work as he critiques the 'Apology' and the 'Journey' through the prism of 'Standpoint theory'.

This work and the next three pieces draw us beyond the immediate purview of the 'Journey,' in order to look at our contemporary life as Christians in Britain, particularly, within BUGB. The next piece is by Michele

---

[8] The Joint Assembly is the annual Baptist Assembly between BUBG and BMS World Mission.

Mahon, whose essay is drawn from a larger piece of research,[9] looking at the role of Black women in ministry within the London Baptist Association. The next essay is by R. David Muir who explores the legacy of Sam Sharpe and how his example (and absence in older Baptist historiography) has influenced and impacted on contemporary relationships between Britain and the Caribbean. The final piece in this section is by Doreen Morrison who offers a powerfully insightful and incisive call for reparations, but in a manner that has been rarely explored in the contemporary literature on the subject.

The final section of the book is comprised of essays that reflect on the future. How do we learn from the past in order that our common life in the future better exemplifies the values of the Kingdom of God? How can Baptists live together across the divide of the Black Atlantic? The first essay in this section comes from, arguably, the most distinguished contributor in the book, Dwight Hopkins. Hopkins' essay reflects on the ministry of Martin Luther King Jr., and assesses his legacy and example for faith-based justice making initiatives in the future. Richard Kidd's essay is a personal reflection outlining how his own growing consciousness towards justice issues provides a microcosm for the wider developments one hopes will emerge within the church and in the wider society. The issues raised in Kidd's essay are mirrored in many respects by Malcolm Patten's piece, which analyses the telling factors and characteristics that contribute to healthy, multicultural churches within BUGB and beyond.

Tim Judson's piece is a more creative, reflective piece representing his skills as a talented songwriter. His contribution is a heartfelt plea for mutuality and solidarity between people. Rhea Russell Cartwright is the youngest contributor to this text and she writes on how someone from the younger generation conceives of justice issues in the immediate future. Given the challenges and opportunities for the future, we are pleased that Lynn Green, the General Secretary of BUGB has outlined her vision for the future and the ways in which leadership perspectives can shape and contribute to that visioning. The final piece in the book comes from the leadership of the JBU, and is written by Karl Johnson, the General Secretary and Merlyn Hyde-Riley, the Associate General Secretary. Their work offers a timely challenge from the former mission field on the need to establish constructive partnership within the orbit of justice making and equity. It is a fine conclusion to this book.

Finally, I would like to conclude this introduction by thanking a number of individuals for their significant contributions that have enabled this book to come to fruition. In the first instance I would like to thank one of my

---

[9] See Michele Mahon 'Sisters With Voices: A study of the experiences and challenges faced by Black women in London Baptist Association Church ministry settings.' *Black Theology: An International Journal* Vol.13, Issue 3, 2015, pp.273-296

Introduction

co-editors, Wale Hudson-Roberts, the Racial Justice Coordinator for BUGB. It was during the early months of 2014 that Wale approached me and inquired as to the possibility of creating a book to mark the tenth anniversary of the 'Apology' and to build on the then oncoming bicentenary. Wale's determination that there should be a book of this kind was pivotal in the process of its development.

Wale Hudson-Roberts would not want me to thank him publicly by name without also recognising the contributions of the Racial Justice Group. The group, comprised of Pat White, Anna Ratcliff, Sivakumar Rajagopalan, Joe Kapolyo and Gale Richards, provided the necessary affirmation and support that helped in the early gestation of this project.

My thanks also, quite naturally, to both Wale Hudson-Roberts and Gale Richards, who have assisted me in putting this book together. Your insights, experience and insider knowledge of the Baptist tradition enabled me to make sense of the task in assembling this book. Many thanks!

My penultimate thanks are clearly directed to the many contributors to this book. All edited collections, such as this one, are only as good as the people who both agree to write and then deliver their pieces for the wider benefit of others. I offer my heartfelt thanks to all of you who have helped to make this book what it has become. I trust that you are pleased with our contributions in this work and the whole collection of which you are a part. Thank you!

I am also grateful to the millions of nameless and faceless Black bodies who fought for freedom and refused to accept the anomaly of being considered only partially or not fully human. Not for them such hypocrisy of partial freedom. Thanks also to the likes of Sam Sharpe, George Liele and many others whose names we do know, who set the example for others to follow. These individuals were able to link their Christian faith to their social condition in order to create the nascent seeds for the development of Black liberation theology that came to life towards the end of the 20th century.

My final thanks, quite naturally, are directed to God, whose mighty presence in the midst of all of the aforementioned has been the glue that has held everything together. It goes without saying that without God, nothing that is, could be, and so for simply being God, I thank God for everything. It was the love of God in Christ that helped our ancestors to make sense of their seemingly insoluble crucible of misery during the epoch of slavery. This book is a salutation to the goodness of God and the boundless grace of the risen Christ and the empowering presence of the Holy Spirit that sustained oppressed and constricted Black bodies across several centuries.

We hope that *Journeying to Justice* is a fitting tribute to the challenges of the past, the critical insights of the present and our anticipated hopes for the future. Ultimately, I hope that this book will one day inspire those who have yet to take their first breath. May your lives be characterised by a reality that is marked with a greater infusion of justice for all peoples, whether within BUGB, the wider UK, amongst our friends and family in Jamaica and across the Caribbean, indeed across the world.

Journeying to Justice is a tribute to the spirit of total liberation for us[10] that continues to inspire all who yearn for the full life promised by Jesus in John 10:10. This book is for you!
Peace,
Anthony G. Reddie
Lead Editor

---

[10] Dwight N. Hopkins *Head and Heart: Black Theology - Past, Present and Future* (New York: Palgrave Macmillan, 2002), pp.77-90

Part 1: Pre-Apology

Baptists and Emancipation in Jamaica
Noel Leo Erskine

In this essay, I propose to look at the role of churches in Jamaica in relation to slavery and emancipation, with particular emphasis on the contribution of Baptists in that ongoing narrative. An underlying theme is to examine the role of two Black Baptist church leaders in Jamaica, George Liele, and Samuel Sharpe, highlighting their different approaches to emancipation. I would like to investigate, in the language of Bob Marley, whether George Liele's ministry may be characterized as 'fighting for survival,' while the ministry of Samuel Sharpe should be understood as 'fighting for emancipation.'

Winston Lawson in his pathfinding book, *Religion and Race: African and European Roots in Conflict: A Jamaican Testament*[1] calls attention to the emergence of Historic, mainline churches in Jamaica, and the flowering of the Native Baptists. According to Lawson, three Historic mainline denominations, Anglican, Methodist and Baptist, highlight the role of colour and class in colonial Jamaica, and provide a context for the struggle of enslaved Jamaicans toward emancipation. In a society in which culture and religion were knitted together, the Anglican Church represented upper class Whites, while the Methodist Church comprised primarily of Free Blacks and Brown persons who were not welcomed in Anglican churches and were required to sit in the back of those churches. Baptists, however, worked primarily among Free Blacks and those who were enslaved. In Jamaican ecclesiology, as in Jamaican society, there were two cultures – European and African – two cosmologies and two theologies that influenced the social ethics and morality of the populace.

Mapping the Journey
In this particular context, there was a correlation between the ethos of plantation society and the Anglican Church. The Anglican Church was the planter's church and their primary motive was that of economic gain. Enslaved persons discovered early that there was a correspondence between higher sugar prices and the brutalization of their bodies. The sad truth in Jamaica during the slavery era is that there were pastors in several of these churches who owned enslaved persons. This, in part, explains why missionaries, and many church leaders were not for the overthrow, and abolition of slavery as an institution. Several Historic mainline churches, in step with the British

---

[1] See Winston Lawson *Religion and Race: African and European Roots in Conflict: A Jamaican Testament* (Frankfurt: Peter Laing, 1996)

parliament, advocated a gradual approach to the freeing of Black persons from the deathly grip of slavery.

There were pastors and missionaries in these churches who had a sense of dis-ease with slavery. However, this did not mean the changing and challenging of the structures of slavery. The church's response was to advocate for a gentler, kinder master. Many churches felt that one way to ensure a kinder, gentler master was to press for the Christianization of enslaved persons. A Christian slave, they believed, would be obedient, dutiful, diligent, and would serve his master as he or she would serve Christ. The hope was that a change in attitude of the enslaved person would elicit a kinder disposition from the master.

Colonial Jamaica was not at peace with promises from missionaries that Christianity would make enslaved persons submissive and subordinate. The problem, the master class argued, was granted Christianity made the enslaved person more dutiful, but what if enslaved persons caught on to the dangerous possibilities of freedom that the Christian scriptures advocated? Then, the kindness of masters would not be enough; enslaved persons would press for freedom. It was at this level that the master class understood Christianity as a double-edged sword. On the one hand, it may produce a dutiful servant and on the other hand, it may give rise to one who yearned for freedom.

The immediate fear of planters was that freedom would mean insubordination, revolts, running away and some notion that slavery was wrong and not in keeping with the Bible's teaching about God's will for Jamaicans of African descent. Lawson reminds us of the close collaboration between the Anglican Church and the State in that salaries for the Anglican clergy were paid from the Colonial Treasury, and it was understood that the Anglican Church was an instrument in the hands of the colonial government. There was no resident bishop of the Anglican Church in Jamaica until 1824, who could reign in the excesses of priests in their mission to the colonial government.

Worship was in the service of keeping things the way they were and not aimed at social transformation. 'Faith and practice seem never to have cohered for them with any consistency that might even raise the questions of social justice and humanity, as they collaborated with the exploitation of the natural and human resources of the country.'[2] There was such a critical disconnect between the practice of the clergy of the Anglican Church and the gospel of Jesus Christ that enslaved persons concluded, 'Master left him god in England.'

---

[2] Winston Arthur Lawson, *Religion and Race: African and European Roots in Conflict: A Jamaican Testament* (New York: Peter Lang Publishing, 1996), p.59 Much of the inspiration and argumentation for this essay is drawn from Delroy A. Reid Salmon's *Burning for Freedom* (Kingston: Ian Randle, 2012) and Noel Leo Erskine's *Plantation Church* (New York & Oxford: Oxford University Press, 2014)

It is widely agreed that, during a large portion of the eighteenth century, a majority of Black people in Jamaica did not attend traditional Black churches. Enslaved persons were not welcomed in the White man's church. James Phillippo, the British missionary who spent twenty years in Jamaica comments:

> Not only were they oppressed and bowed down by the operation of unjust and cruel laws, but there was yet another circumstance connected with the condition of the colored and black population, in some respects still more painful. The most inveterate prejudice existed against them on account of their color. Hence they were universally prohibited all intercourse of equality with whites, and if of such an opprobrious distinction they ventured to complain, they were often insultingly told that they were 'the descendants of the ourang-outang', that their mothers hunted the tiger in the wilds of Africa; and that but for the generosity of their sires, in place of possessing freedom and property, their lot would have been to dig cane-holes beneath the discipline of the driver's whip. At church, if a man of color, however respectable in circumstance or character, entered the pew of the lowest white man, he was instantly ordered out.... With people of color, indeed, the whites, like the Egyptians in reference to the Israelites, held it an abomination to eat bread.[3]

According to missionary Phillippo, 'race' was an overarching rubric that governed the relationship of White people to 'Colored' and Black people. It made no difference whether enslaved persons were in the fields offering their bodies to make profit for the enslaver or at church seeking to worship. In either context, the master-servant, superior-subordinate, dynamic held sway. This means that in essential ways the ethos, and theology that guided faith and practice held sway in all churches that had White leadership. The planters influence was not limited to the plantation where labour by enslaved persons was enforced.

Planters also controlled local legislatures; they made the laws, and they also controlled the churches' relationship to enslaved persons. In instructions given to missionaries to foreign countries from the Wesleyan Methodist Committee, it was stated: 'Your sole business is to promote the moral and religious improvement of the slaves to which you have access, *without in the least degree in public or private, interfering with their civil condition'.*[4]

It should not surprise us, then, that enslaved persons preferred to worship among themselves, and often resented having to worship with White people, because of the ways in which religion was used to reinforce the subordination and subjugation of Black people in relation to social masters. Due to the fact there were some plantations where Black people were not

---

[3] James M. Phillippo, *Jamaica: It's Past and Present State.* (London: John Snow, 1843; reprinted, Westport, CT: Negro University Press, 1970), pp.147-148
[4] Cited, *Religion and Race: African and European Roots in Conflict : A Jamaican Testament*

allowed to have their own worship service or preach they would steal away into the woods and practice their own religion in secret. Black people preferred to worship among themselves and they craved Black preaching, where they could hear the Bible interpreted from their own frame of reference. Wherever Black people were they had an irrepressible need, and desire, to worship God in their own way.

There were many enslaved persons, especially fresh shipments from Africa, in the second half of the eighteenth century, who did not speak English and resisted attempts to learn English. This provided a covering for them to resist the efforts of the missionaries who sought to introduce them to Christianity.

Additionally, there were masters and overseers who were conflicted concerning the efficacy of the Christian religion to produce a docile slave. What if enslaved persons caught on to the dangerous teaching of the Bible regarding the equality of all persons before God? Is it possible for an enslaved person to be slave and Christian at the same time? Was it wise to allow the missionary to share the dangerous book that was the Bible with enslaved persons?

Many missionaries in their attempts to assuage the fears of the master class, and at the same time respect and abide by the instructions of missionary agencies in Europe, taught that the best slaves were those who were baptized and taught to serve their masters as they served God. Enslaved persons who caught on to the contradiction of the church's teaching concerning being slave and Christian, outwardly went along with the church's programme. They entered into Christian conversion, were baptized, but refused to relinquish their African cosmology and theology.

With the badge of colour as the defining mark of enslaved persons, churches began to teach that conversion to Christianity meant freedom not from the control of masters, but freedom in the afterlife. Toward the latter part of the seventeenth century, the primary reason for enslavement was the badge of colour. The economic argument that Africa had an inexhaustible supply of labour for plantations began to give way to the religious argument that God made Black people 'to make a crop' and to serve White people. In navigating the cruel world of slavery, Black people would often appropriate the teachings of the master's religion, which led the missionary to believe that Black people were 'becoming Christian'; that is, setting their African world-views aside as they embraced missionary teaching.

Black Baptists
The Baptist church provided the first missionaries to enslaved Jamaica in the early 1780s, and what is of keen interest, is that they were Black Americans. These Baptist missionaries were former slaves from the United States, namely, George Liele, Moses Baker and George Gibb. When it is remembered that they worked among the enslaved and free Black population prior to the first British Baptist missionaries coming to the island, as a result of their invitation in 1813,

their contribution to the struggle for emancipation is ground breaking. Richard Burton puts the issue in perspective for us:

> The self-styled Black Baptists seemed to have made most head way among the slaves first of Kingston and then of the plantations, whereas the White Wesleyan Methodists who followed them seem to have made their first converts mainly among Free blacks and Coloreds of Kingston who had previously been forced to sit in the back pews or organ loft of the city's Anglican church. Both Black Baptists and White Wesleyan Methodists trained black and colored lay preachers for future proselytizing, but it seems clear that from the outset there was a split in style, form, manner and church organization between the 'Euro-Christianity' taught by the Whites and their nonwhite trainers and the 'Afro-Christianity' taught by the Black Baptists. ... there can be little doubt that it was the Black Baptist preachers who urged slaves to seek immediate freedom, while their Wesleyan Methodist counterpart enjoined them, in effect, to wait until freedom was given them.[5]

According to Burton when White Baptist missionaries arrived from Britain in 1814 and tried to take over the Black Baptist Church, a rupture ensued between the 'Native Baptists' and British missionaries.

> The Black Baptist preachers and their congregations split off to follow their own style of worship, which, giving a Christian form to long-established Myalist practices, emphasized music and dancing, 'spirit possession,' prophecy and speaking in tongues.[6]

We are reminded that Black Baptists had twenty-eight years of autonomous leadership in their style of Christianity that emerged and could not easily surrender their 'Afro-Christianity' for a 'Euro-Christianity' that was out of touch with the indigenous culture.

Richard Burton refers to the early Baptist churches in Jamaica as Black Baptists. Winston Lawson refers to the same community as 'Native Baptists' who merged their reading of the Bible with Myalist practices. The Baptists were the first to reach out to enslaved Jamaicans, and one reason for their successes among the population was the loose structure of the Baptist church, which enabled them to use newly converted lay leaders to supervise African converts. Samuel Sharpe, whose leadership in the 'Baptist War' set Jamaica on the course to emancipation, is one of the foremost of these church leaders to emerge. The flexibility in the Baptist ethos and organization allowed the inclusion of African traditional practices.

Another important leader of the Native Baptists was George Lewis, who rejected the White version of Christianity in favour of his own, more African style. Lewis was born in Africa and like George Liele, was a slave in

---

[5] Richard D.E. Burton, *Afro-Creole: Power, Opposition and Play in the Caribbean* (Ithaca and London: Cornell University Press, 1997), p.37
[6] Ibid., p.37

Virginia. After the American Revolution he was brought to Kingston where his owner allowed him to combine his work with preaching in the parishes of Manchester and St. Elizabeth.

George Liele: Fighting for Survival
It is to the leader among the Black Baptists that we now turn. Liele was an enslaved man born in Virginia about 1750 to African parents, themselves enslaved. Their names were George and Nancy. George Liele was a slave of Henry Sharp, who lived with his master in Brooke County, Georgia, during the American Revolutionary War. He was converted by a White Baptist preacher in about 1775. Licensed to preach by the congregation in which he was converted and baptized, he was allowed to preach on plantations in the vicinity. George Liele was about twenty-three years old when he was converted to Christianity. Speaking of his conversion Liele states:

> This state I labored under for the space of six months.... I felt such love and joy as my tongue was not able to express. After this I declared before the congregation of believers the work which God had done for my soul, and the same minister the Rev. Matthew Moore, baptized me, and I continued in this church about four years, till the (e) vacuation.[7]

Liele acknowledged his call to preach, and after a trial sermon before the congregation, he was ordained to the Christian ministry by Rev. Matthew Moore. When the British forces prepared to leave the Savannah area for Jamaica, in December 1782, not being content to live under the new republican form of government, George Liele borrowed about seven hundred dollars from Colonel Moses Kirkland, and accompanied the British, with wife Hannah and four children. Sometime after his arrival in Jamaica he was charged with sedition for preaching from Romans 10:1 'Brethren, my heart's desire and prayer for Israel is that they might be saved.' The charge brought against Liele for which he was imprisoned is that he was 'exciting the slaves to rebellion.' Liele, while in prison, equivocated between notions of survival and liberation. Should he continue to speak out against the evils of slavery and challenge the forces of oppression, to let God's people go free or should he work within the system of slavery and cooperate with the status quo? The choice was between survival with dignity or emancipation.

    The story of Black Baptist churches in Jamaica as midwife of emancipation or of survival with dignity is always present. A look at the ministries of Black Baptist ministers, George Liele and Samuel (Daddy) Sharpe places in sharp focus these choices that are always present when Christian churches navigate difficult choices in the context of slavery and emancipation. Liele's choice, while in prison, was to opt for survival rather than to press for emancipation from slavery. This choice sheds light on his

---

[7] Charles O. Walker, 'Georgia's Religion in the Colonial Era, 1733-1790,' *Viewpoints: Georgia Baptist Historical Society 5 (1976):* pp.17-44 (p.33)

character, as a leader among his people in Savannah, Georgia, and Kingston, Jamaica.

Liele, one of the first Black persons to introduce Christianity to enslaved persons in the United States, and in Jamaica, represents an interesting model of one who was committed to the survival of his people and his family. Liele believed that Christianity offered the best path to freedom, even if spiritual freedom was seen as a necessary step toward physical freedom. The truth is that often masters and missionaries, alike, were disappointed with the result of enslaved persons, as they would often combine Christian and African practices. In many instances enslaved persons were not willing to abandon Africa nor were they willing to ignore Europe.

In colonial Jamaica, Africa and Europe competed for the souls of Black people. When the lives of enslaved people were understood from the perspective of missionary teaching, Jesus meant conformity, obedience, and even an acknowledgement of subordination and subservience to the master. One answer to the question, 'Where do I stand in relation to Jesus?' was survival within the context of slavery. It was believed that Jesus softened the harshness and terror of slavery because a kinder, gentler slave produced a master who was less inclined to brutalize the enslaved person. Jesus did not yet mean fighting for emancipation, or breaking the chains of slavery. If spiritual chains were removed from their 'souls', the physical chains remained in their minds, and on their feet.

One lesson that George Liele teaches us is that the answer to the Jesus-Africa question, namely, 'Where do I stand in relation to Jesus?' or 'Where do I stand in relation to Africa?' was contextual for enslaved persons. Of course there were enslaved persons who chose to return to their master even after 'freedom was come'. For the most part, however, Black people were committed to a hermeneutic of freedom, and survival with dignity was interpreted as an aspect of that freedom.

George Liele is often written off as an 'Uncle Tom' or one who too easily embraced a Euro-missionary perspective, of a gradual approach to emancipation that suggested enslaved people 'wait until freedom is given'. It must be said that there were no clear ways in which enculturation and acculturation worked for George Liele. George Liele, the father of Baptist missions in Jamaica, worked among enslaved populations in Jamaica, ten years before William Carey preached his inaugural sermon in 1793, and set sail for India. Liele referred to himself and fellow Baptists as Ethiopians. He established 'The Ethiopian Baptist Church' in the capital city, Kingston. His identity as Ethiopian and the name of his church, clearly reference Psalm 68:31 ('Let bronze be brought from Egypt; let Ethiopia hasten to stretch out its hands to God' NRSV).

The charge for which Liele was imprisoned, for preaching from Romans 10:1 in the Race Course (a park in Kingston), was 'for exciting the slaves to rebellion'. Liele developed a pragmatic and contextual approach to the faith in which he believed. In the American context his confession of Jesus Christ as saviour gained him his freedom as well as opportunities to preach;

but in the Jamaican context the same faith landed him in jail. After Liele's experience in jail one wonders to what extent he often said what he believed the authorities wanted to hear, or did what was needed in order to survive the cruel world of slavery.

Within a relatively short time after he was licensed to preach and given freedom to travel as an itinerant preacher in America, Liele staked out a theological position, declaring where he stood in relation to Jesus. One is also led to inquire if there is a double entendre in his claim, 'I requested of my Lord and master to give me a work, I did not care how mean it was, only to try and see how good I would do it.' Was this Liele's way of suggesting that there was a master above his earthly master, one who would call the activities of his earthly master into question? Was this a clever way of using the master's language and theology to call into question the master's claim of authority and right to the enforced labour of Black people? Was this his way of saying, 'I seek work from a greater master, one to whom I am ultimately accountable, and whom I seek to please while at the same time showing respect for the role of the master?'

In December 1777, Liele founded a Black Church in Yama Craw, on the outskirts of Savannah, Georgia. He linked this church through a covenant to the church he founded in Kingston, Jamaica in 1783, which he named the 'Ethiopian Baptist Church'. After his experience in prison in Jamaica, Liele produced a covenant titled: '*The Covenant of The Anabaptist church,*' which begun in America, December 1777, and in Jamaica, December 1783.

There are twenty-one articles of this first covenant shared in a Black Baptist church in Jamaica. I will not list all the articles of the covenant, but will highlight four in order to give a flavour for articles enjoined on Baptists in Jamaica by the father of Baptist Missions, George Liele.

> (X) We hold not to shedding of blood. (Genesis 1x.6; Matt. Xxvi. 51-52.)
>
> (XII) We are forbidden to swear not at all (sic). (Matt. V. 33 – 37; Jas.V.12.)
>
> (XV) We permit no slaves to join the Church without first having a few lines from their owners for good behaviour. (1 Peter ii. 13-16; 1 Thess. iii.13)
>
> (XVII) If a slave or servant misbehave to their owners they are to be dealt with according to the word of God. (1 Tim. i.6; Eph.vi.5; 1Peter11. 18-22; Titus ii. 9-11.)[8]

It is rather difficult to identify these articles of the covenant as representing the customs or interests of African-Jamaicans, during the latter portion of the eighteenth, and early decades of the nineteenth century. The logical conclusion to be drawn from the disconnect between the ideals and provisions of this document, which Liele informs us were read once per month at worship

---

[8] Ernest A. Payne, 'Baptist Work in Jamaica before the Arrival of the Missionaries.' *Baptist Quarterly Incorporating the Transactions of the Baptist Historical Society, New Series, 7 (1934-1935):* pp.20-26, (24-26).

service, and the contextual situation, is that it was imported from his congregation in Georgia and ratified by the congregation in Jamaica. The former was, at first, comprised predominantly of fellow African Americans, who migrated with him to Jamaica. John Palmer Gates who has done an in-depth study of the life and times of George Liele puts the issue before us:

> George Liele was probably the first person to do religious work among the slaves in Jamaica. Up to this time there was not very much effort expended to preach the gospel even to whites .... Some of the Negroes were undoubtedly not far removed from their primitive state.... Not infrequently drums were heard that beat out the rhythm for crude sensual dances which, to the whites at times, were dangerously suggestive of earlier African drum beats in preparation for going on the war path. Belief in witchcraft, the use of charms and other superstitions were common among them.... Even after he was relatively well established as a local preacher he was charged with teaching sedition and thrown into prison. After being loaded with irons and put into stocks, during which time he was not permitted to see his family, he was tried for his life and acquitted. It seems he had preached on the text, 'brethren, my heart's desire and prayer for Israel is that they might be saved.' (Romans 10:1)[9]

It is clear that what was at stake in the articles of this covenant was the survival of Liele and his church. According to Gates, Liele was tried for his life, and this covenant was one reason for his acquittal as it was first submitted to the Jamaica legislature for their approval prior to its adoption by Liele's church. Liele went to extraordinary means to secure a bell for his church, not to inform parishioners of times when church service would commence, but to inform masters and overseers, when church service would begin and end.

> As a result Liele won the confidence, not only of masters and overseers, but of several influential men in Kingston. One of these was Stephen Cooke, a member of the Assembly, who, although he preferred the discipline of the Methodist Church, contributed to the building of Liele's sanctuary and later wrote to Dr. Rippon in London in order to help Liele secure funds from the England Baptists.[10]

What are we to infer from Liele's catering to people in power, who were committed to keeping slavery in place? Did he place his own survival above his own people's emancipation from slavery? Was the covenant a smokescreen to throw the planter class off guard, while Liele knew full well that his parishioners would not abide by the conditions of the covenant?

There are two ways to understand how this first covenant, produced by an African American preacher, functioned in the Caribbean. The first thing to keep in mind is how Caribbean people functioned in relation to what they would have perceived as a church that had the blessing of the dominant culture.

---

[9] John Palmer Gates, 'George Liele : A Pioneer Negro Preacher,' *Chronicle 5, no.3 (1943):* pp.118-129, 123, 124
[10] Ibid., pp.124-125.

Journeying to Justice

The church planted by Liele was not an African church, which was concerned primarily with the question of keeping alive African traditions and religious practices in Jamaica. The name of the church, the 'Ethiopian Baptist Church', and his sermon from Romans, chapter 10:1 give an indication that there was an early attempt by Liele to combine the questions, 'Where do we stand in relation to Jesus?' with the African question, 'Where do we stand in relation to Africa?' This approach not only sought to merge issues of survival with that of emancipation, but it meant that the church combined questions of salvation and social justice.

It is clear that Liele began a new tradition in Jamaica. He introduced something new, namely, how to make the church available to enslaved persons in Jamaica as a centre for worship and the practice of African ways of being in the world. Perhaps he joined issues of salvation and social justice without meaning to threaten the system of slavery in Jamaica. Did his change of heart, placing his own survival above the liberation of his own people from the clutches of slavery, indicate that the gospel of Jesus became for him a tool of social control?

The hard question is why would his people endorse or support his capitulation to the status quo? One answer is that Caribbean people in general, and Jamaicans, in particular, have always had membership in two churches. On the one hand, they have always supported the church that highlights, 'Where do we stand in relation to Jesus?' This church has always represented status for them as it has always been aligned with the dominant culture. Jamaicans have always been proud to identify as Baptist, Methodist, or Anglican, although they know full well that these churches, during slavery, often sabotaged and actively worked against their best interests.

It is of first importance to understand the double entendre at work in Liele's covenant; on the one hand it was intended to satisfy the Jamaican legislature, masters and overseers, and on the other, it was a framework for the local populace that they would 'take with a grain of salt'. Liele's congregation knew that things were not necessarily the way they appeared or in the parlance of Jamaican people, 'Things ain't what they seem to be.' Caribbean theologian William Watty places the issue before us:

> Weak and defenseless, kidnapped and alone, the survival of the black man has been due mainly to a combination of outward conformity to white demands and inward skepticism of white systems. In a situation where those who taught him religion had the same origins and largely the same presuppositions as those who held at his head the loaded pistol, his response was to assent readily and publicly with the necessary 'yes Massa,' and to feign acceptance of the ready made imported canons of belief and conduct, but in *camera* he whispered to his fellow captives 'but it ain't necessarily so'.[11]

---

[11] William W. Watty, 'The De-Colonization of Theology' in Idris Hamid (ed.) *Troubling of the Waters,* (Port of Spain, Trinidad: W.I. Rahaman Printery, 1973), pp.49-50.

What was at stake, according to Watty, was the survival of the church and the circumstances of slavery, which dictated that Liele would appeal to a framework in which acceptance was feigned and enslaved persons understood as, 'that it ain't necessarily so.' What made it possible for Black Baptists to agree with Liele was the knowledge among them that membership in Liele's church did not preclude their secret meetings where they would give birth to plans to move from survival to liberation. We turn now to one of the leaders who placed Jamaica on the course to fight for emancipation.

Fighting For Emancipation
The Baptist War (or Christmas Uprising) of December 1831-January 1832 led by Samuel (Daddy) Sharpe, a deacon of Burchell Baptist Church, in Montego Bay, points back to earlier uprisings in Jamaica that aimed at overturning the system of slavery. The Maroon rebellion of 1760 led by the Ashanti warrior and Obeah man Tacky, was one of the bloodiest revolts staged by African-Jamaicans. Led by Tacky, the warriors prepared for war by mixing rum with gun powder and grave dirt. Blood drawn from the arm of each participant was added, and then the mixture was drunk in turn by each warrior. The drinking of this mixture meant the covenant to fight until death. This was certainly a part of the back drop for the Baptist War aimed at taking on the colonial government in a quest for the overthrow of the institution of slavery.

An additional reason for the Baptist War, according to Winston Lawson, was sparked by news from England that the Anti-slavery society was committed to immediate emancipation and that the House of Commons in April 1831 had taken steps to abolish slavery. A rumour ensued among the enslaved population that freedom should not be delayed any longer as it was granted by the King and his ministers in England, but was being withheld from slaves by White people in Jamaica.

> They were therefore ready and anxious to take hold of the news from England in 1831 that abolition was imminent. Anyone, therefore, who stood in the way of their realizing their dream of freedom from an unworkable and demoralizing circumstance, be they planter, politician or preacher would be denounced as Knibb and his colleagues were at Salter's Hill on that fateful December 27 when the accumulated pressures of alienation and the frustrated resentment of pacification and acquiescence to the status quo, made them declare with bitter disappointment, that 'the man must be mad to tell them such a thing'.[12]

The straw that broke the camel's back was the Jamaican Assembly voting in February 1831 to reduce the number of free days slaves were able to enjoy at Christmas. Lawson contends that the Jamaican Assembly could hardly have

---

[12] *Religion and Race: African and European Roots in Conflict – A Jamaican Testament.* pp.153

picked a more contentious issue, as the Christmas holiday had special significance for Black people. It is understandable that plans to counter that move by the Assembly would have begun shortly after the announcement to abridge the number of days allowed at Christmas.

> It is difficult to imagine a more provocative measure, and one may surmise that serious preparations for an uprising at Christmas began not long afterward, with Sharp in particular using the relative freedom he enjoyed as a deacon of the Black Baptist Church to move from plantation to plantation and, under the cover of prayer meetings, 'holding secret intercourse with those slaves whose cooperation he wished to enlist'[13]

Like cool breeze from the Caribbean ocean, word spread across the island, especially among the Baptists, that the free papers from the King of England would be delivered to Jamaica on Christmas day, but White people would hold it back. It was believed by Black Baptists that Rev. Thomas Burchell, who was in England, was summoned by the King of England to take the 'free papers' to Jamaica in time for Christmas.

> ...the crisis of white authority was revealed when on the Salt Spring estate, just before Christmas, a driver refused to flog a slave woman caught with 'a piece of sugar cane in her hand', when constables were brought to restore order, the slaves repelled them with cutlasses drawn. Christmas itself passed uneasily if tensely, but on 27 December, the day scheduled for the resumption of work, thousands of slaves in the west of the island simply downed tools, declaring that 'we won't be slaves no more; we won't lift hoe no more; we won't take flog no more. We free now...no more slaves again'[14]

     The Baptist War of 1831, led by Daddy Sharpe, signalled the beginning of the end of slavery in Jamaica. Black Baptists fighting for emancipation in and around Montego Bay brought to a climax the long struggle of African-Jamaicans for emancipation from imperial rule. The struggle over the years took the form of enslaved people running away, many, as in the case of the maroons of Jamaica, fleeing to the hills and organizing periodic attacks on the British. The focus of this war, however, was Black Baptists organizing to withdraw their labour. As a result of this, the brunt of their attack was on the institutions of the plantation. A total of 120 buildings on the estate were torched as Black people insisted that they were human beings who had a right to emancipation; they had a right to withdraw their labour, and attack the institutions that kept them in slavery. More than 20,000 African-Jamaicans were involved in this uprising. The focus was not a call to arms but for enslaved persons to withdraw their labour and crush the monster of slavery.

---

[13] *Afro-Creole: Power, Opposition and Play in the Caribbean.* p.86
[14] Ibid., p.88

The leader was Daddy Sharpe, who although a deacon of the local Baptist church, had a large following among the Native Baptists. Daddy Sharpe gave witness to Black Baptists stating that they were family, which opened the door to Daddy Sharpe's extraordinary leadership.

Edward Hylton, one of Daddy Sharpe's followers, tells of being in the hills and receiving a message from Daddy Sharpe to attend a meeting at Johnson's house on Retrieve Estate in St. James. The gathering took the form of a prayer meeting. After the meeting, Daddy Sharpe, William Johnson, who became one of the leaders fighting for emancipation, Hylton, and a few others, remained behind.

> After a while Sharpe spoke to them in a low, soft tone so that his voice would not be heard outside. According to Hylton he kept them spellbound while he spoke of the evils and injustices of slavery, asserted the right of all human beings to freedom and declared on the authority of the Bible, that the White man had no more right to hold the Blacks in bondage than Blacks had to enslave the Whites[15]

The meeting went late into the night as they agreed on a strategy to overturn slavery. They covenanted not to work after the Christmas holidays but to seize the right to freedom in faithfulness to each other. 'If backra would pay them, they would work as before. If any attempt was made to force them to work as slaves they would fight for their freedom. They took the oath and kissed the Bible.'[16]

What Daddy Sharpe intended was a non-violent protest that would be expressed as a labour strike. The plan was that on the day after the Christmas holiday an overseer or driver would go to the 'busha' on each estate and inform him that slaves would not work until they agreed to pay their wages. The bushas were to be kept on the estate until they agreed to pay wages for work. Philip Curtin suggests that what happened was the Native Baptists skilfully detached the Baptist Missionary Society from White missionaries, and were using the Baptist organization as a European trade union leader used the bargaining power of the workers.[17] Later developments indicate that this was indeed the case. On December 27 William Knibb, visiting Moses Baker's chapel at Crooked Spring, now Salter's Hill, tried to persuade Black Baptists that rumours about freedom having been granted were untrue. His words were received with immense dissatisfaction, many persons left the chapel, offended. Others remarked: 'The man...must be mad to tell them such things.[18] Missionary Knibb stated:

> I am pained – to the soul, at being told that many of you have agreed not to work anymore for your owners, and I fear this is too true. I learned that some wicked

---

[15] Hazel Bennett and Phillip Sherlock, *The Story of the Jamaican People*. (Kingston, Jamaica: Ian Randle Publishers, 1998), p.214
[16] Ibid.
[17] Philip D. Curtin, *Two Jamaica's* (New York: Atheneum Press, 1970), p. 86
[18] *The Story of Jamaican People*, p.216

person has persuaded you that the King of England has made you free. Hear me! I love your souls and I would not tell you a lie for the whole world; I assure you it is false, false as hell can make it. I entreat you not to believe it, but go to your work as formerly. If you have any love for Jesus Christ, to religion, to your ministers, or to those kind friends in England who have helped you build this chapel, and who are sending a minister for you, do not be led away. God commands you to be obedient.[19]

Black Baptists saw through the hypocrisy of missionary Knibb and his theology of obedience. They responded that they had worked enough already and declared they were slaves no more.

Daddy Sharpe and his freedom fighters interpreted the struggle for emancipation through the lens of liberation. Missionary Knibb said he loved their souls. Sharpe and his compatriots understood the body as a site for liberation. It is reported that when Daddy Sharpe was apprehended he said that he had rather die than be a slave. The price paid by Daddy Sharpe and his people for emancipation was very high. In the aftermath of the Baptist War, 600 African-Jamaicans were killed by British forces. In their defence they killed 14 White people. The seeds for the destruction of slavery were sown. On the 1st August, 1834, a partial freedom was granted to British colonies throughout the Caribbean, with the abolition of slavery following on the 1st August 1838.

It is quite clear that the Baptist movement that George Liele initiated in Jamaica went in directions he could not have imagined. A central distinction between the position Liele advocated and that practiced by the Native Baptists had to do with perspective. While Liele benefited from being a member of a Christian community in Georgia and earlier Virginia, he was able to interpret the world, slavery and African religions, from an African frame of reference. For example, he preached a sermon in Jamaica from Romans 10:1 'Brethren my heart's desire and prayer for Israel is that they might be saved.' In this sermon he compared the plight of African-Jamaicans to Israel in Egypt. The sermon was regarded by authorities as incendiary, and as a consequence, he was imprisoned. The laws of Jamaica made it extremely difficult for this Black Baptist to fight for emancipation. In 1802 a law was passed stating that if a free Black person was found guilty of preaching sermons advocating freedom of enslaved persons he would be committed to prison and kept in hard labour. Liele made peace with the planter class by agreeing to work within a system dictated by the laws of Jamaica.

On the other hand, the converse was the case for Native Baptists who while committed to Baptist organization and freedom, opted to work outside a system engineered by the planter class. The Native Baptists interpreted the world and Christianity from an African frame of reference inspired by Myal

---

[19] John Howard Hinton, *Memoirs of William Knibb* (London: Houlston and Stoneman, 1847), p.118

religion, as was the case with Daddy Sharpe, who challenged both Baptist ecclesiology and plantation practice, in his quest for emancipation.

Liele introduced Black Baptists to a radical version of Christianity, which they interpreted through Afrocentric lenses. In a context of slavery, two expressions of Baptist faith emerged. Baptist orthodoxy, which seemed important to Liele, and Native Baptist ecclesiology that was important to Daddy Sharpe, and departed from Liele's teaching at critical points, embracing a hermeneutic of emancipation. Without Liele neither would have emerged.

Black British History: A Critical Reappraisal
Paul Walker

Things have changed and are not as they once had appeared. The details of the history of Black people in Britain have become clearer and better defined over the past few decades. The discovery that people of African descent were in the United Kingdom for at least 1800 years, has challenged the assumption that their presence is the result of migration from Britain's colonies, during the mid twentieth century. It is sometimes recognised that ports, like London, Liverpool and Bristol, had long established Black communities because of seafaring and the slave trade, but generally, Black people in Britain is thought to be a recent occurrence. This, however, is not the case.

There was a Black person in Britain as early as 210 AD, and by 250 AD, a division of Moors were defending Hadrian's Wall.[1] Henry VII and VIII employed a Black musician. During the early modern period, Black people are often depicted in art and literature, Shakespeare's play, *Othello* being one example. Until recently, however, some had argued that such representations were not based on the actual presence of Africans, but rather on myths and legends. Recent research has, however, challenged this assumption. Catherine of Aragon brought Africans to Tudor England in 1501 as part of her retinue after Henry VII arranged her marriage to Prince Arthur as a way of establishing trade relations with Spain. Relations with Spain broke down because of "strained existing commercial arrangements, including slavery", so England sought other methods of acquiring African slaves.[2]

An example of an African being in Britain during this period is Sir Peter Negro who was in the army between 1545 and 1550. Sir Peter eventually became an officer and was involved in the taking of Leith, Scotland in 1547, for which he was awarded a knighthood by the Duke of Somerset, Lord Protector.[3] Negro's presence in England may not have been so unusual as during late medieval and early modern times there were Africans in military service throughout Europe. Sir Peter Negro's status during the mid Tudor era is, however, an exception as most Elizabethan and Stuart Africans lived in

---

[1] Peter Fryer, *Staying Power: The History of Black People in Britain* (London: Pluto Press, 1984), p.1. Edward Scobie, *Black Britannia: A History of Blacks in Britain 1555-1833* (Oxford: University Press, 1977). Paul Edwards, 'The Early African Presence in the British Isles', in J. S. Gundara and I. Duffield, (eds.), *Essays on the History of Blacks in Britain* (Aldershot: Avebury, 1992).
[2] See Tamara Lewis, "Like devils out of Hell': Reassessing the African Presence in Early Modern England', *Black Theology: An International Journal*, Vol. 14, No.2, 2016), pp.108-121.
[3] Ibid

menial condition.[4] A group of West Africans is known to have come to England in 1555, brought directly from Africa to England.[5] In 1562 John Hawkins set sail for the coast of Guinea where he captured three hundred Africans.[6]

Until slave trading became illegal in the British Empire in 1807, some ships' captain brought Africans back for personal profit or use, which resulted in a small Black population in Britain. The practice continued illegally afterwards, although between the early modern period and the beginning of the nineteenth century, Britain's Black population remained small.[7]

The Eighteenth Century

In the eighteenth century the numbers of Black people in Britain begin to grow, so that

> Scattered from Devon across to Kent was a handful of Black pages and laundrymaids (sic) and the like: young slaves used as household servants and status symbols in the mansions of English noblemen and gentry.[8]

The demand for sugar and rum increased during the eighteenth century, which increased the economic driving force of the slave trade.[9] Then as the eighteenth century progressed there began a small inward migration of African, African-American, and Caribbean people to Britain, some brought by owners returning from the Americas or the Caribbean, although an increasing number came as travellers, fugitives, students and anti-slavery campaigners. David Killingray writes

> It is now estimated that by 1770 there were 5,000 Black people in London and altogether 10,000 in the British Isles. Most were concentrated in the major

---

[4] Ibid
[5] Fryer, *Staying Power*, pp. 4-5. F. O. Shyllon, *Black People in Britain 1555–1833* (Oxford: University Press, 1977), p. 6. Winthrop Jordan, *White Over Black: American Attitudes Toward the Negro, 1550-1812* (Chapel Hill: University of North Carolina Press, 2012), p. 5.
[6] Shyllon, *Black Slaves in Britain*, p. 3.
[7] Fryer, *Staying Power*, p. 14. An example being Erddig, the stately home in Clwyd, which had a Black slave, whose portrait is reproduced on one of their postcards. There are numerous other examples. Kenwood House, North London, a portrait of Princess Henrietta of Lorraine, by Sir Anthony Van Dyke, dated 1643 has a small Negro page boy looking up in wonder at her.
[8] Fryer, *Staying Power*, p.14. Fashion was largely responsible. Having one or two slaves became a status symbol, as was the consumption of the newly available bitter drinks, tea and coffee, which were made more palatable by the addition of sugar. Sugar was also needed for the manufacture of chocolate. This fuelled the demand for slaves to work on sugar plantations.
[9] See James Walvin, *Black Ivory: A History of British Slavery* (London: Fontana Press, 1993); James Walvin, *Questioning Slavery* (London: Routledge, 1996).

trading ports of London, Bristol and Liverpool, but they were also found in towns and villages throughout Britain.[10]

They arrived for different reasons, by various routes, and many became involved in the nascent abolition movement, thereby, playing significant roles in Britain's history, contributing to political, church and social life in Britain. These were amongst the first of many who came over in the next one hundred and fifty years.

Amongst those who left a significant footprint in history were Ukawsaw Gronniosaw, Phillis Wheatley, Ignatius Sancho, Ottobah Cugoano, and Olaudah Equiano. All were Africans, except Wheatley, who was African-American. These well known people were only a few of the Black community in Britain at the time. Others were Yahne Aelane, (anglicised name Joseph Saunders); Boughwa Genansmel (Jasper Goree); Cojoh Ammere (George Williams); Thomas Cooper; William Green; George Robert Mandeville; and Bernard Elliot Griffiths. All were co-signatories with Equiano and Cugoano on a letter from nine "Sons of Africa", published in the *Diary* newspaper in 1789, declaring that 'thanks to God the nation at large is awakened to a sense of our sufferings ...' Others who signed public statements were Daniel Christopher, John Christopher, James Forster, John Scot, Jorge Dent, Thomas Oxford, James Bailey, James Frazer, Thomas Carlisle, William Stevens, Joseph Almaze, John Adams, George Wallace and Thomas Jones.[11]

The best known of these is Olaudah Equiano because of his autobiography, *The Interesting Narrative of Olaudah Equiano, or Gustavus Vassa, the African. Written by Himself.*[12] In his lifetime the book went through eight British editions and six more followed in the 22 years after his death. Equiano's life story is regarded as the single most important literary contribution to Abolitionism.[13]

Born in eastern Nigeria about 1745, he was around 11 when he and his sister were captured and enslaved. He experienced the horrors of the Middle Passage

---

[10] David Killingray, 'Black Baptists in Britain, 1640-1950.' *Baptist Quarterly*, Vol. 40 (April 2003), pp. 69-89. Norma Myers, *Reconstructing the Black Past: Blacks in Britain 1780-1830* (London: Frank Cass, 1996), ch. 2.

[11] *The Diary; or Woodfall's Register*, No. 24 (April 25th 1789) and Shyllon, *Black People in Britain*, App. ii.

[12] Vincent Carretta, *Olaudah Equiano, The Interesting Narrative and other Writings* (Harmondsworth: Penguin Classics, 1995). See also James Walvin, *An African's Life: The Life and Times of Olaudah Equiano 1745-1797* (London: Cassels, 1998).

[13] Olaudah Equiano was 'The Face of Freedom in the Millennium Dome', *The Observer* 8th August 1999, p. 23. Although whether in the fiasco that surrounded the whole project that ever came to fruition I do not know! The article was written by David Dabydeen whose novel, *Harlot's Progress* (London: Vintage, 2000) is based on Equiano's life (first published by Cape in May 1999).

and after a brief time in Barbados was shipped onwards to Virginia.[14] He managed to save enough money to buy his freedom, and in 1767 he returned to England, where he became a hairdresser. He subsequently became a sailor and travelled widely, spending another spell in the Caribbean, and after many adventures, returned to Britain in 1777. A practising Christian, he offered himself for ordination, hoping to become a missionary to Africa, but the Bishop of London refused to ordain him. Equiano became involved in the abolitionist movement with Grenville Sharpe and Thomas Hardy, and from 1787, its work became the centre of his life. He travelled extensively around Britain speaking on abolition and published his famous Life Narrative in 1789. He visited Birmingham in 1789 and received a warm welcome from the many high class abolitionists and also from the working people.

The majority of Black people who came to Britain were involved in the anti-slavery movement, but there are examples of those of a criminal persuasion that were exceptions to the general trend of philanthropy and Christian probity. Joseph Mountain (1758 - 1790) is one such example. Born into slavery in Philadelphia in 1758, his life narrative begins when he sailed for England, arriving in May 1775. Mountain went to London, met other criminals with whom he travelled across London and the south of England with 'a hand organ and various other musical instruments' as a cover for 'highway robbery'. Wanted in London, they travelled to York and Newmarket, continuing to rob people and coaches. Returning to London, Mountain boarded 'the brig *Sally*, as cook…' He sailed to Lisbon and back and then to Jamaica. Back in London, he and two other criminals started highway robbery again, travelling to Coventry, Newcastle, Warrington, Lancaster and Liverpool, then to Plymouth, with another accomplice, to rob naval officers.[15]

The Nineteenth Century
As the eighteenth century passed, the dynamics behind the Black presence in Britain altered. Whilst the keeping of Black people as personal slaves, servants in big houses and fashion accessories for the wealthy, continued, the struggle for abolition and the ending of the legal Slave Trade, in 1807, changed the pressures that were causing the movement of Black people across the Atlantic. The struggle for abolition, the personal and communal suffering of which they had been a part changed the internal psyche of Black people and the external dynamic that had governed slavery. The sheer injustice of slavery and the various slave revolts that had taken place, particularly in San Domingo, later Haiti, in 1781,[16] caused a significant number of people of African descent

---

[14] Doubts have now been expressed about Equiano's African birth. See Carretta, *Olaudah Equiano,* and James Walvin, *An African's Life: The Life and Times of Olaudah Equiano 1745-1797* (London: Cassels, 1998).
[15] Mountain's life narrative is available at http://docsouth.unc.edu/neh/mountain/menu.html (Accessed November 2015)
[16] C. L. R. James, *The Black Jacobins: Toussaint L'Ouverture and the San Domingo Revolution* (London: W. H. Allen, 1980) originally published in 1938.

to begin to act in their own interests, against slavery and its injustices. People of African descent began opposing slavery and racial injustice by informing people in Britain of the horrors of the institution by speaking in churches and chapels, at anti-slavery gatherings and writing their own life narratives.[17] By doing so they produced, along with British abolitionists, a growing group of people who were determined to bring an end to slavery.

Thus, the pattern of movement of Black people within the Atlantic triangle altered. The norm had been for Black people to find themselves in Britain, via capture in Africa and shipment to the Americas in huge numbers. Although there is little doubt that the slave trade continued illegally, after 1807, pioneer African Americans, Caribbeans and Africans emerged who came to Europe and Britain under their own agency, to further the anti-slavery cause. Many were fugitives, others liberated slaves, sailors, academics and ordinary people, who had a vision for the eradication of slavery, and who were willing to put that commitment into action. These people got involved in various forms of resistance like escape, gaining literacy and education, lecturing, writing and publishing, bringing forth polemical arguments against slavery. These forms of campaigning and resistance found expression in Britain through newspapers, theatrical performance, sometimes in music halls, investigative writing, editing newspapers, preaching and engagement with the political and parliamentary system. All of the aforementioned was in the cause of abolition.

The result was that growing numbers of people from the Caribbean, America and Africa came to Britain because it was both a safe haven and the centre of the abolitionist cause. Numbers increased with emancipation in the Caribbean in 1834, and also because of the social and political situation in America, in particular the Fugitive Slave Act of 1850. This law required the capture of and return to their owner of any fugitive slave even from states where slavery was illegal.[18] This resulted in fugitive slaves coming to Britain to avoid capture, with most becoming involved in the anti-slavery movement.

The nineteenth century saw a big rise in the abolition movement on both sides of the Atlantic and it particularly flourished in British non-conformist chapels. The fugitive and liberated slaves who came to Britain as part of the Abolition movement, which aimed to erect 'a moral cordon around America that would isolate her from the international community',[19] were mostly Christians. They pursued their abolitionist strategies through the many anti-slavery organisations, most of which were organised and dominated by Baptists, Quakers and Methodists. Some examples are given below of people who came to Britain during the nineteenth century as part of the Transatlantic Anglo-American abolition movement.

---

[17] Audrey Fisch Ed. *The Cambridge Companion to the African American Slave Narrative* (Cambridge: University Press, 2007).
[18] Kolchin, *American Slavery*, p. 84.
[19] Blackett, *Building an Antislavery Wall*, p. 6. James W. C. Pennington, *The Fugitive Blacksmith* (London: 3rd edition, 1850).

We now turn to some of the less well known Black people whose presence in our churches has been unearthed in recent research. The first discovery I made, which resulted in the discovery of others, was of Revd Peter Stanford who was minister of Hope Street Baptist Church, Highgate, Birmingham UK from 1889 - 1895. Born in Hampton, Virginia, around 1860 he was five at the end of the American Civil War. As the plantation system collapsed the orphaned Stanford was taken in by Native Americans, who eventually passed him to a Quaker group who took him to an orphanage in Boston.

From here, he was adopted by a Mr & Mrs Stanford, who were coal merchants. After what he describes in his life narrative, *From Bondage to Liberty*, as 5 years of ill treatment, he ran away and eventually ended up living with a children's gang on the streets of New York City. He converted to the Christian faith and was noticed by some prominent abolitionists, including the Revd Henry Highland Garnet, Harriet Beecher Stow and her brother, Revd Henry Ward Beecher. They help him to attend Suffield Baptist Institute, Connecticut, where he completed his studies before being ordained in 1878 as pastor of Zion Baptist Church, Hartford, Connecticut. Zion Baptist was a mission church for African Americans who had come from the Southern States before and after Emancipation.

In 1882 Stanford went to Canada where he was briefly pastor of a church in Hamilton, Ontario and then of the Horton Street Baptist Church, London, Ontario, where he was editor of the *Christian Defender* newspaper. He arrived in Liverpool in May 1883 and afterwards went to London where he was employed as an evangelist by a Rev. Mr. Baxter, editor of the *Christian Herald*. He subsequently spent time in Bradford and Keighley, in West Yorkshire. He settled in Birmingham in 1887. On August 13th 1888, he married an English woman, Beatrice Mabel Stickley, at the Baptist chapel in Smethwick. In May 1889, Stanford became the minister of Hope Street Chapel, Highgate, Birmingham. In that same year he published his life story *From Bondage to Liberty*, probably to counter accusations that he was a charlatan. Stanford took over another church in Priestly Rd., Sparkbrook, Birmingham, whilst continuing the work at Hope Street.

It can seem remarkable that a church in a working class district of nineteenth century Birmingham should call an African American ex-slave as its pastor. The City had, however, a world-wide reputation for justice, equality and enterprise, and had been at the forefront of the campaign to abolish slavery. After slavery had ended in the United States, Birmingham had many organisations which supported freed slaves, especially through its many Non-conformist chapels that flourished in the city. Birmingham was, therefore, a place where a person like Stanford could find an appreciative welcome. Stanford's passionate advocacy for racial justice and his commitment to progress through hard work would have made him attractive to many chapels in the City.

In the 1890s Birmingham became a centre of the campaign against the lynchings of African Americans, probably due to a visit of Ida B. Wells in

1894. Stanford was well known as 'Birmingham's Coloured Preacher' so would have been an obvious choice when anti-lynching campaigners in Birmingham wanted someone to go to the USA and report on these gruesome activities. Thus, at a public meeting in May 1894, it was resolved that Stanford should visit the United States and report on the situation.

In September 1895 Stanford returned to Boston, Massachusetts and began his investigation into lynchings, which revealed that, despite emancipation and Reconstruction, the injustices Black people faced were largely unchanged. He found that the number and form of lynchings were worse than the reports in England had indicated. After his investigation Stanford published his book *The Tragedy of the Negro in America* in which he gave details of how Black people arrived in America, the injustice they suffered in slavery and the horror of lynchings. He attempted to explain the phenomenon of lynchings from an historical and social perspective using both eye-witness descriptions and statistics to illustrate his arguments.

At the same time as Stanford was researching lynchings he founded St. Mark Congregational Church, Roxbury, Boston, the first African American church in that district. He was an early ecumenist and organised the Interdenominational Ministers' Association in Boston. From St Mark, Stanford went briefly to minister in New York City. He returned to North Cambridge, Massachusetts and founded the Union Industrial and Stranger's Home for homeless women and children. He served as Vice President of Christ's Medical and Theological College, Baltimore, and as the Vice President for Massachusetts in the National Baptist Convention. He died on May 20th 1909 of kidney failure.

This re-discovery of the Black presence in Britain is producing varied leads to other possible avenues of investigation. Connections and threads abound. One such connection is with the wider slavery, racial justice and anti-lynching discourse of the late nineteenth century. Ida B. Wells-Barnett (1861-1930), an African-American woman of striking courage and conviction, was one of the principal leaders of the anti-lynching crusade in the USA. Raised in Mississippi after the Civil War, Wells worked her way through Rust College and taught for a time in a school in Memphis, Tennessee. A writer, she became part owner of a newspaper, the *Memphis Free Speech*. In May 1892, in response to an article on a local lynching, a mob ransacked her offices and threatened her life if she did not leave town. Moving to Chicago, Wells continued to write about lynchings. While investigating these murders, she would go directly to the site of a killing, despite personal danger, eventually publishing in 1895 *A Red Record*, the first documented statistical report on lynching.[20]

A forceful speaker, Wells lectured widely in North America and Great Britain. She toured British cities, speaking in Birmingham in 1893. This was during the time Stanford was the minister in Highgate. Did they meet? It

---

[20] Ida B. Wells-Barnett, *On Lynchings* (Amherst, NY: Humanity Books, 2002).

seems likely. Were her visit and the speaking engagements part of what galvanised the great and the good of Birmingham to take notice of the issue of lynchings in the southern states? I suspect so.

During her stay in Birmingham she resided at 66 Gough Road in Edgbaston.[21] Gough Road later became one of the places where Caribbean people settled when they first came to Birmingham as part of the mass migratory movement during the post World War II period. It is strange and possibly significant that the places where Black people lived and worked in the nineteenth century became the very places where they subsequently settled in the twentieth century!

These examples of the presence of Black people in Britain over the centuries, centred on my own context of Birmingham, indicate that it is very likely that many other people of African heritage are yet to be re-discovered in cities, towns, and villages across the country. We now turn to the 20th Century, during the earlier parts of which, people of African heritage continued to be involved in social reform. These include World War I and following that, the Pan African movement and World War II and eventually, Caribbean migration as part of the Windrush epoch.

The Twentieth Century
As the nineteenth century passed the Black presence in Edwardian Britain continued to grow and change. As previously noted, the context and issues to be addressed altered slightly as the motives, perspectives and commitments of Black people focused on different issues than in previous times. Even after the struggles of earlier centuries the underlying issue of racial justice remained. There was a continued struggle for justice and fair treatment for Black people in Britain. Slowly, the British Empire began to face the issues raised by colonialism, independence and Pan Africanism.

One indication of the nature of the British Empire was the diversity of countries that were represented at the new King's coronation in 1902. 'Kings, rajahs, presidents, chiefs, emperors and prime ministers were summoned to witness the coronation.'[22] The rulers and the ruled, from the far flung reaches of the British Empire, were in attendance. Troops and dignitaries from India, Africa and China; people from Canada, Australia, New Zealand, the Caribbean, Fiji and Malta paraded and the whole image of Britain as global empire with many peoples under its rule was spectacularly reinforced. Changes were, however, in the air. Resistance to colonialism was fermenting and would soon begin to affect political and social attitudes in Britain.

As is revealed by the pioneering research of Jeffrey Green, many of the Black people who were in Britain during the Edwardian period were

---

[21] Alfreda M. Duster, (ed.), *Crusade for Justice: The Autobiography of Ida B. Wells* (Chicago: University Press, 1970), p.101.
[22] Jeffrey Green, *Black Edwardians: Black People in Britain 1901-1914* (London: Frank Cass, 1998) p.1.

entertainers, musicians, actors and sportsmen.[23] The significance of the church continued, however, as seen in the life and work of Revd James Harley (1873-1943). Born in Antigua, Harley studied in America before coming to England in 1907 to study theology at Jesus College, Oxford, after which he had a number of curacies, eventually being ordained priest in 1911. At some point around 1915 he 'responded to a call to undertake secular war work... trained as a toolmaker... and worked in a munitions factory.'[24] He subsequently became a local politician.

World War I
The First World War brought people from all over the empire to fight.[25] Caribbean soldiers first joined the Allied troops in France in 1915. Although even in those extreme circumstances there was opposition by British Army commanders to Black troops being part of 'White' regiments and fighting in the front line. This opposition soon altered when massive losses and the intervention of King George V forced a change of attitude.

By 1914 there was a great deal of loyalty in the Caribbean towards British institutions, and support for Britain's war effort was strong, although some people had reservations about involvement, believing it to be a 'White man's war'. Reformers in both South Africa and the Caribbean saw the war as an opportunity to press for constitutional change and representative government, a cause which had become strong by 1914. So patriotism was very much often linked with hope for future reforms.

The pro-participation arguments of local Caribbean newspapers gave weight to the representation from colonial Governors to the British establishment. Although British officials did not want Black men serving on the Western Front, pressure from the colonies and the huge death toll, resulted in the British government approving the creation of West Indian contingents, and recruitment soon began in earnest. There was no conscription, except in parts of West Africa.

Rather, recruitment organisations employed moral persuasion along with vague promises of glory, discipline, exercise, the possibility of honours and hints of free land, at the end of the war. Recruiters also spoke of the economic advantages of enlisting, which were effective in a situation where unemployment was high, the cost of living constantly rising, and wages being depressed. Thus, the groups most open to promises of paid work, even if it was in war, were plantation workers and the massed ranks of the unemployed.

The West India Regiment (WIR) was an infantry unit of the British Army, whose soldiers were normally stationed in the colonies of the Caribbean between 1795 and 1927.[26] The British West Indies Regiment (BWIR) was

---

[23] Green, *Black Edwardians*,
[24] *The Church Times*, October 2nd, 2015.
[25] Robert N Murray *Lest We Forget* (London: Hansib Publications, 1996)
[26] Roger N. Buckley, *Slaves in Red Coats: The British West India Regiments, 1795-1815* (Yale University Press, 1979).

formed in 1915 from local volunteers to fight overseas. There was widespread enthusiasm on the islands to help the war effort, and the cost of sending the Regiment to France, was raised from public subscription. Two thirds of the total recruitment of 15,200 were Jamaican. The Regiment served in Palestine, Italy and on the Western Front.

By the middle of 1916, men rejected in England as unfit or who had been wounded began to return. The promises that recruiters had peddled were soon seen as bogus, when it became clear to the men and the public, that no preparation for the invalids and returnees had been made. Moreover, those men discharged as unfit or undesirable were not entitled to any benefits or pensions, while those who were entitled to benefits experienced excessively long delays before they received assistance. In Jamaica the men were given a few shillings, a cheap suit and free railway transport home. Transportation problems meant that some had to remain in Kingston for several days, which exhausted their money before they even left for home. This caused deep dissatisfaction because most had no other form of support and, having relinquished their jobs to fight for King and Country, they were left in destitution and poverty.

Caribbean participation in the war was a significant event in the still ongoing process of identity formation in the post-emancipation era of Caribbean history. The war sowed the seeds for profound socio-economic, political and psychological change, and greatly facilitated protest against the oppressive conditions in the colonies. Resistance to colonial rule was increased by the adoption of the nationalist ideologies of Marcus Garvey, and others, throughout the region. The war also laid the foundation for the nationalist upheavals of the 1930s in which World War I veterans were to play a significant role.[27]

World War II

With the Second World War we reach a better known period of Black history in these islands. The population of the Caribbean colonies was around 14 million in the late 1930s, 16,000 of whom volunteered to fight in the Second World War. Over one hundred were women who were also posted overseas, eighty joined the Women's Auxiliary Air Force (WAAF) and thirty the Auxiliary Territorial Service (ATS). About six thousand Caribbean men joined the Royal Air Force and the Royal Canadian Air Force, serving as fighter pilots, bomb aimers, radio operators, gunners, ground staff and administrators. Thousands of Caribbean seamen made their contributions in the Merchant Navy, one of the Second World War's most dangerous services.

One thousand volunteers for army service were formed into the Caribbean Regiment, which went overseas in 1944 and saw service in the Middle East

---

[27] A. A. Cipriani, *Twenty-five Years After: The British West Indies Regiment in the Great War 1914-1918* (Originally Trinidad Publishing Company, 1940; also Karia Press, 1993). C. L. Joseph, 'The British West Indies Regiment 1914-1918', *Journal of Caribbean History*, Vol. 12, May, 1971.

and Italy. In addition, Caribbean men served in the Royal Engineers as highly skilled technicians. Upwards of 40,000 Caribbean people opted to join the various branches of the civilian war effort in the United States. 236 Caribbean volunteers were killed or reported missing during the Second World War; 265 were wounded. Caribbean air force personnel received 103 decorations.

Post World War II
At the end of World War II, people returned to the Caribbean with a complex mixture of feelings, experiences and broadened horizons. As a consequence of these lived experiences, the Caribbean now seemed dull and woefully short of opportunities. The economic situation in the Caribbean had worsened. The returnees' awareness of a wider world and richer possibilities overseas, contributed to both the post-war campaign for independence and the hope of many to try their hand in Britain, as family and friends heard of their experiences. The need for post war reconstruction led to calls for people from the Caribbean to come to Britain to fill the labour shortage, which led to that now iconic journey of the *Empire Windrush,* which arrived at Tilbury docks on the 22nd June, 1948 after picking up people around the Caribbean, although the greatest number of the 492 passengers were Jamaicans. The experience and details of this event have been well documented and do not need further elaboration.[28]

Conclusions
So what does all this add up to? Well it is clear that a whole dimension of British history has been overlooked and many pieces of local history connected with Black people have been forgotten. Contrary to popular belief there have been Black people in Britain since at least the third century; their presence here did not begin with the arrival of the *Empire Windrush*. Black people have been part of our national story throughout our history, sometimes playing major roles in cultural and social movements, but despite this presence, sometimes in large numbers, they have effectively remained invisible.

It is clear that it was not solely White Europeans and Americans who fought for abolition, as there were also many Black people who exercised their own agency in that struggle. Black people were also missionaries in Africa and there was the equivalent of a transatlantic mission of Black people *to* Britain. This research indicates that the contribution of African, African American and Caribbean people to church and society during the nineteenth century was more extensive than was previously realised. It is also significant that, although there are now a greater number of accounts of Black people and their history in these islands, the specifically Christian aspect has been largely ignored or deemphasised.

---

[28] On this period of migration from the Caribbean see: Mike Phillips and Trevor Phillips, *Windrush: The Irresistible Rise of Multi-Racial Britain* (London: Harper Collins, 1998).

How have Black people been removed or allowed to fade from the picture of our national life? How a fascinating and significant piece of history has been forgotten in less than one hundred years is not easy to explain. Their presence has been largely ignored by most historians and is only now being re-discovered. This rediscovery will ultimately enrich us all as a nation.

Reflections on the Atlanta Trip and its Legacy
Dave Ellis

From the time I was a little boy, growing up in Wolverhampton, there were two places that I never imagined I would visit in my lifetime. One was South Africa and the other was the southern States of America. Little did I know that, from 1999 onwards, God was going to bless me with both experiences. Between the 8th and 11th January, 1999 I attended an international summit of 'Baptists Against Racism,' at Ebenezer Baptist church, Atlanta Georgia. Thinking about the visit I was really excited for a number of reasons. I was going to the church of my great hero, Revd Dr Martin Luther King Jr. I was also travelling to the States for the first time and I was going with a team that I greatly respected. The team consisted of Patricia (Pat) White (Chair of BUGB Racial Justice group); Rosemarie Davidson-Gotobed (LBA Racial Justice Coordinator); the Revd Chris Andre-Watson (Minister of Brixton Baptist and member of the Racial Justice Group); Revd Fred George (Baptist Union President), Revd Anne Wilkinson-Hayes (a Baptist minister and a Bible study leader/speaker at the conference) and myself (Minister of Totterdown Baptist Church in Bristol and Chair of the Keyboard Project, a Bristol Racial Justice group).

Meeting amid the symbols of America's struggle for Civil Rights, this was an international gathering of Baptists, issuing a call for churches to combat racism and ethnic strife worldwide. The conference consisted of around 200 delegates from 30 countries. I was blessed to be attending an International summit of Baptists Against Racism sponsored by the Baptist World Alliance (BWA), a worldwide fellowship of Baptist unions and conventions based in Washington.

The summit was held at the historic Ebenezer Baptist Church, for many, the home church of the civil rights movement, the church of the towering figure that was Martin Luther King Jr. Sessions were also held at the nearby Wheat Street Baptist Church, King's alma mater Morehouse College and at the Carter Presidential Center, where participants were greeted by former President Jimmy Carter, himself a prominent and committed Baptist.

In Atlanta, our group was somewhat conspicuous because as we travelled about on the trains from our hotel to the Church, our diverse team of one White English women, two Black British women, one Sri Lankan man and two Black British men was definitely not the norm. Our group enjoyed each other's company and had very natural conversations with one another in our terribly English accents. I did not see another ethnically mixed group of people like ours talking outside the Conference in Atlanta, Montgomery or in Birmingham Alabama.

Reflections on the Atlanta Trip and its Legacy

The Conference

As I walked into Ebenezer Baptist Church and looked around the sanctuary, my eyes were drawn to the pulpit from which Dr Martin Luther King Jr. had preached. I marvelled at the kind of oratory that could challenge and change a nation and do so without the use of force. His was a revolution of love.

Some of my wide-eyed optimism was brushed away when it was pointed out to me by Baptist World Alliance conference veterans that the conclusions were probably pre-written before we had even arrived at the conference. Anything we discussed would not make an impression on the predetermined outcomes. This would only make the 'God moment' that occurred later in the conference all the more remarkable.

In a session at the Morehouse College chapel, named after her late husband, Coretta Scott King cited the global effect of her husband's legacy, noting a hundred nations that now observe the King holiday.

Coretta Scott King reminded us that churches are no longer as segregated as when her late husband declared 11 o'clock, 'the most segregated hour in America.' Coretta Scott King also noted the apology of the Southern Baptist Convention for the ways in which Baptists had supported racial discrimination, in a resolution of repentance, adopted at the convention's 1995 meeting in Atlanta.

Calling on Baptists to work for an end to violence between people of different faiths, King said, 'We have done much, and we have much more to go, but I see the dim outlines of the beloved community.' It would be our privilege to talk to Mrs Coretta Scott King and shake her hand afterwards.

In the plenary addresses, John Kinney and Douglas W. Waruta focused on the theological and socio-historical bases of racism and on healing through resources of the Holy Spirit. Calling for repentance and true progress to reconciliation, Richard Land was a welcome voice from among the Southern Baptists. Denton Lotz evoked the dream of Baptists committed to reconciliation.

Anne Wilkinson-Hayes would lead a study based around the Bible passage telling the story of the Syro-Phoenician woman in Matthew 15:21-28 and Mark 7:24-30. She spoke of how Jesus broke so many cultural rules in engaging in conversation with this woman from another ethnic background, as well as her gender. Wilkinson-Hayes shared how she had been brought up to be afraid of certain cultures in Britain, but following Christ would persuade her otherwise. Wilkinson-Hayes did the British delegation proud as her talk was well received by the packed auditorium.

The whooping and a hollering from the congregation came when Charles Smith started preaching. Smith, senior minister of Shiloh Baptist Church, Washington, D.C., and chair of the BWA special commission, described racism as 'a human scourge and pervasive evil that permeates every crack, corner and crevice of the known world.' While many governments and corporations get involved to fight racism, 'unless God's people get involved, the problem is not going away.' 'God can convert the chilliest, staunchest and deeply entrenched racist in the world, if we preach the Word of God with power,' said Charles Smith.

Cawley Bolt, and Karl Heinz Walter also provided Bible studies emphasizing gospel partnership amid diversity, the challenge of global justice, cross-bearing to change racist culture, and God's model of social integration. Other regional and special reports noted racism through Hispanic eyes (Osvaldo L. Mottesi), the struggles of indigenous peoples of Latin America (Jorge Lee Galindo), Caribbean racism (Horace O. Russell), and of course, North American racism, economics, and conflict resolution.

There were brief speeches from Jimmy Carter and Billy Graham and a statement of the Atlanta Covenant: 'A Call to Baptist Churches to oppose racism and ethnic conflict and to actively work to establish a united witness for Christ and His Kingdom.' The findings of the summit and proceedings (the belief that spreading the gospel and racial justice are inseparable), plus the venues, participants and themes, all evoked historic memory, most prominently the Ebenezer Baptist Church, which has been so much a part of the civil rights movement. The meeting represented commendable efforts to urge our churches to be inclusive bodies, to be a delight to God, and Christ-like counter-cultural examples to institutions restricted by racism.

The plenary seminars gave expression to some of the regional difficulties faced by groups from around the world. The rights of aboriginals in Australia and Native Americans as indigenous peoples were discussed. Similarly, with Hispanics in the United States, plus there was concern for refugees and migrants in the Dominican Republic and Western Europe, and inter-ethnic conflicts in Rwanda and northeast India. These and many of the challenges linked to racism were reviewed in Atlanta.

The Carter Center
The 'God moment' came when the conference took on a more prophetic edge as we met at the Carter Center. The Carter Center is a policy organization founded by Jimmy and Rosalynn Carter to fight disease, hunger, poverty, conflict, and oppression around the world. Former President, Jimmy Carter, and the great evangelist Billy Graham gave keynote speeches and an address was also given by the Revd C T Vivian.

In the sessions at the Carter Center, Billy Graham reminded us that 'Racism is a dirty word'. He referred to it as a 'deadly poison.' Former President Carter said the dreams of ending racial discrimination 'have not been materialized. There have been legal changes, but too much separation of race and no adequate compensation for years of slavery.' Carter was the honorary chairman of the BWA's Special Commission on Baptists Against Racism.

Describing the Christian church as 'the last rampart of racism,' Carter blamed the continuing racial segregation at the 11 o'clock hour in the United States on the tendency of people to build small communities 'and encapsulate ourselves with people like us, and this puts no burden of Christian action on us.' He called for churches to 'reach out to a neighbouring church that has a different racial and ethnic composition' as a beginning but important step toward better race relations.

Reflections on the Atlanta Trip and its Legacy

To the BWA, Carter said, '...I am pleased that the international community of Baptists has taken such a strong stand against racism. Our Saviour Jesus Christ has called us as one people to be equal before God with no room for racial discrimination or prejudice.'

Revd C.T. Vivian's speech at the Carter Center started off in the most provocative of ways. He said 'I have been involved in the Civil Rights movement a long time, I am just sick and tired of looking at your ugly faces.......The Southern Baptist convention is racist.' When one of the delegates stood up and said 'I have been a Southern Baptist all of my life and I am not a racist', he said 'woman, you are an exception to the rule.'

C.T. Vivian, a civil rights veteran who chairs the 'Center for Democratic Renewal' in Atlanta, also voiced hope in God's power to change people during his address, but said it will not be easy. 'If you're Black in the United States, you become a Christian in spite of Christianity, not because of it,' said Vivian, a former Nashville, Tenn. pastor. Even today, Vivian said, churches have 'never dealt with the depth of (the) sin' of racism. After sending missionaries to Africa for centuries, European and American Christians need to receive Black missionaries to 'help them face their most atrocious sin,' he said. Racism is the greatest barrier to missions in a world that is three-fourths 'dark to black,' Vivian said, identifying the 'symbol of the white Jesus' as both a symptom and cause of racism. Noting that Jesus was from the Middle East and undoubtedly had dark skin, he observed: 'We're so racist we can't even tell the truth about God. We have to make him white to even live with him. Why can't the church stand to have God as anything else than white?'

Vivian said while seeing Jesus as a person of colour would mean a lot to Black people, it raises a serious question: 'Could White people remain Christian if they had to bow down to a Black Jesus?' 'Why are we still dealing with a 16th-century problem at the end of the 20th century?' Vivian asked. 'We have not gotten rid of racism within the church and without the culture that surrounds the church. Those who want to help find there is no place to go.'

Chiding the Christian church and Baptists for the continuing problem of racism, Vivian said, 'Racism destroys more people in more places of the world than any other single factor. ... No person of colour under racism will ever know what they might have been, done or become for themselves, their family or their people. We have no values that are not daily being compromised by racism.'

Vivian described racism as 'the greatest barrier' to winning most of the world to Christ. He called for Black missionaries to come to Euro-American countries 'to save them from their most atrocious sins' and praised Billy Graham for making this evident in his worldwide evangelistic efforts. Vivian continued by stating 'The black church is now in control of itself, and this was given because we are Baptists. Without this, we never would have this great drive for peace and justice.'

Vivian offered several practical ways Baptists can fight racism and called for, among other things, 'a racist-free Baptist church.' He called on theologians 'to make powerful statements around the world' against racism and for every Christian teacher educated in a Baptist school to have a course in anti-racist education. 'Our work can save us all, if we choose to do it,' Vivian said.

The Prophetic
The prophetic part of the conference came when BWA chairman Denton Lotz, moved by C. T. Vivian's speech, apologised to the British delegates for a comment he had made earlier in the week and he asked the delegates for their forgiveness. Then the conference got down to the real business of constructing the Atlanta Covenant that had been worked on by all the delegates of the 30 nations represented at the summit. Whatever had been rumoured to be pre-written was disregarded as the delegates drafted and affirmed a lengthy statement. The Covenant declared a 'decade to promote racial justice' beginning in 2000 and urging BWA member unions to promote efforts to eradicate racism and fight against ethnic conflict worldwide.

The covenant notes that while Baptists have 'a rich heritage of commitment to international mission' and have made significant contributions in areas of health care, education and church planting, 'racism has tainted these efforts.' The Covenant urged Baptists to be 'agents of reconciliation.' The Covenant urged Baptists to examine ways in which their 'evangelism, Christian education and economic structures perpetuate racism, and work aggressively for change.' The challenge was to create 'a renewal of worship and cleansing from racial sin' in Baptist churches 'and a commitment to holistic and interracial mission and evangelism.'

Additional goals were 'to work for the elimination of unfair trade and [for] a just world economy, the protection of the rights of aboriginal and tribal peoples and to study the affirmation of the relationship between gospel and culture.' There was a call for integration 'in churches, especially in North America and Europe, where worship is largely still segregated.'

The Covenant committed Baptist churches to 'racial justice as an integral part of proclaiming Good News; [to] promote economic development as a way forward to racial justice; use multi-racial images and idioms in worship; and develop church educational programs that promote a Christian lifestyle that demonstrates justice and racial harmony.'

The Visits
We visited a number of significant places concerning America's struggle for racial justice. One of the standout visits was to The Martin Luther King Jr. Center in Atlanta. The centre included a museum dedicated to preserving the memory of Dr King Jr., which had many artefacts from his life. We saw the letters, sermons, speeches, commendations, Nobel peace prize, gifts from different nations, suits and ministerial clothing, all associated with Dr King. There was a section of the museum dedicated to Mahatma Gandhi who

inspired Dr King with his peaceful protest against the British Empire in India. It was a very awe-inspiring place.

We went on a trip to Alabama and visited Martin Luther King Jr.'s first church, called Dexter Road Baptist Church in Montgomery, Alabama, where he began to put his ideas of civil rights action into practice. This coincided with Rosa Parkes' refusal to move from her seat for a White person on a bus in 1955. The rest, as they say, is history.

Following this visit we went into Birmingham, Alabama, to the 16th Street Baptist Church where a bombing took place that killed four little African American girls in Sunday school on 15th September 1963. One of the memorials in the church is a stained glass window designed by artist John Petts. It depicts a Black Christ with his arms outstretched, his right arm pushing away hatred and injustice and his left arm extended in an offering of forgiveness.[1]

When we left the church we went across the road to the Birmingham Civil Rights Institute, a large interpretive museum and research centre. Using multi-media and historical artefacts, the museum depicts the struggles of the civil rights movement in the 1950s and 60s.

As we sat in the museum's gallery, a film was played about the experiences of Black people during the process in which slavery was being abolished in the United States, from 1863 onwards. In the period, a few concessions were shown towards equality for the African American slaves after the 'Emancipation Proclamation,' but then, little by little, segregation came in the South and completely took away those rights.

As we went through the museum, I could not reconcile the impact of seeing the actual bars of the prison cell of the Birmingham jail where Martin Luther King was imprisoned. Next to it, in life-size projection, they played the 'I have a dream' speech – I watched it four times and was moved by the whole mesmerising impact of the speech. It was a tremendously humbling experience to be there; we all received a greater appreciation of the struggle of oppressed Black people in the deep south of America.

Preaching at Peachtree Baptist Church
Throughout the Conference we had heard the repeated claim that the biggest form of racism seen in America is in the segregation in Churches on a Sunday morning when people go to their own churches and do not really mix. I preached in a mixed church on the Sunday, at Peachtree Baptist Church, a fairly rich church in the Atlanta suburbs. I was told that from a membership of 125 people, the annual offering was over $1 million. I was then surprised when I saw an old Black man polishing the brass on the front doors, while a rich White older lady in a fox fur scarf (which still had the fox's head on it) walked into the church and said good morning to me. It set off my prejudices; for in my head I was thinking I was back in 'Gone with the Wind' territory. This

---

[1] The murderers of the four girls were not convicted until 2001.

thought was further confirmed when the Pastor told me that if I had tried to enter that church 40 years ago as a Black man, they would have hung me in the porch and said they had done a good days work for the Lord!

Fortunately, the Pastor told me about the current vision of the church. He said they had a sister church down the road, which folded because it did not want to embrace the whole community. At Peachtree Baptist they were determined that this would not be their fate. Their change in outlook and vision was to make themselves more inclusive in ethnic and cultural terms. To this end they had employed their Senior Pastor from Miami, alongside a Black female associate minister, who was a former lawyer from New York. Her husband was a federal judge, which is one rung below a Supreme Court Judge. The leadership of this church was overseen by intellectually powerful and committed people.

When I looked at the ethnic composition of the people in the service, it reflected a very diverse community of youngsters and adults. After the service the Pastor asked me to wait in order to meet the Church that used their building in the afternoon. This turned out to be a Hispanic Church with about 50 members, which had planted over a dozen churches in Central and South America. It was wonderful to meet both congregations that day.

As a postscript to that visit, when I came back to the conference I saw one of the Black pastors crying. I asked him what was troubling him and he said in another part of downtown Atlanta, for the first time in his Church's 120 year history, they had a White preacher and he, as the Pastor, was being heavily criticized by a section of his church for breaking this sequence in the life of this congregation. He found this very hard to swallow, as what should have been a day of rejoicing, would be reduced to an issue of colour. It reminded me that there are two sides of the community with their own prejudices that need to be broken, healed and reconciled as the body of Christ.

Conclusion

The BWA produced a book reflecting on what was achieved in the 10 years following the conference. When we finished the 1999 Baptists Against Racism conference and linked hands with the 200 delegates from 30 countries singing the great Civil Rights song 'We shall overcome one day' I, in my heart, truly believed there had been a shift, and dared to dream that a new brighter and better day was coming. I continue to pray that this dream will one day be realised.

25th Anniversary Ordination
Johnathan Hemmings

This sermon was preached on the 26th October, 2014, at Perry Rise Baptist Church, London.
Text: St Matthew 16: 13-17

Introduction
The people of God are a people of God's own choosing and a people of God's own making for God's own purpose. They are, therefore, the outworking of God's grace. This is how the Church has understood itself over time. Jesus declared 'you did not choose me, but I chose you and appointed you to go and bear fruit' (John 15:16).

The writer of Ephesians recites, 'For it is by grace that you have been saved through faith. It is the gift of God. Not of works that is of our own doing.' 'We are God's workmanship created in Christ Jesus for good works which God prepared in advance for us to do' (Eph. 2:8-10).

The people of God are entirely and absolutely a people of God's own choosing and of God's own making for God's own purpose. The purpose is to bear witness to God in the world. It is to represent God in and to the world. 'You are a chosen people, a royal priesthood, a holy nation belonging to God, that you may declare the praises of him who called you out of darkness into his marvellous light' (1st Peter 2:9). We are a people of God's own choosing, of God's own making, for God's own purpose. This is where the story of Israel is represented by our Old Testament reading (Genesis 35: 1-15) as it intersects with the New Testament reading.

Both speak of a people chosen by God, being formed and shaped by God, for God's own purpose, to bear witness to God in the world. This is where the Baptists of Great Britain and Baptists in Jamaica find their stories intertwined with each other.

They both are stories of peoples of God, who are entirely the work of God's grace, called to fulfil God's purpose of bearing witness to the love and kindness and goodness of God in and to the world.

It is in this context and against this backdrop that I invite us to understand our text for today. It was for the purpose, the ministry of making God known, that Jesus chose and prepared his disciples. It is as part of this process of preparing them, shaping them for the task of being God's witnesses in the world that he asked them two questions. Two critical questions! The whole scene feels like an examination room, as Jesus sought to see what they had learned from being with Him, from being taught by Him. How were they being shaped?

The two questions asked:

- Who do men say that the Son of Man is?
- What about you? Who do you say that I am?

Put another way:
- What are men saying about me?
- What do you know about me?

I suggest that these are the questions that need to be answered by the people of God in every generation, those called by God and being shaped by God to bear witness to God in their space and time. They need to be answered by the church today, called to bear witness to the God revealed in Jesus Christ by the power of His Spirit, in this post-Christendom, postmodernist age. What are postmodernists saying about this God and what does the post-Christendom Church know and say about this God? This needs to be answered by every one of us who claims to be numbered among the people of God. Those who are of God's choosing, and God's making for God's purpose. It is critical for us to ask ourselves these questions because they really reflect two possible ways by which we may represent God in the world. What are those ways?

1. We can represent God based on what others say, or
2. We can represent God based on what we *know*

If I were to name these two ways, I would name one *ideology* and the other *theology*.

We may represent God, bear witness to God either by embracing ideology, that is, what people are saying about God, or by doing theology, that is, discerning what God has to say about God's self, and believe me, there is a world of difference between the gods of ideology and the God of theology. They are not the same. Can I just spell out why it is so important for us to make the distinctions?

1. People have always had much to say about God, based simply on their ideas about God. Persons who don't know God but have a lot to say about God, they are ideologues. I am sure we can all see how dangerous it is when our knowledge of God is based solely on human ideas about God. The danger in this is that our god might be nothing more than the figment of people's imagination. The world is never short on ideas about God. The Church must always guard against being guided by ideology and not by theology.

The truth is that the witness of the Church has, over time, been seriously compromised by ideologies that we have allowed to supplant theology, guided by ideas about God, rather than knowledge of God. The problem with human ideas is that they have and will always be conditioned by time, and space, by culture and tradition and special interest. Human ideologies are not free from political, social, ethnic and economic considerations and interests. The god who is as a result of human ideas, is a god of our own making, a god who can fit into our own social, political and economic systems and arrangements, a god who will legitimise our culture of greed and pride, a god who makes us comfortable with systems and institutions that are often diabolic and iniquitous. It was ideology that that led the church to embrace slavery and to be complicit in the holocaust. Caesarea Philippi was known for its idols, the god of human makings. Jesus chose this scene to do his examination maybe so that his disciples could see that the ideas people had about him were among the idols, which they had to dispense with, and put away. It was that which Jacob demanded of his household as he sought to respond to God's calling and choosing to become the people of God (Genesis 35:2).

To represent God by the ideological constructs of human beings is its own form of idolatry. Israel knew and the Church has known the temptations to create our own gods who will bless and legitimise our prejudices and our intolerance, and our acts of injustice and pride. Gods to sympathise with our political and economic arrangements even when they do not reflect the values of God's Kingdom.

It is not difficult to know when we are serving the gods of ideology. The gods of ideology make strangers and enemies of the other. This god always divides and excludes. This god of ideology is to be found wherever you find racism, sexism, and classism. It is these gods that make an issue of our cultural and ethnic differences. Some religious differences of this longstanding ideological divide still remain in the church but they are joined by new ones. Ideologies developed to reinforce our preferred positions. So these days the church is divided along the lines of evangelicals and liberals, conservatives and fundamentalists. Are not these labels developed among ideological lines to stigmatise others? Ideological labels to exclude and divide and diminish the other. Ideological labels may be good to make some groups marketable but they do not represent the Kingdom.

2. We ought to represent God based on what we know about God, hence the importance of the second question - *Who do you say that I am?* It is not based solely on human idea but rather on God's own revelation of God's self to us –'Flesh and blood did not reveal this to you'. This *is* where the theology begins. Experiential knowledge is basic and fundamental to the doing of theology. If this text does nothing else it should underline how absolutely important it is for the Church, the people of God, to do theology. It is to engage in rigorous reflection on the ways in which God chooses to make God's self known to us.

Our principal source is the 'Word of God'. We must spend time reflecting on the 'Word of God'. One of my concerns about the church in our time is the ways in which the 'Word of God' is being marginalised in the life and worship of the Church. So often when we consider worship is running too long it is more often than not the sermon that is in need of cutting. Much of the singing, which seems to be the central feature of our worship, is with songs that replace the hymns that embodied the theology of the Church. Many of the songs of today are designed to make us feel good about ourselves.

When we alienate the Word we alienate God, because we don't encounter God making God's self known to us. We must not underestimate the difficulty there is in doing theology amidst the preponderance of ideologies that exist about God. The Church must always be mindful of the propensity to fall back into idolatry of ideology, even when God reveals God's self to us. Is this not what Peter's upbraiding of Jesus represents? A slipping back to ideology by refusing to accept what God had further to say about God's self, refusing a knowledge of God that was demanding.

The ideologies of this world are seductive. Cheap grace, they call you to model a Christ, to represent God without any sacrifice, without any suffering. No need to love, or forgive. It is only a serious doing of theology that will guard against the Church lapsing back into the ideological representations of God that compromises its witness. Theology, then, is not this private preserve of the experts, but is grounded in our shared experiences of God. It is for the doing of theology why we should not forsake the assembling of ourselves together.

We need to spend time reflecting on the ways in which God reveals God's self to us in ways that defy our expectations and presuppositions of God, rejecting many of our ideas that too often are conditioned by cultures and are reflective of our interests and biases, our preferences and prejudices. Theology must involve the sharing of experiences because no one experience fully represents who God is. It should, therefore, be an ecumenical enterprise in just about every sense of the word. When we try to confine God to ours only, we are being ideological and not theological – reflecting the closedness of ideology and not the openness of theology. If we are going to seriously engage this process we need to throw away the gods we have been carrying.

How are we, who are God's people, by God's own choosing and God's own making for God's own purposes, representing God in this postmodern, post-Christendom world? How are we bearing witness in the places where we work and worship, where we live and play?

We must be absolutely careful that we do not represent the gods of our own choosing, of our own making, for our own purposes. Rather, let us through the rigorous doing of theology, strive to better discern so that we may more faithfully bear witness to the God made known in Jesus Christ, by the power of the Spirit.

What do men say about me? What do you know about me? Amen.

Part Two: The Apology

In Search of Freedom
Karl E. Henlin

Sermon preached on the occasion of the Joint Baptist Assembly, at the Brighton Centre, Brighton, England, the 4th – 7th May 2007

Introduction
Your theme *'in search of freedom'* is salutary, not only because of its obvious relationship with the 200th celebration of the ending of the trade in slaves, but more so, because it speaks to the ultimate quest of human beings in every generation, namely, *'freedom'*.

The theme speaks about a search, and for me, that in itself is an admission that real freedom is always an unfinished project and thus represents something of an elusive target. Real freedom in all of its definitions is always being realized, and our task is this, to be always engaged in programs and practices that will aid in the actualization of freedom, in our time. *In search of freedom* is an invitation never to rest on our laurels and never to become complacent. It is an invitation and a challenge, never to be found congratulating ourselves, but instead to make every commitment to be used as an agent of real freedom in the world. The theme is to be saluted because it accepts that freedom is a work in progress, for there is always something else to be done, something more to be accomplished and something other for us to experience.

We who gather in this session today have been invited on a journey that has rehearsed the roles played by protestant missionaries, and particularly Baptist missionaries, in ensuring that not only did the trade cease but also that slavery as an economic system was also to be abolished. I join in giving God thanks too for men such as William Wilberforce but also for the resistant movements led by men such as Sam Sharpe and Cudjoe, and with them, countless numbers of slaves who refused to accept that this was their given lot in life.

TEXT – St. Luke 4:18-19
So we come to the passage that forms the basis of this presentation today. We are being invited by this text into a service already begun, and Jesus, the home town boy, has been invited to read the scriptures. Is he given a pre-chosen passage or is he free to choose? Whatever it is, he is loudly applauded for his eloquence because the words have been pronounced with beauty and meaning.

> The Spirit of the Lord is on me, because he has anointed me to preach

good news to the poor. He has sent me to proclaim freedom for the
prisoners and recovery of sight for the blind, to release the oppressed,
to proclaim the year of the Lord's favour.

But alas, the moment that begun in tranquillity is about to be transformed into chaos, for the previously celebrated reader is eventually hounded out, chased down and driven to the woodlands by a once worshipping congregation now transformed into a murdering mob. What has happened here? Jesus has dared to interpret the scriptures he has read. 'Today this scripture is being fulfilled in your hearing'.

In a real sense these are the words with which Jesus launches his career and they are set to become a kind of mission statement. The words taken from the prophet Isaiah speak about God's agenda in God's world and they speak of the ways in which Jesus imagines and envisions his life's work. It is clear that Jesus intends that by his life's mission, those against whom the world's forces are set and those who are the least and the disadvantaged are to expect drastic change and reversal of their conditions of and status in life. This theme of freedom was to become the sole driving force of the mission of Jesus because Jesus knew what we also know, that in life there are forces at work that seem always to be compelling us to suppress and to oppress others and too that there are forces at work that seem always to suppress and oppress us.

The freedom, of which we speak, then, is more than a freedom from, though it is that also, but it is freedom to become. It is a freedom to live life according to the purposes of God, for that is true life. So Jesus says 'I am come that they might have life and have it more abundantly' (St. John 10:10). Such a life I dare to say is life conscious of God's purpose, life lived in obedience to God, patterned after the life of Jesus and lived in the power of the Spirit. In a real sense that is freedom! It is living in the purposes of God, obedient to the Father, in the likeness of the Son and by the enabling of the Holy Spirit. The passage inspires three questions that will aid us in our search for freedom.

1. What is Jesus saying?

There really could have been no more appropriate text for us gathered over these days contemplating the theme *'in search of freedom'* and all the time understanding that there is an urgent warrant laid upon our lives as Disciples of Christ. What is Jesus saying? We know that Jesus lived at a time when the Roman superpower occupied Palestine, and also at a time of social desolation in Palestine.

What this meant to the life of the ordinary peasant Jew was economic hardship and instability. When you combine a lack of agricultural land proportionate to the population, with natural catastrophes and competing tax systems, what emerges is the preponderance of a new poor who were often emigrants, bandits, revolutionaries and beggars. These are the people who figure prominently in the life of Jesus as presented in the gospels, the socially insignificant, the poor and the hungry, the diseased, the disabled and the outcasts.

We are privileged today to be able to look back at the life of Jesus and what do we see? We are confronted by a man who is moved by his social location and is never satisfied to ignore the social realities of the oppressed but who actively engages their cause as his own. So what is Jesus saying except this?

Jesus speaks about the year of Jubilee....to preach the acceptable year of the Lord. What's Jubilee all about? We know it, do we not? Leviticus 25:1-24 provides the answer and perhaps we will now understand the tumult in the synagogue. A jubilee year is a sabbatical year on a grand scale and then we learn this:
- The soil is to be rested
- Debts are to be cancelled
- Slaves are to be freed
- Capital is to be redistributed

It is a program that envisions radical social change, a kind of levelling of the playing field. It is a program that has social equality as its aim; a kind of equality that is bent on preserving human dignity, community and solidarity. No wonder Jesus had to run for his life!

It would soon become obvious that Jesus intervened in every reality that robbed people of their dignity and removed them from experiencing community, by restoring them into experiences of solidarity. It was a ministry of reversal. What Jesus was saying is that there can be no authentic ministry and mission, no missionary engagement and search for freedom that does not seek actively to engage the oppressive contexts in which God's children live and exist. His was a ministry of compassion to the most vulnerable and any mission and any ministry which ignores this or else merely spiritualizes them, is a mission largely based on human preferences and a blinkered vision of God.

2. What are we hearing

But what are we hearing as Jesus speaks? Our hearing is largely affected by our own social and theological location. As Jesus read the scriptures, the gathered community heard wonderful congratulatory words. They were nice sounding words; the kind of words that make for great sound bites. But they are words rife for misinterpretation and Jesus used the opportunity to interpret. The congregation is aghast! And why? Because they were hearing words set to disturb their world and their world view. Jewish people gathered are hearing about God's intention for outsiders and they are hearing of God's activity in the circumstances of those whom they least expected. *They are hearing about God's grand action of reversal!*

Some of us are aware that debates rage about whether or not Jubilee was ever actually realized? We need not be detained today by this diversionary tactic except to say that even if it has never happened, what Jesus speaks about comes to us as a standard after which we must strive, a goal towards which we must journey, and an ideal for which we must dream and work. These are not idle words but instead are words set in motion by the ministry of Christ.

Christians in every generation must strive and search for the kingdom values and motifs to become real in our time. What are we hearing in a world sold out on individualism? We hear a word in this that speaks to the personal relationship that people can and ought to have in Christ and yes that is a kind of real freedom. In a world in which people are enslaved to their passions, their desires and their habits, Jesus does offer the kind of freedom that creates a new person in Christ. But there can be no avoiding the reality that Jesus uses the Jubilee motif that is radical and revolutionary. It speaks about *renunciation, restoration and redistribution.*

What do we hear when Jesus speaks words like this today in the 21st century, when we are gathering to commemorate the ending of an evil program that brought disruption and separation and also loss of selfhood to millions of people? What do we hear and what did the slaves hear? There was the attempt, and this by some who were missionaries, to have the slaves interpret these words as that which promised a better life in heaven up above. It was the desire of the masters that slaves attend religious instruction with the hope that it would make them more docile and obedient.

Sadly, wherever freedom texts were read, some missionaries under instruction, would invite the slaves to spiritualize these texts and thus to define freedom merely as a freedom in Christ from personal sin or else even to assign these texts as ones that were only applicable to European people. It was true that like as for Jesus, whenever slaves dared to interpret these texts in ways contrary to their masters' will, they too would be taken to the hill and there was no escaping death. *But they were in search of freedom!*

Refusing to accept slavery as God's purpose for their lives, they heard the scriptures pointed at their own space and location, and thus reconfigured the faith once offered to them. Illiterate, impoverished and disempowered, still they understood that God was at work in their spaces, and thus these slaves discerned by the aiding of the Spirit of God, a freedom motif. *The faith presented to them as a tool of bondage became an instrument of freedom.* Perhaps instead of hearing *'obey your masters'* they heard *'obey your maker!'*

God was at work, however, not only among those who lived as slaves on the plantations, but also here in England. William Wilberforce made it his life's work to lobby Parliament to bring an end to the trade in slaves until that act was passed. No doubt, inspired by his own faith convictions, he too heard in the words of Jesus a summons to action. Despite his own health challenges, men like our own Hon. William Knibb and James Phillippo, took on this evil monster and through God won freedom for God's children.

The architects of the plantation system heard these same words but missed their meaning because it was a word inviting them to look beyond their narrow self interests and to see God disturbing and disrupting any agenda of human beings that has oppression of others at its heart. For the truth is we all seek to hear God speaking to us in words suited for our comfort, words defending our long held positions, comfortable words, congratulatory words. But not so! And they drove Jesus from their midst!

What are we hearing? We who have gathered are God's people who have one single and ultimate agenda and motive. We listen to a calling way beyond our nationalities and our ethnicity. We serve a higher calling that evades the boundaries of social class, race, colour and achievement. We are God's people! Thus today, we are called to hear God offering to us a new agenda for our mission in the world. We must seek to hear words that will disturb the status quo and disrupt our agenda, words that threaten existing arrangements and words that beckon us to risk all and anything, to be found as obedient and faithful servants. In truth, we must become willing to be unacceptable and unpopular prophets, even in our own country, whether in Jamaica, in Asia, in the Caribbean, in North America or here in England.

3. What shall we do?

The truth is that the trade in slaves and then slavery itself would come to an end only because there was collaboration between the abolitionists and the slaves; I mean collaboration between those on this side and those on the other side. What ought we to be doing? There are some things that we need to *affirm, to agree and to act upon:*

We need to affirm that:
- Human oppression is not something about which Jesus is indifferent. The abuse of power which makes victims of people is not something about which Jesus makes innocuous remarks and platitudinous statements. Rather, he has come to challenge and overthrow the citadel of power that is used to oppress. His death on the cross is a challenge to the structures of power.
- Real freedom requires accepting the humanity of all people and involves a commitment to create wholesome community through a diverse humanity.
- Freedom is divinely inspired, not humanly generated, and thus we are called to reject all prejudices that belittle and demean human potential

We need to agree that:
The end of the Middle Passage was not the end of evil and wrong, and the end of slavery is not the end of evil and wrong, in this world. The evidences abound in our world, whether child slavery, human trafficking and bonded labour are but a few of the examples one could cite. There are matters arising still be to addressed by the world church community, but perhaps specially by us Baptists, who theologically place such high values on freedom.

We have got to partner together with our brothers and sisters across the world where young children are being forced to work against their will in factories and industries. We have got to ask questions about the conditions of work that are producing the goods and services we readily and all too easily consume. Transatlantic slavery gave to Europe an economic advantage based upon un-free labour and has provided the bedrock of the economies of this and other regions. Such an ambition remains an enviable quest for still too many in this liberalized economy.

With some regret I have to say that even in the Caribbean this legacy remains. The descendants of slavery have in some senses turned in upon each other and our murder rates are increasingly aided and abetted by the ease with which guns and ammunition are smuggled from nations far away onto our shores. Plus, in the process, they are making our island homes places from which so many are seeking to leave.

There is a constant brain drain of our human resources as some of our professionals are being enticed to serve in lands far away from home, while the dictates of a world market stifle our agricultural industries. In the process nations such as the one from which I have come, are being mired in debt, the kinds from which there seems to be no end in sight.

Surely, a Europe now de-Christianized, and a Caribbean so economically challenged and vulnerable to the shocks of globalization, together stand in need of freedom.

We need to act:
There is a call, then, to the search for ways that bring this freedom into the lives and contexts of all God's people. This is no time for sweet sounding rhetoric, the kinds that congregations and assemblies applaud. It is a time for radical decisions and a time for radical action.

I am aware of the movement *Set All Free*[1] established by the churches together in England to commemorate the ending of the transatlantic slave trade. This is commendable and deserves the full support of any community meeting under the banner of Christ. Their recommendations are laudable. To these I add the following and this because the abolition of the trade and slavery has not since taken into account the primary victims of this monstrous wrong.

Apology:
The freedom of which we speak, and for which we still search, is a freedom with which, both the descendants of former slave owners and of former slaves must reckon. For it is true that in slavery both the slaves and the masters were in bondage, living in ways outside of the purpose of God. Thus I make this call, that:
- A full apology is offered for what really has been a most monstrous action. The apology is necessary in order that the forgiveness that is on offer can be appropriated, the healing made complete, and the

---

[1] 'Set all free' was an ecumenical project of 'Churches Together in England'. The project sought to challenge the churches in England to action in both commemorating the Transatlantic slave trade and ending modern forms of slavery. The project ran from 2005-2008. Details of the work of 'Set all free' can be found in Richard S. Reddie *Abolition: The Struggle to Abolish Slavery in the British Empire* (Oxford: Lion, 2007)

chapter closed. This has been raised before by us, with your leaders, but perhaps the time has come to reconsider this matter again?

Compensation:
- Compensation of a kind to show real remorse is necessary as the fruit of repentance to show how completely they have repudiated the monstrosity of slavery and its ill-gotten gain. It would be a great symbol to reveal a sincere reality. In this regard the subject of debt relief for debt ridden two thirds world nations must remain a subject on the agenda of the developed world.

All this is not to perpetuate the sense of victimhood among people of African descent or to make ourselves the 'White man's burden' or else to give legitimacy to the notion of the African who always needs the help of the White people. It is to challenge that legacy and to close that chapter once and for all. Without it, chattel slavery and the slave trade that supported it, remains an open sore.

Conclusion
So how is all this to be done? It is all possible when a community of the Spirit becomes open to the new things that God's Spirit brings; for Jesus did say 'the Spirit of the Lord is upon me.' To root out evil cannot end with fixing the circumstances created by evil or ending the captivity with which people are captured. There is a deeper, more inner struggle, which is required as well, one which involves the deep recesses of our inner being, the centres of consciousness and motivation. It is a deeply spiritual battle. And that freedom for which we all long is a possibility, for where the Spirit of the Lord is, there is liberty!

Legacies of the Transatlantic Slave Trade[1]
David Shosanya

Introduction
The November 2007 BUGB Council meeting was going to be different: I anticipated it being more like a Baptist equivalent of the 1974 Muhammad Ali vs George Foreman 'Rumble in the Jungle'[2] than a series of polite exchanges. The single agenda item was an extended discussion on whether or not the Baptist Union should issue an apology for The Transatlantic Slave Trade (hereafter referred to as The MAAFA, the Black holocaust). This Council meeting was the culmination of a public request made by The Revd Karl Henlin,[3] a number of representations by UK based Black Baptists, private conversations between BUGB and BMS World Mission and dialogue in public forums about what has since become known as the 'Apology'. There was no appetite for a rematch – in boxing parlance, only a clean knockout by either side would settle the matter!

Blame, Shame and Consequence
The journey to the council meeting began as it always did: a short bus journey to the underground station, a tube to King's Cross St Pancras, then the train to Derby station, a ten minute walk from the station to the bus stop and a 45 minute bus ride to the Hayes Conference Centre, in Swanwick; a total journey time of about three and half hours. Before I knew it, it was time to give my presentation on the legacies of The MAAFA.

As I stood in front of council I became aware of an unexpected - and in all honesty unwanted - softness of heart that temporarily disarmed me. In retrospect I am convinced that the Holy Spirit gently, but firmly, restrained my

---

[1] Many African thinkers have renamed the Transatlantic Slave Trade 'The MAAFA', Africa Holocaust, arguing that its impact is at least equal to if not greater than the Jewish Holocaust. The spirit of the renaming is not to draw comparisons between the two unspeakable evils of the mass extermination of human beings. Rather, it is an attempt to create awareness about the extreme scale and significance of the MAAFA in cultures that seek to minimize its impact while at the same time advocating for a serious recognition for The Jewish Holocaust.

[2] The 'Rumble in the Jungle' was a legendary heavyweight boxing title fight between Muhammad Ali and George Foreman, in Kinshasa, Zaire (now the Democratic Republic of the Congo), in 1974. Further details on this legendary fight can be found in the following link: https://en.wikipedia.org/wiki/The_Rumble_in_the_Jungle

[3] The Revd Karl Henlin was the then President of the Jamaica Baptist Union, who was a guest speaker at the BU Assembly in Brighton, in 2007. His address has been reproduced in this book.

natural instinct and predisposition to fight and made me aware of what was on God's heart. It changed my approach!

Without thinking I found myself saying to Council that the aim of my presentation was not to focus on blame but to explore the consequences and the legacies of the MAAFA. In fact, in my mind it was all about blame! There is a general consensus that something that could not be accounted for by human skilfulness transpired at that moment. Many individuals, with whom I have spoken, presenters and listeners alike, are of the view that those unplanned words ushered in a spirit of grace into what was, to all intents and purposes, a highly charged environment and a deeply contested space.

Shame, Withdrawal and Isolation
I have given some thought to what may have happened and the following diagram has been helpful in shaping my understanding. However, before discussing the diagram I want to draw attention to the work of Dr. Brenee Brown, an American social scientist and researcher.

Brenee Brown has spent years exploring the impact of shame on individuals. In March 2012 she delivered a TED Talk,[4] which is one of the most watched in the history of the event. Much of Brown's findings from her initial research are documented in a best-selling book, *Daring Greatly*[5], in which she speaks about the common experiences of shame as human beings. Her research shows that our discomfort with feelings of shame means we seek to repress them. This leads to 'comparison', 'withdrawal' and ultimately 'isolation'[6].

Reframing Shame
In retrospect, I have concluded that the room was split along the fault line of shame: historic shame (national history), institutional shame (corporate consciousness with corresponding bad practices) and personal shame (individual acts of racism). The individuals that supported the request for an apology for the MAAFA located themselves within the presently unfolding history of a nation whose backward historical trajectory included acts of gross inhumanity carried out against the 'Other' in the name of civilisation and Christianity. They recognised that the history of a nation must be owned by its citizens in its entirety and that a selective appropriation or re-writing of history - only owning the positive aspects of a nation's history - was duplicitous and unsustainable.

Conversely, those individuals that were of the mind that the distance between what took place hundreds of years ago and what was happening in

---

[4] TED talks: Technology, Education & Design, are gatherings bringing together the most progressive thinkers in the world around a particular theme for presentations and conversations to be made and facilitated by experts.
[5] See Brenee Brown, *Daring Greatly: How the Courage to Be Vulnerable Transforms the Way We Live, Love, Parent, and Lead* (London: Penguin Way, 2015)
[6] Brenee Brown, p. 29

contemporary society were to be separated with respect to how one assumed - if one assumed at all - any level of responsibility could or would not allow themselves to see the correlation between the two. It was imperative that we shift the focus from apportioning and inducing blame, which leads to accompanying feelings of shame. Rather, we required a new dynamic that would create the psychological, emotional and spiritual space to explore an emotive and explosive topic more objectively.

As indicated earlier the following diagram, 'Pathways of Guilt & Shame'[7] has helped me to understand what might have taken place when a 'blame' paradigm replaced a 'consequence' one. What I believed transpired is that my White sisters and brothers[8] allowed themselves to recognise and embrace the transgression. However, rather than adopting a defensive disposition and becoming consumed with feelings of shame resulting in either 'rumination', or 'misattribution', they allowed feelings of guilt to surface and were able to confront them. This enabled them to accept that their own 'moral standards had been violated' and subsequently allowed for a sense of 'personal responsibility'. This led to remorse (apology) and ultimately to reconciliation.

The cycle, in order to be redemptive and for each constituency to rediscover faith in the other, will inevitably need to be repeated again and again until full and complete reconciliation is achieved: 'forbearance and apology' are relatively easy in comparison to 'reparations'!

---

[7] www.emotionalcompetency.co/shame.htm

[8] As an individual that has been subjected to the interrogative obsessiveness of others I am reticent to speak on behalf of my White sisters and brothers. All I can do is to offer a personal - but by no means full perspective - on what transpired. This is not an apology for 'interpreting Whiteness' in the context of a inter-cultural dialogue, but a recognition that being investigated, interpreted and 'spoken for' is equally as uncomfortable for White individuals as it is for Black people.

Legacies of the Transatlantic Slave Trade

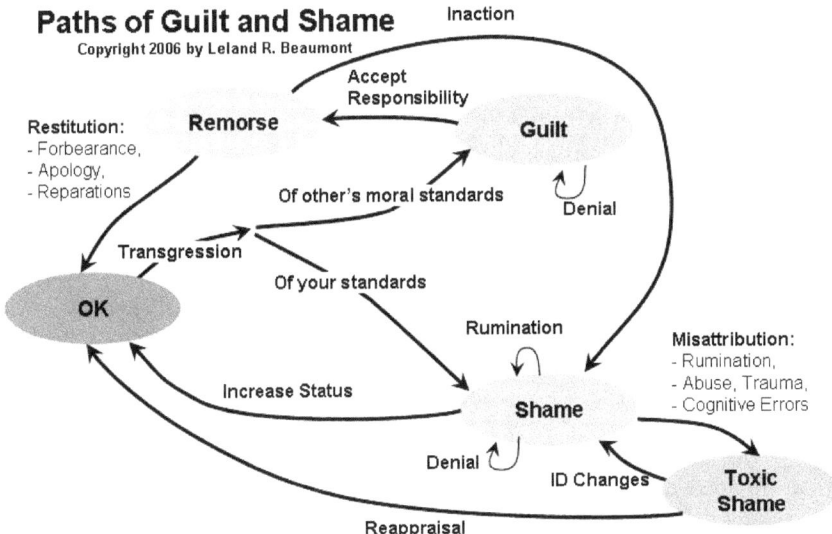

A conceptual hook

In seeking to explore the misguided view American society has of African American males, John O Calmore appropriated the conceptual imagery of a legal case, 'City of Memphis v. Greene', to which reference was made in the Supreme Court. The case centred on a road closure in a wealthy White neighbourhood, undertaken in order to prevent its use as a thoroughfare by African Americans. Calmore argued that metaphorically the African American community was socially and legally constructed as 'unwanted traffic,'[9] and therefore, subject to exclusions of various sorts.

I want to suggest that the metaphor is equally applicable to the UK and that it succinctly captures the attitude(s) that betray the carefully concealed thoughts in and through which the legacies of the MAAFA are located. In short, historically speaking, African and Caribbean individuals and communities in the UK, like African American males, are individually and collectively also constituted and represented in the minds of their White counterparts as 'unwanted traffic'. Consequently, our presence and agency is consistently being contested, and our sense of self assaulted.[10] The legacies of

---

[9] John O. Colmore, 'The Law & Culture Shift: Race & The Warren Court Legacy', *Washington & Lee Law Review* p.59, No. 4 (2002) cited in Athena D. Mutua, (ed.) *Progressive Black Masculinities* (New York: Routledge, 2006), p. 137

[10] The linked dual concepts of 'contested' 'space' are critically important in this regard. The former refers to the idea that individuals and communities that co-habit in a limited space struggle to assert their authentic identity and sense of self in a space where each group is also attempting to do the same. The trouble is that there is often 'not enough' room for all groups to assert themselves equally. Consequently, there is

the MAAFA in the UK are not, therefore, incidental or coincidental, but are a systemic, deliberate and aggressive assault of and on African and Caribbean communities.

Six Legacies of the MAAFA
In reality, there are as many legacies of the MAAFA as there are individual descendants of each displaced individual or community. My hope in November 2007 was to highlight themes under which to locate the legacies by drawing on my experiences as a Black man born and raised in England, alongside my understanding of the constituency being addressed. My hope was to assist my White Sisters and Brothers in Christ to internalise the inextricable link between their existence as descendants and citizens of the UK and the contemporary expressions of the legacies. Six themes or 'hooks' were highlighted and these will be explored in the following pages.

1. Social and Geographical Dislocation
At the heart of this legacy is a sense of 'non-belonging' or philosophically speaking, being in a permanent state of existential crisis.[11] The psycho-social fallout of the forceful removal of millions upon millions[12] of Africans during the MAAFA is seldom acknowledged by White society as a trauma still affecting African and Caribbean communities. The time lapse between 'then' and 'now' conveniently serves as a 'distance regulator' that absolved many White people of personal guilt and, as a corollary, reduces Black people to 'wingers' and irresponsible irritants lacking in moral fibre.

---

a 'contestation' within the space between groups to assert themselves. The space is consequently contested. Micro-Aggressions refer to those apparently benign but in reality extremely damning minute acts of aggression that have a cumulative effect on an individual or a community, and as a result, cause more harm than a 'macro' (major outright) act of aggression. These include subtle but powerful acts of exclusion and barely detectable attitudes of superiority projected onto the 'Other' and myriad similar actions.

[11] There are significant differences between the experiences of African and Caribbean individuals and communities whose formative experiences of self are located in Africa, the Caribbean and the UK. It is widely recognised that individuals that are shaped outside of the UK have a stronger sense of self and are much clearer about their identity, individually and communally. This should not be surprising in that while they too may experience various challenges that are an intrinsic part of life, they are not subject to (at least in contemporary terms, though one could argue that they are historically), the daily assaults on the self that are the various expressions of racism, those of us born, raised and living in Western societies experience on a habitual basis.

[12] We must remember when we are speaking of the number of Africans that were transported to include those individuals who never made the journey through the 'middle passage' and were either cast overboard due to illness, rebellion, as a punishment, as well as those who arrived and died soon after.

Sociological theories such as the 'third generation hypothesis'[13] argue that there is an incremental assimilation into the new culture into which migrants move over subsequent generations. Yet, despite this theory, many British-born African and Caribbean individuals, still find that their experience of racism continues to express itself in passive and aggressive acts of marginalisation, exclusion, discrimination and oppression. As a result, we are consistently reminded that Britain is not home, that we do not belong; it is a place where we are grudgingly tolerated.

In October 2009 I hosted the inaugural 'State of Black Britain Symposium', in Central London. Attendees were asked to complete a survey. One question asked if they felt that they were British. Over 80% of the 250 attendees felt unable to claim a strong sense of being British. The attendees included leading political/civic leaders, academics, faith and community leaders, activists, senior business owners, and representatives from private, public, voluntary and third sector organisations.

What we shared in common, then, and still do today, is a sense that while we may no longer be verbally and physically assaulted with impunity as we once were, we are persistently 'made to feel' that we do not belong. Stephen Small suggests that this feeling of not belonging is an integral part of two problems faced by British Black communities; the first 'is the racialised nature of immigration legislation, which has restricted their entry into the country', and the second is 'the perception on the part of White English people that Black people are somehow 'not English' even if born in England.'[14]

Land as an intrinsic component to understanding self

These problems are compounded by a lack of identifiable space that we can call our own. John Mbiti in his seminal work, *African Religion and Philosophy*[15] has noted the importance of land to Africans. He points out that 'the land provides them with the roots of existence, as well as binding them mystically to their departed.'[16] The Western mind can easily underestimate the importance of the departed. The ancestors are an indispensable component of what it means to be a person. In African cosmology the ancestors are an intrinsic and indispensable part of the community whose existence continues in the Zamani (the unlimited past) through ritual and communal recollection of the departed.

Mbiti points out 'that while the departed person is remembered by name he is not really dead: he is alive, and such a person I would call the living dead.'[17] Mbiti continues by saying that 'to move Africans by force from the

---

[13] See the following link for a brief explanation of this theory: http://www.issacharministries.co.uk/images/presentation.pdf
[14] Stephen Small *Racialized Barriers: Black Experience in the United States and England in the 1980s* (London and New York: Routledge, 1994) p. 61
[15] See John Mbiti *African Religions & Philosophy* (London: Heinemann, 1990)
[16] Ibid, p.2
[17] Ibid, p.25

land is an act of such great injustice that no foreigner can fathom it.'[18] He continues by pointing out that:

> ...even when people voluntarily leave their homes in the countryside and go to live and work in the cities, there is a fundamental severing of ties which cannot be repaired and which often creates psychological problems with which urban life cannot as yet cope.[19]

Clearly land is significant, it is more than just a geographical location or physical space. Rather, through the interconnectedness of the departed, ancestors and the living descendants, 'space' becomes place, 'space' that is infused and suffused within a meaningful story. Land, therefore, becomes the intersection between the departed and the living. Together, they collectively constitute community, which is a foundational value of African culture that is captured in the concept of Ubuntu: 'I am because we are.'

It is worth noting, although perfunctorily, that this cosmology of the importance of land and the centrality of the ancestors is more than mere sentimentalism. It is both conspicuously evident and deeply embedded in, in fact intrinsically necessary, to even a rudimentary understanding of the Hebrew Scriptures and the self identity of Israel as 'the people of God' and an autonomous nation (Gen 17:8; 13:14-17; 15:7, 17-21; 17:7-8; 24:7; 26:2-5; 28:12-15; 35:10-12; 48:4 and 50:24).

2. Identity Disorientation

The idea of identity disorientation is closely linked to the construct of social and geographical dislocation. It is a natural consequence of 'not belonging,' which raises the inevitable question of one's identity: 'who am I?' The question of identity is one of the five existential life questions; the other four being: 'where do I come from?', why am I here?', what is my purpose?' and 'what contribution can I make?' Answering these existential questions is difficult enough in the first instance. This is without the additional challenges of having to negotiate the burden of racialised, systemic socio-political and cultural dynamics that present additional layers of complication and serve to aggressively, though covertly, undermine one's sense of identity.

One can add to the systematic, ideological warfare on the personal and corporate identity of African and Caribbean individuals and communities, a covert but concerted assault on the self identity of such people in Western history, which still finds expression in our current context.

An example of this would be the creation and emergence of the pseudo-scientific literature of the 17th or 18th century representing itself as a credible reality about the inferiority of African and Caribbean women and men. Peter Fryer has carefully documented the way in which parts of the British scientific community created and promoted spurious theories about the inherent

---

[18] Ibid, p.25
[19] Ibid, p.27

inferiority of African people, coupled with the alternate belief in the superiority of White people.[20] It is conceded that many of these theories have been proved to be unscientific and have lost credibility over the passage of time. However, it would not be difficult to put forward a cogent argument that defended the proposition that such beliefs are not unconsciously held by the majority, and consciously by a further minority of White people, often to their own consternation, when they finally realise this truth!

Brainwashed
Tom Burrell, the former owner of the largest African American owned advertising agency in the US, wrote a book called *Brainwashed*. His goal was to use his 45 years of experience in advertising to interrogate and explain how 'propaganda' has been used through various media to convince Black people of their inferior status when compared to White people. Burrell quotes Dubois who argued that:

> ...in the propaganda against the Negro since emancipation in this land, we face one of the most stupendous efforts the world has ever saw to discredit human beings, an effort involving universities, history, science, social life and religion.[21]

Black Skin, White Masks
The roots of identity disorientation emerge for many African and Caribbean people as a result of the legacy of colonialism. One of the best texts I have read on this subject was written by the renowned Martinique psychiatrist Franz Fanon. In *Black Skin, White Masks,* Fanon concluded that the effects of internalised and racialised ideological conditioning inflicted on the mind of the Martinique young man induced in them an inferiority complex that left many with a misguided sense around their true identity. This is not a phenomenon that is unique to Martinique. Almost every African or Caribbean person that is both consciously aware of and truthful about their own internal dialogues around identity and sense of 'personhood' would be able to testify that this is an issue with which they have had to wrestle. Fanon concluded 'that the fact of the juxtaposition of the white and black races has created a massive psychoexistential complex.'[22]

The Crooked Room
Melissa V. Harris-Perry, an American TV host and academic, has drawn on insights from cognitive psychology, in particular, research conducted on 'field dependence' in her analysis of American society. Harris-Perry draws on a

---

[20] Peter Fryer, *Staying Power: The History of Black People In Britain* (London: Pluto Press, 1984)
[21] Tom Burrell, *Brainwashed: Challenging The Myth Of Black Inferiority*, (New York: Smiley Books, 2010), p.1
[22] Franz Fanon, *Black Skin, White Masks*, (London: Pluto Press, 1991), p.14

study where a crooked chair is placed in a room and an individual is asked to sit on the chair and align themselves vertically.[23] What researchers discovered was that some subjects could only arrive at what they thought was a place of alignment in relation to their surroundings. What was particularly surprising was that some subjects were as much as 35 degrees dis-aligned but thought themselves to be perfectly aligned!

Harris-Perry suggests that this is the experience of African American women in America when they confront race and gender stereotypes. I would argue that what African American women experienced in the crooked room, is also true of African and Caribbean individuals and communities wrestling with subjective understandings of self, while seated in a crooked chair of White society.

3. Infra-Structural Exclusion

It is now 50 years this year since the British parliament passed the first 'Race Relations Acts'. The existence of such legislation implies a corporate recognition that discriminatory practices have and continue to significantly disadvantage and exclude African and Caribbean individuals and communities by creating artificial 'glass ceilings' and reduced opportunities.

Racialised identities

Stephen Small has convincingly argued that excluding African and Caribbean communities from fully participating in and making a contribution to society, is not benign. Rather, it is intentional, and is based on acts of marginalisation. He argues that:

> ...racialised barriers and boundaries were created to secure political and economic goals; the former blocked Black access to resources and power, while facilitating non-Black access; the latter demarcated the acceptable terrain (political, economic, social) which could be traversed by Black people, while keeping all terrains open to non-Blacks.[24]

He continues:

> ...in creating racialised identities for themselves Anglo Europeans have also given rise to racialised identities for people of African origin, though for the latter it is one which has for the most part grown in opposition to injustice, exploitation and oppression. It is an identity which is not without its problems.[25]

---

[23] Melissa V. Harris-Perry, *Sister Citizen: Shame, Stereotypes & Black Women In America* (New Haven: Yale University Press, 2011), p.29
[24] Stephen Small, *Racialised Barriers*, p.15
[25] Ibid, p.15

White Privilege

Small's descriptions of the way one ethnic group is given access to resources and the other denied, graphically illustrates the manner in which privilege is structurally embedded within society to advantage White people.[26] Essentially, this is about bestowing benefits on White people that are withheld from African and Caribbean people. This field of enquiry has recently become more in vogue, with the introduction into the academy of a number of courses that interrogate Whiteness and investigate White privilege.

Peggy McIntosh has described White privilege

> ...as an invisible package of unearned assets that I can count on cashing in each day, but about which I was "meant" to remain oblivious.

McIntosh asserts that

> ...white privilege is like an invisible weightless knapsack of special provisions, maps, passports, codebooks, visas, clothes, tools, and blank checks.[27]

Given McIntosh's comments it is reasonable to conclude that Whiteness is an intentional ideological construct that disadvantages Africans and Caribbeans while privileging White people. One of the consequences of White privilege is that it portrays and reinforces a distorted and pathological view of Africans and Caribbean people that falsely represents us as inadequate or incapable. Blackness or Black people are constructed in contrast to Whiteness, which is portrayed as adequate and capable. Black people, therefore, are unable to assume or be given (itself another disrespectful and paternalistic assumption) a visible presence within or to represent 'the system' for fear of failure. Often, where we are present our agency is undermined to such an extent that it is barely recognizable, if at all.

Conversely, where we are visible that visibility is very often a convenient location on which to project and deflect the dysfunctionality of the system that is present by virtue of our place within it. Our strong sense of community, the intrinsic and intuitive sense of our interconnectedness, manifests itself in an unconscious or unspoken sense of shame and responsibility that both adds an unnecessary burden to and sense of responsibility for structural and societal ills.

It was pointed out earlier that racialised barriers were intentionally constructed to privilege White people and disadvantage or exclude African and Caribbean individuals and communities. This subtle nuance could easily be ignored or overlooked if we fail to realise that structural exclusion is about

---

[26] Ibid, p.15
[27] Peggy McIntosh, *Unpacking the Invisible Knapsack*, online Pdf. See the following link for access to this work.
https://www.pcc.edu/resources/illumination/documents/white-privilege-essay-mcintosh.pdf

whether or not one's presence can be translated into an expression of personal agency in the light of situational dynamics.

4. Historical Amnesia

Perhaps the best way to illustrate this idea is to retell a story. Having just left school I decided to study for a BTEC in Business Studies. I recall being seated in a finance lecture when the topic of conversation strayed onto racism. The lecturer, a White man, spun round from writing on the board and with an arrogant smirk on his face, stated with 'unquestionable' confidence, as if it was an indisputable fact, that 'Africa had no history before the MAAFA'. In effect, he was saying that, in historical terms, the continent of Africa had no history worth recognising before colonisation, and its peoples had made no noteworthy contribution to civilisation. I had never heard any person make such an emphatic statement about Africa and Africans before, although I was aware that it is consistently implied in the history syllabus of the British educational system.

It was not until arriving at university and joining the African and Caribbean Society that I became more familiar with African History. Through the process of greater consciousness, I discovered the African contribution to literature, science, mathematics, engineering, physics etc. Finally, my amnesia was beginning to be reversed. I refer to this as amnesia because, in recollecting conversations within the home between the educated elders, many of whom had studied in England in the 50s and 60s and had gained post graduate degrees, I had been exposed to discussions about the African contribution to civilisation, which the brutal impact of racism had had the effect of eroding from my mind.

It was not that I did not know but that I had forgotten. Or, rather, I had been made to forget as the 'system' conditioned me to erode what little recollection I had of pre-colonial African history. I was brainwashed into believing in the achievements of Western civilisation. One is reminded of the African proverb that says 'until the lion has his or her own storyteller, tales of the hunt will always glorify the hunter.'

This is a sad reality with which I continue to wrestle. I sometimes still find myself reverting to that internalised pathology about Blackness and struggling with the powerful conditioning to believe that Africans have contributed nothing to the world in all spheres of human existence aside from music and sport. Internalised pathology is covertly reinforced in collusion with infrastructural exclusion, particularly within the educational system. This is the point made earlier about infrastructural exclusion not being solely concerned with denying us access, but simultaneously, it is also about misrepresenting and distorting how reality is portrayed.

5. Spiritual & Temporal Dichotomies

Until very recently (with the exception of the Black prophetic tradition), African and Caribbean Christians have bought into the heretical theology of 'the Curse of Ham.' As a consequence, this has kept us in a disempowered mindset that has added to the structural evil of economic powerlessness, as 'the will of God for Black people'. Thankfully, liberation theologies are skillfully unmasking the truth of this spurious belief as the practical outworking of a global system of White privilege.

The truth is that what the Revd Dr. Vernon Johns once said of Negro religion, that 'it is 40 percent emotionalism, 30 percent hilarity, 28 percent hysteria and 2 percent miscellaneous,'[28] is increasingly and speedily losing traction in African and Caribbean Christian communities, if it remains at all! Martin Luther King, Dr. Johns' successor at Ebenezer Baptist Church, was also critical of Black expressions of religious faith in his day and lamented that it

> ...emphasised emotion rather than ideas and volume rather than elocution

and that

> ...many ministers preached only about the afterlife, rather than about what the role of the church could play in improving present day society.[29]

Historically, Black expressions of faith have been overly preoccupied with 'getting into heaven', at the expense of inhabiting the space between 'socio-political reality and eschatological hope,'[30] as outlined by Jurgen Moltman. As a result there has been a monumental failure to prophetically address the injustices that define that space, particularly those injustices that are a direct consequence of one's ethnicity and culture.

6. Internalised Pathology

Internalised pathology is covertly reinforced in collusion with infrastructural exclusion, particularly within the educational system. This is the point made earlier about infrastructural exclusion not just being about not allowing access, but simultaneously misrepresenting and distorting how reality is portrayed. Fanon's window into the colonial mind is instructive in this regard in that his writings offer a perceptive insight into the dynamics of an internalised pathology. He suggests that 'the colonised is elevated above his jungle status in proportion to his adoption of the mother country's cultural standard. He becomes whiter as he renounces his Blackness, his jungle.'[31] His objective is, therefore, not simply to understand the malady but to 'help the Black man to

---

[28] William Dwight Mckissic, Snr, *In search of Blacks In The Bible* (New York: Renaissance Productions, 1990), p.11
[29] Martin Luther King, cited in David Carrow, *Bearing The Cross*, (New York: Vintage Books, 1986), p.37
[30] Jurgen Moltmann, 'Political Theology', *Theology Today*, 28:6, 1971, pp.6-23 (6.)
[31] Franz Fanon, *Black Skin, White Masks*, p.18

free himself of the arsenal of complexes that has been developed by the colonial environment'.[32]

Being consistently and unconsciously conditioned by (mis)representations of one's self is to be subject to the most callous act of social, emotional, psychological and spiritual violence that erodes one's self-esteem. More than that, it induces (and that is the pernicious nature of this covert ideological warfare) a deep seated sense of shame that, if not checked, will leave an individual or community with feelings of powerlessness and non-being.

Insights from Feminism

One of the perennial debates in Western societies focuses on representations of idealised projections of women's bodies. This pathology leaves many women with distorted views of themselves, which leads to many forms of dysfunctional behaviours, including diseases like bulimia and anorexia - maladies that are on the increase. It would be easy to say, and some do, that women should 'get a grip' and resist the unrealistic expectations of society, and to be themselves, meaning accepting their bodies as they are. However, taking time to interrogate and deconstruct the toxic cocktail of media and other influences that lead women to succumb to damaging messages about the need to have perfect bodies can simultaneously offer valuable insights into internalised pathologies in relation to 'race'. Three points are worth noting in this regard and are briefly considered here. There are three independent but interlocking realities that constitute the context that allows pre-designed and damaging messages to be articulated and internalised.

1. A perilous/spurious narrative that purports to present a distorted perspective as the truth. It has been pointed out earlier that concerted efforts have been made to caricature African and Caribbean individuals and communities. The basic assumption that informs the thinking behind this point of view is that men and women are not equal. Women are to be used by men as objects of pleasure or service by virtue of their inferior status.

2. A powerful mechanism through which to disseminate that 'truth'. Men have controlled the means of mass communication and utilised this power in order to promote our propaganda. Consequently, the dominant narrative has been the one that we have created and sought to disseminate and impose on women. More recently, the rise of the feminist movement has challenged and resisted this narrative.

3. Women have been excluded from controlling the media that promote the lie and so this distortion becomes accepted and internalised. Conversely,

---

[32] Ibid, p.30

women have been excluded and have struggled to retain a sense of reality and personhood in the face of a tirade of uncomplimentary messages aimed at undermining their sense of self.

The parallels are clear for all to see. It is the same three interlocking realities that underpin and facilitate the pathological (mis)representation of African and Caribbean communities in Britain.

Conclusion
Despite the abolition of The MAAFA, evident within the United Kingdom are a number of legacies that are the result of its existence. While it is granted that it may not be the expressed intention of White British communities to be racist and exclusionary and/or oppressive, the fact is, as a result of their cultural heritage, this is almost inescapable. A White person denying that they are racist is comparable to a person swimming in a pool and claiming not to be wet! The reality is that context shapes and informs what an individual becomes and what she or he thinks. The fact is, then, that White communities are implicated by virtue of the structural sin that continues to shape British society, which continues to allow White people to experience a level of privilege from past injustices. The 'Apology' in 2007 was but the start of a long process and not the end in itself.

The Apology: A Journey Towards Justice
Wale Hudson-Roberts

Introduction
I am grateful to our early Black Baptist pioneers, Revd Fred George, Revd Dr Desmond Gordon, Miss Pat White[1] and Mrs Rosemarie Davidson-Gotobed[2] for the foundations they established. Without their commitment and skills the 'Apology' might not have come to birth. I write with them and many others in mind.

The UK's role in the slave trade is a matter of 'deep sorrow and regret', Prime Minister Tony Blair stated in March 2007. In a statement marking the anniversary of the British parliamentary Act abolishing the slave trade, the former PM said slavery was among history's 'most shameful enterprises.'[3] His comments were heard in a video message at a commemorative ceremony that took place at Elmina Castle in Ghana, which served as Sub-Saharan Africa's first permanent transatlantic slave trading post. Many Africans and Caribbeans were disappointed that the former Prime Minister's statements fell short of an apology. After all, slave-owning planters and merchants, who dealt in slaves and slave produce, were among the richest people in 18th century Britain. Profits from these activities helped to endow All Souls' College, Oxford with an extensive library, to build scores of banks including Barclays, and to finance the experiments of James Watt, inventor of the first efficient steam engine, plus many other activities as well.

Four months after The Prime Minister had offered this statement of regret, the then General Secretary of the Baptist Union of Great Britain (BUGB), was asked at the meeting of the Baptist World Alliance in Ghana to offer an apology on behalf of BUGB. This occurred during the Reconciliation Service with other Baptist Unions to mark the 200th anniversary of the abolition of the slave trade Act. Since the matter had not been discussed at BUGB Council, or widely in the Union, he felt unable to apologise. Instead, he offered the 'Prayers of Lament' that had first been used at the Baptist Assembly in the UK. Sitting in the slave castle, he personally felt the need to apologise for the appalling wickedness of the slave trade, but, as a servant of the Union, he believed BUGB Council had to make its own decision.

A decade earlier, in June 1997, the Jamaica Baptist Union (JBU) Executive sent a resolution to Baptist Missionary Society[4] which read:

---

[1] Former Moderator of the Baptist Union of Great Britain's Racial Justice Group.
[2] First person to be appointed as Racial Justice Co-coordinator.
[3] See the following link for media coverage of Tony Blair's comments. (Accessed 3rd June 2016)
[4] Now renamed as 'BMS World Mission'.

> Today the effect of slavery and colonialism continues to have a dehumanizing effect on the people of the two thirds world and migrants to the United Kingdom. The violence of racism continues to destroy, denigrate and undermine the lives of millions of people, both victims and perpetrators of this cancerous social scourge. As a church we affirm our oneness in Christ and our solidarity with humanity being persons created in the image of God. Any form of injustice, whether racial or economic, threatens God's image in humanity. As corporate humanity, we are participants in the process of slavery. A social practice which led to much anger, bitterness, self-hate, emotional imprisonment, family instability, up-rootedness and deprivation.

This resolution called upon the church community in the UK to provide leadership to the rest of the country by making a public declaration of repentance of the atrocities of chattel slavery, repentance of the acts committed by her fore-parents in the name of development and progress; repentance of the acts of exploitation, economic and racial injustice.
In February 1998, the BMS replied as follows:

> Your letter was given careful attention and took much time. Many points of view were expressed and we were entirely united in our denunciation of, and opposition to, any policy or course of action that fails to treat all people as of equal value. We are intolerant of any attitude which discriminates between those God has created equal and we are encouraged by the clear statements to that effect that have been made by many church leaders in Britain in recent time. I have been asked to write to enquire from you if there is a specific reason why the Jamaica Baptist Union has raised the issue with us at this particular time. Perhaps something has been said or done which led your Executive Committee to form this resolution? In order that we could wisely progress this matter from this point it would be helpful for us if you could indicate any particular 'trigger' for the resolution and your letter.[5]

The Revd Trevor Edwards, former JBU General Secretary, in a letter dated May 1998, made the following four robust points in his response:
Firstly, the relentless racism experienced by Caribbean migrants residing in the UK. Secondly, racism is both a justice matter and a mission issue and needs, therefore, to be addressed. Thirdly, job opportunities are limited for the Caribbean migrants when compared with UK residents. Finally, the disproportionate number of Black people in prison and mental institutions should not be ignored. Despite conversations with BMS, and other Baptist bodies, concerning a helpful response to the issues raised, yet again it was the JBU who reignited and breathed urgency into this important matter.
During his sermon at the 2007 Joint Baptist Assembly[6], the Revd Karl Henlin (President of JBU), whilst drawing his sermon to a close, urged British Baptists to offer 'a full apology for what really has been a most monstrous action'. He said,

---

[5] The BMS
[6] This sermon is reproduced in its entirety in this text.

'The Apology' is necessary in order that the forgiveness that is on offer can be appropriated, the healing made complete and the chapter closed. This has been raised before by us with your leaders; perhaps the time has come to reconsider this matter again.

In the immediate aftermath of the sermon, it was difficult to know what those gathered at the Joint Assembly, were thinking. What is indisputable, however, is that his challenge changed the course of race relationships in BUGB. His message emboldened Black Baptists to grasp the nettle and seek an apology, also helping some White people to better understand the call for an apology.

It was not long after Mr Henlin's challenge that BUGB Trustees agreed for the Racial Justice Working Group, moderated by Pat White (herself a Jamaican), to 'develop a process for a conversation concerning an apology' at BUGB November 2007 Council.

Pat White and I were aware that many Council members were apprehensive about participating in what some felt was a potentially 'incendiary' conversation. To develop a process that encouraged maximum participation, in an anxiety-filled climate, would bring its own unique set of challenges. Suggestions from the Racial Justice Working Group and Revd Dr Kate Coleman, Revd Kumar Rajagopalan, Revd Dr Myra Blyth, and Mrs Christine Hudson-Roberts were helpful. They helped us draw up a list of excellent presenters and themes ahead of the 'Apology' debate.

On Monday 12th November 2007, Jonathan Edwards, the General Secretary of BUGB opened the 'Apology' conversation. He encouraged Council to listen carefully to one another and to do so with deep respect. We were reminded that we live in a society that was still deeply racist. He also acknowledged that, for some Council members, it would be difficult to frame words of apology for events which had taken place long before they were born. He was painfully aware that there was also the risk that the issue could be divisive, but urged that in the presence of God, we listen to what 'the Spirit was saying to the churches', even as we listened to one another.

Graham Sparkes, one of five presenters selected by the Racial Justice Working Group, was the first to present. He acknowledged that despite the achievement of a handful of courageous Christians and parliamentarians in the 19th Century, the 'spirit of slavery' lived on, as exemplified in the continuing campaign to end unfair rules. Reminding us that Mali, for example, was dependent on its staple crop of cotton, but because the USA continued to export its subsidised cotton, the poor Mali farmers could not obtain an adequate price to export their crops.

My presentation followed, in which I spoke of the racism deeply rooted in British society and of the continuing resentment felt, especially by the younger Black generation, in this nation. Council watched a video of the experience of Doreen Lawrence, the mother of Stephen Lawrence, who was murdered by White youths in South London. Council watched as she spoke of her hurt at the callousness of the police, emergency services, and ultimately of the courts, which failed to convict those charged. The video continued with the names and photographs of the numerous young Black people killed recently in Britain. It concluded with Martin Luther King's, 'I have a dream' speech.

A screen presentation by Richard Reddie, Director of the 'Set All Free' Project demonstrated the legacy of the slave trade to Britain, not just at its height, but through succeeding generations. Britain grew rich on the trade, to become the world's leading power, even after the abolition of slavery. All aspects of industry and cultural development had been fuelled by the triangular trade: ships to West Africa to transport thousands of slaves to the plantations in the Caribbean, who subsequently supplied the plantation owners with goods, and then returned to Britain with produce from the plantations, such as sugar and tobacco. Richard Reddie reminded us that the Industrial Revolution was powered by this trade of capital and banking, exports and imports.

The Revd David Shosanya, the fourth presenter, had been present when Caribbean and African church leaders had confessed their own resentments and hurts to one another.

> They had not engaged in a culture of blame but recognised the continuing consequences of their actions - an ongoing psychological disconnection from the land, family and from who they are. Africans spoke of 'ubuntu' - that which makes us what we are, our 'humanness', our 'belonging'.

David Shosanya argued that many young Black people suffered from a feeling of 'invisibility'. They felt as if they did not belong to British society and that they had no history, no land and no culture.

The final insightful presentations came from the Revd Joe Kapolyo and the Revd Dr Richard Kidd. Both men are theologians, and have been College Principals, but have very contrasting life histories. Joe Kapolyo lived in rural Zambia when it was colonial Northern Rhodesia, and Dr Richard Kidd was a student in both Oxford and Cambridge. However, coming to personal faith in Christ and commitment, alongside a conviction of Baptist principles, emphasised their individual value to God and to their fellow women and men.

Richard Kidd suggested that emphasis on personal and individual commitment could, in itself, be a stumbling block making it difficult for a Christian to see how s/he could apologise for 'sins of the fathers'. Joe Kopolyo focussed on the Old Testament concept of shared responsibility. On the matter of ubuntu, both David Shosanya and Joe Kapolyo were of the same mind. The theology of ubuntu suggested that humans practised their behaviour within community based relationships. Therefore, both joy and suffering were shared in equal measure by the community. Both men concluded that ubuntu was consistent with an apology.

Summing up, Richard Kidd suggested that if he was willing to make an apology for the engagement of his forebears in the transatlantic slave trade he would be allowing himself to become vulnerable. As a corollary, this would lead to him sharing in the pain of others, whilst realising that this would incur some guilt and the need for repentance because he was a beneficiary of the past.

Joe Kapolyo admitted that he had been sceptical of the value of such an apology. He had seen, however, the liberating effect of the 'Apology' by the Japanese for the crimes against the Koreans and the impact of the 'Truth and Reconciliation Commission' on South Africa's efforts to reconcile the oppressor and the oppressed. Furthermore, he had also witnessed Tony Blair's apology for the Irish Potato Famine and the Southern Baptist apology for their share in the sins of segregation, and in these actions, he realised the necessity for an apology and its power for liberation.

Small group discussions followed the presentations. This gave space and time for members of Council to reflect on the content of the presentations, consider the legacy of slavery and whether an apology from Council members would contribute to the healing and liberation of Black Baptists.

The comments from these discussions were summarised in a number of key themes raised by the Revd Viv O'Brien:

- It was clear that God had been speaking to the members through the presentations and the groups.
- Some had understood the pain of others for the first time.
- There was a general recognition for honesty before God and each other.
- The need to confess the sin of racism to God and to those who had been hurt/affected by it.
- The language of repentance needed to be concretised.

A plenary followed, during which the following comments were made.

> There had been times when I had been disappointed as a Baptist because I had not been fully included in the family as a member of the ethnic minority, but I have been stunned by the language and intense listening of this Council and for the first time I felt heard and healed.

> I am grateful to Council for its willingness to expend so much time on the matter of the Apology. An Apology, however, would only be the beginning and the start of a new way of working towards greater unity and deeper humility in listening to one another.

> His Black colleagues were most grateful to Council members for listening and it was apparent that the hurt still felt by many had been heard and understood.

> I had come to Council feeling the difficulty of apologising for what we did not personally do, but if Jesus took the blame for sins which were not his, so should we.

> Whilst he had not been part of the slave trade, it had now come to him that the trade was part of himself, which shaped who and what he was and he needed therefore to confess to God and to apologise to those who still suffered in any way from the barbaric trade.

Those who had found it difficult to frame an apology for something they were not personally involved in, might look at Daniel and his whole-hearted confession of the sins of which he had not been a part, and for us we could not offer before the Lord an apology which cost us nothing.

As a result of the General Secretary suggesting that no formal Resolution be tabled in advance, it was necessary to ask a small group to formulate an appropriate resolution under the leadership of Richard Kidd, who then presented a form of words to the Council. Richard Kidd's proposal, seconded by David Kerrigan, read as follows:

> *As a Council we have listened to one another, we have heard the pain of hurting sisters and brothers and we have heard God speaking to us.*
> *In a spirit of weakness, humility and vulnerability, we acknowledge that we are only at the start of a journey, but we are agreed that this must not prevent us speaking and acting at a Kairos moment.*
> *Therefore we acknowledge our share in, and benefit from, our nation's participation in the transatlantic slave trade.*
> *We acknowledge that we speak as those who have shared in and suffered from the legacy of slavery and its appalling consequences for God's world.*
> *We offer our apology to God and to our brothers and sisters for all that has created and still perpetuates the hurt which originated from the horror of slavery.*
> *We repent of the hurt we have caused, the divisions we have created, our reluctance to face up to the sin of the past, our unwillingness to listen to the pain of our Black sisters and brothers and our silence in the face of racism and injustice today.*
> *We commit ourselves, in a true spirit of repentance, to take what we have learned from God in the Council and to share it widely in our Baptist community and beyond, looking for gospel ways by which we can turn the words and feelings we have expressed today into concrete actions and contribute to the prophetic work of God's coming kingdom.*
>
> (italics added for emphasis)

This Resolution was unanimously agreed, after which each member of Council bowed in silent prayer and personal commitment.
It was then proposed:

> In the light of our discussions concerning the transatlantic slave trade and the statement that arises from the discussions, Council asks the Mission Executive, Trustee Board and other appropriate bodies to continue to develop ways of promoting racial justice within BUGB and wherever possible in the world beyond.

Most Council members would agree that what happened was unexpected. Few members of Council anticipated an apology. I have often reflected on this significant occasion when hearts and minds merged, melted and were bowed before the voice of God. I am in no doubt that God was present and that the final outcome was influenced by the Holy Spirit.

The following year a small delegation comprising Pat White, the Revd Jonathan Edwards, the Revd Alastair Brown and myself, represented BUGB and the BMS World Mission by taking the 'Apology' resolution to Jamaica. This was an appropriate destination, in part, due to its relationship with British colonial history, also in part to the ongoing relationship between the JBU and British Baptists. Even though the 'Apology' was officially accepted by Revd Karl Johnson[7], Revd Dr Steve Jennings[8] and Revd Karl Henlin, my sense was the JBU was keen to know how the resolution was going to address racism in British Baptist churches and support the JBU, a former British colony, in its mission endeavours.

Concerning the former, a strategy to challenge racism and develop a truly multicultural Baptist Union, was birthed by Revd Ian Bunce (former Head of the Baptist Union Mission Department) and me. This was an attempt to convert the words of the 'Apology' into action. The strategy was entitled the 'Journey'. Its main strategic priorities were:
- Building Multicultural Congregations
- Training
- Multicultural Events
- Establishing Culturally Inclusive Structures
- Youth Leadership
- Baptist House

The aforementioned were the outcome of extensive research, which I undertook alongside Rosemarie Davidson-Gotobed and Revd Graham Sparkes. Yet even the 'Journey's' continuing work has not curtailed the amount of racism that Black and minority ethnic people experience in our Baptist Churches, Colleges and Associations. Converting the 'Apology' into action has been a painstakingly slow process. I am of the conviction that this is, in part, due to White privilege and a misunderstanding of the term 'multicultural' among many British Baptists. As a result we may have to wait some time before experiencing 'the fruits of the 'Apology'.'[9]

In the immediate aftermath of the 'Apology' there was a significant amount of positivity and excitement in the air. Many Baptists were proud that our church was the only British Christian denomination to make a public apology for the enslavement of Africans; but over time the desire for an inclusive Union has dissipated, among some, and consequently undermined the Union's *Five Core Values*.

The Five Core Values
The 1996 BUGB Consultation called for increased work on issues of living justly in our contemporary world. This resulted in a Task Group being put in

---

[7] General Secretary of the Jamaica Baptist Union.
[8] Former President of the Jamaica Baptist Union
[9] Revd Karl Johnson

place to reflect on what we learn about Christ and the call of God for us to 'act justly, to love mercy, and to walk humbly with our God.' (Micah 6:8). The resulting document – *Five Core Values for a Gospel People* – was created, outlining the call to the Baptist Union to be an *inclusive, sacrificial, prophetic, missionary and worshipping community*.

In the next part of my essay I intend to look at the Union's Five Core Values, through the lens of racial justice. Given the constraints of space, I will not be able to explore each of the Five Core Values, in turn. Alternatively, I will look at what I consider to be the key issues, in the context of this book project, in which my insights are shared with others. The purpose in using this particular methodology is not only to critique our Union's response to the 'Apology', but to explore and consider ways in which we can better build on the 'Apology' and strive to 'become one team.' (Using the language of our renewed culture of one team)

Interpreting Key Aspects of the Five Core Values
An Inclusive Community: Challenging Baptist understanding of 'Multicultural'

In his book, *Ministry for a Multicultural Church*[10], Robert Schreiter defines a multicultural church simply as 'many cultures together in one church.' This definition is to my mind a misnomer. Regrettably, it is a definition that many Baptists have also adopted. A truly multicultural community must be more than a reflection of ethnic and cultural diversity. Rather, it is one that prioritises how it addresses White privilege, hierarchy and also embraces cultural tension; these are the key ingredients to creating a multicultural community. A truly multicultural space is where the existence of the 'other' is respected as a matter of fact; where relationships refuse to be infected by racism. It is one where 'powerless' and 'powerful' cultures are encouraged to find their true identity with each other in Christ.

The term 'multicultural' recognises the inherent worth in human diversity, and challenges the inequalities of worth, which are so often attached to human constructed hierarchies. Therefore, a multicultural Union is one that reflects justice in strategy, policy, procedure, liturgy, theology, worship, and above all, creating culturally sensitive, listening, learning, and transformative relationships.

More than most, St. Paul understood the meaning of 'multicultural'[11] and the necessity for racial justice to underpin all truly multicultural Christian communities. Paul's conversion helped him accept that God's purpose in Jesus was to break down the distinction between Jews and Gentiles, thereby, creating one new humanity. It was the radical conversion of Paul that opened his eyes to see that Gentiles are also worthy of embrace and inclusion without having to first become culturally and religiously Jewish. His revelatory

---

[10] See Robert Schreiter - http://sedosmission.org/old/eng/schreiter.htm
[11] What I am suggesting here is that St. Paul understands the essence of the nature and the practice of multicultural, while acknowledging that this term did not exist in his time or epoch.

experience on the Damascus road enabled him to become a committed and passionate advocate of Christ's multicultural Church in which Jews and Gentiles were treated with dignity and equal respect.

His commitment to inclusion was expressed in terms of justification by grace through faith, which was also applied to cultural and ethnically based justice issues that plagued the Church (Gal.2: 15-16). Whatever the challenges of living out the practice in reality, there can be no doubt that Paul's original teaching of justification by faith strongly influenced the self understanding of the early Church, which was multicultural, with Jewish Christians, Africans, Greeks, and Roman citizens seeking genuinely to embrace and respect each other in worship.

For Paul, a multicultural inclusive ecclesia is more than a smattering of cultural differences in a defined space. The gospel imperative for the multicultural community is demonstrated in his imagery of the Body of Christ and the two creedal marks of oneness and catholicity. Both highlight the subject of unity in diversity. This appears to be central to Paul's multicultural vision. Paul's vision is of a common dependence of all members of the body on Christ alone, who is the head. It is given expression in terms of the mutual dependence of all members of the body, on each other, which 'conjure up a multicultural ecclesial vision of equality and justice for all.'[12]

In the quest for the Baptist Union to become a truly multicultural entity, racial justice needs to be a key element in its theology, and strategy. Justice questions relating to the equal sharing of properties, resourcing with justice and generosity, how decisions are made and by whom, are key issues for the Union. These processes need to be aware of the hermeneutical prism through which the Bible is interpreted and must incorporate an analysis of differing styles of leadership and worship. These are all key questions that Council, the Baptist Steering Group, our Colleges and Associations need to explore seriously.

To describe ourselves as multicultural requires us to rejoice in the diverse gifts of the human family and reject the sin of racism, which maligns the Christian community. We need to challenge institutional racism at all levels of the Church and society, and welcome and include liturgical diversity in worship.

A Sacrificial Community: Challenging White Privilege

One of the characteristics of institutional racism is its lack of willingness to critique White privilege and power. This understanding is well articulated by Peggy McIntosh, who wrote of White privilege from the perspective of a White person. In her writing she states:

---

[12] See Katalina Tahaafe-Williams' unpublished PhD Thesis for a more detailed exploration on the challenges of being a 'Multicultural Church' – *A Multicultural Church: Multicultural Ministry as a tool for building the Multicultural church.* (Birmingham: University of Birmingham, 2012).

As a White person I realised I had been taught about racism as something which puts others at a disadvantage but had been taught not to see one of its corollary aspects, White privilege which puts me at an advantage.[13]

So, White privilege is a term for societal privileges that benefit White people in Western countries beyond what is commonly experienced by minority ethnic people under the same social, political or economic circumstances.
McIntosh notes a number of conditions in which racial inequalities favour White people, from renting or buying a home without question to walking freely without suspicion; from driving an expensive car to purchasing bandages in 'flesh' colour. She concedes that she sees:

> ...a pattern running through the matrix of White privilege, a pattern of assumptions which were passed onto me as a White person. There was one main piece of cultural turf; it was my own turf and I was among those who could control the turf. My skin colour was an asset for any move I was educated to want to make.[14]

Even though the 'Apology' has contributed significantly to facilitating deeper cross-cultural relationships among many Baptists, it has not even begun to assist British Baptists to address the 'elephant in the room', namely, to reflect, review, and repudiate White privilege. This remains a perennial issue.
By the time this book is published, I will have been in my post as Racial Justice Coordinator for over 13 years. Over the last two years my workload on matters of racism has escalated - with 2015 being the most demanding[15].

African and Caribbean Baptist ministers have been keen to inform me of the racism they have experienced. At least once a month I have been asked to offer advice on a racist allegation committed by a church member. One of the primary drivers responsible for such behaviour is White privilege. White people believing that they have the right, because of their ethnicity, to be in positions of power and influence alone. When they feel that their positions are being challenged by minority ethnic people, their responses can sometimes be racist towards the people they feel are threatening their privileged position. This can sometimes mean that even in the most culturally diverse congregations, some White people feel the need to remain in positions of influence and power. Often, when a minority ethnic person has been called to be the pastor of a church, the White congregants, uncomfortable with a

---

[13] Peggy McIntosh – see http://ted.coe.wayne.edu/ele3600/mcintosh.html (Accessed the 3rd June 2016)
[14] Peggy McIntosh – see http://ted.coe.wayne.edu/ele3600/mcintosh.html (Accessed the 3rd June 2016)
[15] This book was in its early stages of preparation when the British electorate voted to leave the European Union. The rise in racialised intimidation and violence has been marked since the 'Brexit' vote. See http://www.aljazeera.com/news/2016/06/brexit-increase-racist-attacks-eu-referendum-160628045317215.html

Black or Asian person as their leader, will find a 'more suitable' fellowship in which to worship.

White privilege can also justify limited participation in racial justice issues. So, for example, where it concerns the 'Apology', many White Baptists conclude that it is a metaphor for a post-racial Union. As a Black person of African descent, I believe that privileged White Baptists should do everything possible to collaborate with those whose ethnicity is not naturally laden with respect and power, and as 'Baptists Together', we need to address the sin of racism in church and society.

White Baptists need to remember that the 'Apology' recognised itself as the beginning of the process and not the end. If the 'Apology' does not transform the heart and mind and challenge White, western theology and unearned White privilege, then it is simply a perfunctory experience, and not an act of repentance.

A Prophetic Community: Martin Luther King's understanding of a prophetic church
Martin Luther King refused to relegate following Christ to the private, spiritual realm or to the arenas of personal piety. Also, the conviction that one can change society by converting individuals was not an agenda promoted by him. For King, individual and social salvation had to occur simultaneously. The experience of rebirth must, according to King, translate into just institutions, structures, policies and laws. The Church at its best always addresses both individual and social salvation, thus justifying its existence as both the conscience of the State and the best symbol of the Christian community. King's legacy should stand as a reminder to British Baptists that being a prophet has no relationship with patriarchal domination or apolitical neutrality in the face of structural injustice. The real prophet speaks truth to power, challenging the actions of government and church when they undermine the Gospel message.

The scriptures have much to say about a prophetic community. The psalmists articulate at some length the essential character of God. God upholds the cause of the oppressed and defends the fatherless, the widow and the refugee. God's concern for the poor is woven through many psalms and marks the overarching message of the Hebrew prophets. The texts are clear; the poor are dependent on God. The prophets did not speak into a vacuum. The powerful have made unjust laws and oppressive policies that degrade and deprive the poor of their dignity and rights, and it is into that context that the prophets proclaimed, 'thus says the Lord'.

The prophets exercised clear advocacy on behalf of the vulnerable and held the rulers to account for their unjust practices. They spoke up for the marginalised, critiquing a form of religion unconcerned for the weak and the vulnerable. The prophets' messages and various legislative measures serve to reveal God's heart towards the vulnerable. The prophet is committed to helping humanity appreciate that all people, not just some, are created in the image of God, and are inherently and intrinsically beautiful.

So, the salient question that confronts Black Baptists and the whole Baptist Union of Great Britain is this: As a result of the 'Apology' do Black Baptists feel that we are now worshipping in a culturally liberated Union? Are we part of a Union committed to building the totality of our humanity? Is this a Union reflecting culturally diverse worship, preaching, theology and other aspects of what it is to represent the Kingdom of God? Is this a Union willing to make sacrifices for the creation and nurturing of genuine multicultural relationships; where the cultures of the all people in the union matter, are validated, valued and respectfully embraced?

Personally, I am in no doubt that the 'Apology' has made some difference to our common Baptist life in Britain. Many British Baptists are becoming increasingly aware that the theological injunction; to act justly, also applies to Baptists from minority ethnic communities. 'The Obama factor' (the notion that Obama's rise to the White House is a metaphor for a post-racial America), has become an unhelpful hindrance in moving forward the agenda for racial justice in BUGB. The notion that as a Union and a nation, we are now in a paradigm when racism has ended is a sentiment expressed by many British Baptists, as it relates to the 'Apology'. Is it no wonder, then, that many Baptists are of the opinion that the 2007 Apology in itself constitutes a post-racist Baptist Union? My retort to my colleagues holding this position continues to be that the 'Apology' is the beginning of the process and not the end.

The 'Apology' was a collective confession of racial injustice informed institutional sin. As the sin of racism has been unwittingly, and often consciously, permitted to live and breathe within our institution for decades, it will possibly take decades to be readdressed. History itself reinforces this. Historical and contemporary movements[16] challenging the sin of racism and other unjust practices, have some interesting commonalities.

Firstly, in each movement, there is a disparity between the investment of time in the struggle for justice and just societal outcomes. The Suffrage movement is an example worthy of mentioning; despite their persistent cry for voting and other rights, many women still earn less than men, for doing comparable jobs.

Secondly, in some cases it has taken decades for these movements to contribute to changes in unjust policies and laws. Even though a number of these changes were passed some years ago, on any given Sunday morning, for example, America remains among the most segregated continents in the world. Each of these movements, while not existing in exactly the form in which they were initially created, nonetheless, their continued activism reveals the unchanged nature of the injustice to which they sought to respond. That these movements could only bring about limited societal change highlights the need for our Union to continue being relentless in challenging racial injustice.

---

[16] The social movements I have in mind include The Arab Spring, Black Consciousness movements, Disability Rights, Global Justice, The Black Lives Matter campaign, Women's Suffrage, The Civil Right Movements, and many others.

We have to hope that because of the 'Apology' successive generations, including the generation of son and untold numbers of young Baptists, 'will not be judged by the colour of their skin but by the content of their character.' The fruits of the 'Apology' for our Churches, Colleges and Associations, will be judged not by us, per se, but by successive generations. Our present Baptist generation, therefore, cannot afford to engage in post-racist or colour blind rhetoric. We do not have the time for such forms of escapism or naivety. Post Apology, we need to work even harder in rooting out all forms of racism, in order to create a Baptist movement that speaks and lives prophetically, speaks of sacrifice and lives sacrificially; a movement that embodies racial justice in the very core of its being.

A White Guy Talks 'Race'
Steve Latham

Introduction: White Theology

> 'Why can't they just get over it?' 'Why do they keep bringing it up?' 'It was so long ago.' 'I wasn't even born when slavery happened.' 'We don't bear any responsibility for what happened in the past.' 'They've got a chip on their shoulder.' 'We need to stop talking about racism, and just work together.' 'Raising the issue will only make things worse.' 'Why do they have to have their own churches?' 'Shouldn't we all be united?' 'Why can't we just all 'get along'?' 'Isn't Christianity colour-blind?'

Frequently, when confronted by the claims of Black Christians, and their academic cousins, in Black theology, White Christians, pastors, and theologians take refuge in defensiveness. We give excuses. We try to move on. We admit there has been racism in the past, but assert that we need to progress beyond that now. We argue that because we were not personally involved in historical racist incidents, then we bear no share of guilt. Hence the objections by some White pastors, for example, to the Baptist Union's apology for the slave trade. In another incident I witnessed, two White pastors, uncomfortable at being challenged to consider their own racial attitudes, displaced their anxiety, and began making sexist remarks against the female workshop convenor.

However, being able to face up to our historical responsibility is essential for being able to move on. For this, we need to recover the Biblical sense of corporate solidarity in sin. This has two aspects: the historical and the sociological. Firstly, Daniel and Nehemiah, for example, repented before God for sins their people committed before they were born (Neh. 1.4-11: Dn. 9.4-19). Although we were not personally responsible for past sins, such as slavery, we do benefit from them, as the historical long term prosperity of our nation derives from it.

Secondly, racism does not simply lie in the past, but there are sins of racism happening now; and insofar as we are part of a group, which practises racism, then we are implicated in it, and must accept responsibility, in terms both of repentance and practical action against it.

Many Black sisters and brothers, of course, want to help us move past being immobilised by our guilt-feelings, to actually do something practical about racism. We do not want to remain stuck in guilt. Confronting guilt, however, is still an essential precondition for moving forward, beyond it.[1]

---

[1] James Baldwin, 'The White Man's Guilt', *Ebony* (August 1965), pp. 47-48

Facing up to the discomfort of discussing racism is inescapable if we are to learn how to overcome it. Even in writing this essay, I am again reminded of my own complicity in the sin of racism. This is necessary, even as we are repeatedly plunged into fresh situations, which expose the raw edges of prejudice, stereotyping, and discrimination.

The aforementioned often inhabit the heart of even the most 'right on' liberal Christian. Going 'past blame', as bell hooks puts it,[2] does not mean avoiding responsibility. It is not for the White believer to demand forgiveness, to demand that the debate moves on. It is for the Black believer to graciously offer forgiveness, and to declare precisely when the moment might come to move on, if it comes at all, in the contemporary sphere.

One of the greatest obstacles to the White person realising their own culpability, is that our own 'Whiteness,' is so invisible to us. The problem is always other people. 'They are Black; we are ordinary.' 'They have a culture; we are normal.' 'They are ethnic; but we don't have an ethnicity.' We consider to be 'commonsense' what is actually part of our culture. However, when anything appears natural or 'neutral', then we know we are in the presence of a particular ideology.[3]

In reality, our culture is socially constructed, although not always consciously and over time.[4] What counts as 'White culture' is, therefore, not normal but a human creation. It has been elevated as the norm in our culture, so much so that we do not even recognise it any more.[5] This is a historical process, as new ethnic groups are progressively incorporated into an enlarged conception of 'Whiteness,' for political reasons.[6] Although, most of this literature originates in North America, it remains true that racism has also been historically formed in Britain too.[7] This affects our theology. Our theology is also 'White', made by and according to White norms of debate and rationality, embodying the questions of a White academia and ekklesia.[8]
To address this requires constructing a critical White theological engagement, to deconstruct the norms of theological discussion, exposing its 'White'

---

[2] bell hooks, *Writing Beyond Race. Living Theory and Practice* (New York: Routledge, 2013), pp. 26-8
[3] Slavoj Žižek, *In Defense of Lost Causes* (London: Verso, 2009), p. 21
[4] Peter L. Berger and Thomas Luckmann, *The Social Construction of Reality* (London: Allen Lane The Penguin Press, 1967)
[5] Jeff Hitchcock, *Lifting the White Veil. An Exploration of White American Culture in a Multicultural Context* (Roselle, NJ: Crandall, Dostie & Douglass Books, Inc., 2002)
[6] Nell Irvin Painter, *The History of White People* (New York: W. W. Norton & Company, 2010), pp. 201-211, 359-373, 383-396
[7] Ann Dummett, *A Portrait of English Racism* (Manchester: CARAF Publications, 1984)
[8] Tom Beaudoin and Katherine Turpin, 'White Practical Theology', in Kathleen A. Cahalan and Gordon S. Mikorski (eds.), *Opening the Field of Practical Theology. An Introduction* (Lanham, MD: Rowman & Litchfield, 2014), pp. 251-269

origins, and directing it into a relevant liberatory praxis.[9] This will need to be provoked through a dialogical encounter with the insights of Black theologians, such as Anthony Reddie.[10]

Learning to recognise ourselves for what we are, i.e. 'White', and conceptualising it in a way that opposes the unquestioned supremacy of the norms embedded within it, means we need to actually meet, and listen to, the 'other'. For how can we be saved unless we hear the liberating word preached by the other (Romans. 10.14-15)? For me, conscientization began in university, studying South African Black Theology. Heart transformation, however, occurred through encountering people during ministry in the inner city.

Here, I became aware of the hidden recesses of prejudice, within my own heart. Today, we still need to prepare White pastors for ministry in multicultural areas. For this, they will need immersion, through placements in multicultural churches. These can be supplemented through 'Racism Awareness Workshops'. During formal seminary studies, specialised modules, for example in Black theology, can be helpful; but this may marginalise anti-racist concerns within an academic ghetto. So we need to insist on including Black theologians within regular modules alongside the usual suspects. Furthermore, we must not expect our Black believers to take sole responsibility for challenging racism in teaching contexts. White Christians need to take the initiative in addressing what is a White problem.

Liberation through the Black Christ
One theme arising from Black theological reflection is that of the Black Christ. Clearly this concept or symbol resonates existentially with the lived experience of Black people throughout the world. In this way, the exploitation and oppression of racism is both borne, and overcome, by Jesus on the cross and in the resurrection. Can this same symbol, however, be a source of liberation for White folks as well?

On a personal note, studying Black theology introduced me to the concept of the Black Christ. Spiritually, the Black Christ has been a presence in my own devotional life, also. Before I began ministry, I went on retreat and had a vision of Christ, who appeared as a large Black man, emerging out of the sea, and asking me to join him as he fed people scattered on the beach. While this risks parody as a typical piece of White paternalism, it remains for me one of the defining moments of my own calling, to be a servant of the Black Christ.

On the other hand, the Black Christ is suspect in the realms of systematic theology. Surely, by stressing the particularity of the Black experience, we are in danger of losing the universality of Christ himself?

---

[9] Chris Shanahan, *Voices from the Borderland. Re-imagining Cross-cultural Theology in the Twenty-first Century* (London: Equinox, 2010), pp. 228-234
[10] Anthony G. Reddie, *Is God Colour-blind? Insights from Black Theology for Christian Ministry* (London: SPCK, 2009), pp. 48-52

Instead, systematic theology attempts to define some objective idea of who Christ was and is. Yet, this claim represents a particular social location, of 'Whiteness' as somehow normal, unquestioned. Black theology consequently challenges this assumption of academia as a neutral space from which to make Olympian pronouncements.[11] A supposedly objective picture of Christ, however, is one which is ignorant of its own cultural conditioning. The abstraction from particularity, in which systematic theology engages, may indeed be essential to concept formation; however, the process must be one which nurtures, rather than negating, the social experience of each person. For this, the artificial distinction between systematic and practical theologies must be removed, through self-aware reflection on our contextual embeddedness.

It may be objected that Christ was not historically 'Black' – that is, of African descent. To portray him thus would, therefore, be to do violence to the actual reality of his lived existence, and to remake him in the image and interest of a particular social group. The claim could be then made that Black theology is merely repeating, in reverse, the mistakes of colonialist and imperialist theologies.

Here, the image of Christ was re-made in order to justify and naturalise the position of European rulers as themselves representatives of the Divine image. Of course, Christ was not White, blonde-haired and blue-eyed. He is, however, still depicted as such, in stained-glass windows, posters, book illustrations, and Sunday school materials, in churches throughout the country. These images, sadly, can still be found in many BME congregations, which have internalised the racist stereotypes, with the membership often preferring traditional pictures of Jesus over more diverse ethnic and cultural images.

It is at this level, of popular religion, that the issue of the Black Christ first hits home. Even where churches attempt to be relevant through using data-projection to illustrate sermons, there is still shock value in displaying non-European images of Christ. While Black believers experience devaluation through their own religious invisibility, White believers also miss out through this Europeanization of Jesus. In contrast, the Black Christ confronts us with our own particularity, and liberates us from the narrowness of our own positionality.

Furthermore, rather than undermining the universality of Christ, the symbol of the Black Christ actually reinforces and guarantees it. By judicious use of the doctrine of the Incarnation, we can discover fresh riches in our experience of Christ, both personally and socially. Essential to any doctrine of the Incarnation is the idea of *kenosis* (Phil. 2.6-8). There is, however, a socio-political aspect to *kenosis*. Specifically, Christ took on the form, or experience, of a servant in his self-emptying. There is, thus, a sociological class base to the Incarnation. Although he was rich, he became poor, for our sakes, for our liberation and salvation (2 Co. 8.9). Christ does not only identify with humanity as such. In particular, he identifies with the poor and oppressed.

---

[11] Basil Moore, 'What is Black Theology?', in Basil Moore (ed.), *Black Theology. The South African Voice* (London: Hurst & Company, 1973), pp. 5-7

Such an understanding roots Black theology within the wider methodological and schematic frameworks of 'Theologies of Liberation'. It is saved from spiritualised, magical, thinking by emphasising that, as one of the oppressed, Christ created and led a social movement of liberation among the poor, the 'anawim', the people of the land, which continues as we speak. In relation to Black theology, Christ is therefore, said to be 'Black', precisely because he takes on himself the condition of all the 'wretched of the earth',[12] the marginalised and alienated from mainstream society. Because Black people are, *qua* Black (irrespective of personal wealth), excluded, then, Jesus must be 'Black'. Furthermore, this is so, not only symbolically, but ontologically, as Christ takes on and shares the experience of oppressed people. He shares their being, and they share his. The Incarnation, therefore, requires that Jesus be 'Black'. Orthodox theology grounds anti-racist theological orthopraxis.

Therefore, far from being a threat to Christ's universality, the notion of the Black Christ suggests a way to reconcile the dynamic tension between his universality and particularity, because there is a cultural as well as a political dimension to the particularity of Christ's Incarnation. Irenaeus' doctrine of 'Recapitulation', for example, pictures Christ summing up in himself the whole of human nature, and then ascending bodily to heaven so that this very human nature is now resident in heaven, sitting on a throne.[13] In order to do this, however, Christ had to become a particular human being, a specific person. One cannot become a human being in general. To say that Christ recapitulated human nature in general remains an idealist abstraction, a Gnostic heresy, unless he was incarnated as a single individual.[14]

It is in his very particularity, by being someone in particular, that he represented the whole human race in all our diversity. Christ's universality is guaranteed by his particularity. Historically, Christ was not a Han Chinese woman from the Ming Dynasty, for example, but a Jewish man from the period of Roman occupation. As James Cone wrote, 'Jesus is who he was'. It is his very Jewishness, part of an oppressed people, which provides grounds for asserting his Blackness.[15]

Christ identifies with the oppressed, in his past historical incarnation and in his present historical realisation, today. He is the singularity, which condenses the experiences of the multitude, and then re-institutes itself as a

---

[12] Frantz Fanon, *The Wretched of the Earth* (Harmondsworth: Penguin, 1985)
[13] Henry Bettenson (ed.), *The Early Christian Fathers. A selection from the writings of the Fathers from St. Clement of Rome to St. Athanasius* (Oxford: Oxford University Press, 1956), pp. 81-83
[14] J. Kameron Carter, *Race. A Theological Account* (New York: Oxford University Press, 2008), pp. 24-29
[15] James H. Cone, *God of the Oppressed* (London: SPCK, 1977), pp. 115-136

corporeal movement[16]: AKA the Body of Christ. There can, therefore, be many, multiple, Christologies, to suit our pluralistic, social situation.[17]

While maintaining the particularity of the historical Jesus, the universal Christ of faith will be re-envisioned according to the particular oppressions of sin from which people need to be liberated. In this sense, the Black Christ is Christ-for-everyone. He is the pattern for the owning of Christ by every excluded group, according to their own image. The Black Christ is the universal Christ.

Salvation for White Folks
Taking up W. E. B. Dubois' depiction of the pain in the 'souls of White folks,'[18] we also see that the Black Christ indicates the route towards social salvation for White Christians, as well. Paul, for example, constructed the kenotic, self-emptying, Christ as a discipleship model for the believer (Phil. 2.5-8). The insight has been developed by Henri Nouwen, as a programme of downward social mobility for the Christian, as we reject power and privilege, in favour of identification with the powerless and downtrodden.[19] This, of course, represents a gospel requirement of those who have a position to give up. To balance it, we need Mary's song of liberation where, alongside God bringing down the rulers, God also lifts up the humble (Lk. 1.52). The way the Gospel addresses different social groupings is also different. For one, it means to step lower, for another to come up higher (Lk. 14.7-11).

However, this does not entail indulging White romantic notions. Some want to 'become Black', or to be loved by Black people, suitably grateful for our condescending help. There will always be a gap, something of a painful tension. Identification can never be complete. We will remain 'White', retaining our social location. As Cone points out, however, the issue is what we do with the power we possess, how we orientate ourselves politically. Do we simply accept and enjoy our privilege, or do we actively oppose the system, which has tried to co-opt us?[20]

Likewise, we must avoid any paternalistic attitude of helping those whom we consider lower down the social scale. Instead, as James Perkinson wrote in his ground-breaking book, we must reverse the order of priority. The roles of learner and teacher are turned around, as we submit to the pedagogy

---

[16] Gerald Raunig, *Factories of Knowledge. Industries of Creativity* (Los Angeles, CA: Semiotexte. Intervention Series 15, 2013), pp. 9-16
[17] Volker Küster, *The Many Faces of Jesus Christ* (London: SCM Press, 2001)
[18] W. E. B. Du Bois, 'The Souls of White Folks', in David Levering Lewis (ed.), *W. E. B. Du Bois: A Reader* (New York: Henry Holt and Company, Inc., 1995), pp. 453-465
[19] Henri J.M. Nouwen, *The Selfless Way of Christ: Downward Mobility and the Spiritual Life* (London: Darton Longman & Todd, 2007)
[20] Cone Ibid, p. 220

of Black people.[21] This stance implies, as Justo and Catherine Gonzalez wrote, that the oppressed possess an epistemological advantage.[22] Read from the underside, Scripture reveals a more accurate understanding of the power dynamics in society. In practice, this produces a steady stream of uncomfortable episodes for the White Christian, as there will always be new layers of sin to be exposed to, through tense stand-offs. For the White church leader, in particular, this is a regular occurrence, as church members challenge his or her presuppositions. This posture of corrigibility, however, deriving from a robust doctrine of original sin, is exactly what is needed to ensure any progress in racial justice.

To be authentic, such learning must result in action. Faith must be accompanied by works; moreover, the works spelled out in James's letter include the socio-economic sphere, not just the individualistic sins often cited by conservative Christians (Jas. 1.27-2.17). Regarding racism, Barbara Trepagnier, for instance, has examined how 'well-meaning White people' actually perpetuate racism, even when they claim to be against it.[23] They think of themselves as 'non-racist', because they do not actively commit 'racist acts'. Thus, they feel free from guilt. They also fail to actively challenge racism. Not merely 'non-racism', but 'anti-racism,' is demanded. This takes our practice of *kenosis* to its logical conclusion, since it was Jesus' challenge to structures of exclusion, which led to his own exclusion and death (He. 13.12-14).

Actively confronting racism must entail leaving our comfort zone and entering the conflict zone. It could also lead to our exclusion. Most White Christians, however, seek to defuse conflict; but if we are aiming at God's multi-racial goal, then conflict is inevitable – sometimes with the racists, often between well-meaning White Christians and the Black Christians who challenge them.[24] Complaints and conflicts prompted by those on the underside are necessary provocations for change (Acts. 6.1). This will require a spirituality which is able to analyse the question of power.[25] The lack of promotion for Black church leaders within our ecclesial structures, local and national,[26] will, therefore, require us to be confrontational, as we challenge

---

[21] James W. Perkinson, *White Theology. Outing Supremacy in Modernity* (New York: Palgrave Macmillan, 2004), pp. 185-248
[22] Justo L. Gonzalez and Catherine Gunsalus Gonzalez. *The Liberating Pulpit* (Eugene, OR: Wipf & Stock, 2003), pp. 18-21
[23] Barbara Trepagnier, *Silent Racism: How Well-Meaning White People Perpetuate the Racial Divide* (Boulder, CO: Paradigm Publishers, 2006), pp. 5-7, 47-62
[24] Duane Elmer, *Cross-Cultural Conflict: Building Relationships for Effective Ministry* (Downers Grove, IL: IVP, 1993)
[25] Eric H. F. Law, *The Wolf Shall Dwell with the Lamb. A Spirituality for Leadership in a Multicultural Community* (St. Louis, MO: Chalice Press, 1993), pp. 53-61
[26] Anthony B. Bradley (ed.), *Aliens in the Promised Land. Why Minority Leadership is Overlooked in White Christian Churches and Institutions* (Philipsburg, NJ: P&R Publishing, 2013)

institutional racism, which is the systematic exclusion of minority ethnic people from positions of power.[27]

A truly anti-racist stance, however, will not limit itself to changing power relationships within the church. In addition, we are obliged to prophetically denounce the racist applications of power within society as a whole. The church must, therefore, be involved in immigration, housing, policing and other issues of importance to minority ethnic communities.

Typically, New Testament scholarship depicts the Jewish believers' reluctance to accept Gentile believers as equals in the new covenant (Gal. 2.11-21). White Christians are then challenged, by analogy, to likewise welcome the stranger and the alien (Dt. 10.19). A more accurate analogy for the position of the White Christian in the New Testament, however, would be the actual gentile power, which oppressed the Jews, namely, the Roman Empire.

The scandal of the gospel is, therefore, the acceptance of the oppressor by the oppressed on the equal terms of God's free grace. The beneficiaries of the system, Roman or White, are paradoxically saved through their incorporation into the social body of the downtrodden. We can compare this with Robert Beckford's identification of Black Christians in White-led churches with the house slaves who lived in the 'big house'.[28] In this light, White believers correspond to the servants and employees who ran the plantation, but who have switched sides in a movement aimed at subverting the entire imperial plantation system. As people who benefit from these power arrangements, we are those who 'belong to Caesar's household' (Phil. 4.22).

Conclusion: Black Spirit
In addition, I also feel a bit like Paul who lamented that his own people, the Jews, had rejected the good news (Rom. 9.1-5). For many White people today, talk of the Black Christ, for example, will only further entrench them in their views, that the political and intellectual classes have sold out to the powers of political correctness. How can we erect the 'bridges' needed to build multicultural communities?[29] I am concerned at the cultural denuding and reracination of, particularly, the White working class, alienated from society and from church.[30] Poor White communities may be psychologically compensated for by being allowed entry into the privileged category of 'Whiteness'; but there is a psychic and spiritual price to be paid for such acceptance. Thandeka has written about the 'shame, which occurs within the

---

[27] Maurice Hobbs, *Better Will Come. A Pastoral Response to Institutional Racism in British Churches*. Grove Pastoral Series 48 (Nottingham: Grove Books Ltd., 1991)

[28] Robert Beckford, *Jesus is Dread: Black Theology and Black Culture in Britain* (London: Darton Longman & Todd, 1998), pp. 45-46

[29] Paul Weller, *The Problems of the White Ethnic Minority* (London: CARAF/ONE for Christian Renewal, n.d.), p. 14

[30] Lucinda Borkett-Jones, 'Chav Christianity', *Christianity* (February 2014), pp. 32-35

White heart, as we learn to deny aspects of ourselves in order to fit in with the system of White supremacy.[31]

Salvation must, therefore, apply to both oppressor and oppressed. The Black Christ liberates White as well as Black. As White Christians in South Africa learned, challenged by the Black consciousness movement, 'White liberation' means being set free from our own prejudices, for society itself to be reconstructed on a non-racial foundation.[32] For this, the church is meant to be a pilot project of God's ultimate intention (Rev. 7.9). This, in turn, means standing against alternative constructions of identity and belonging.[33] With the nostalgic melancholy prompted by the loss of empire,[34] White Christians sometimes retreat into the little Englandism of UKIP, with its racialised, anti-immigrant, rhetoric. Christian language is also explicitly deployed by groups like 'Britain First', who claim to be defending 'Christian Britain' against the Muslim threat. Perhaps, we therefore need to revisit the radical British tradition.[35]

In Christian terms, this means revitalising the history of the Lollards and Levellers, dissenters and Non-conformists, who pioneered and preserved a British notion of liberty – what in the U.S., Cornel West calls the 'prophetic tradition'.[36] So, too, it might mean reinvestigating notions of 'Englishness', as debates are joined about our sense of English identity, in the face of the increasing push for Scottish devolution. However, this must be done in a way which opens us up to difference and the 'other' in culture and ethnicity; a radically new conception of national identity based on hospitality and welcome.

Theologically, the concept of the Black Christ also needs to be complemented by renewed Trinitarian and Pneumatological emphases. The main shortcoming of the Black Christ theology is that of one-dimensional Christological approaches, which ignore the distinctively Christian doctrine of the Trinity.[37] It is understandable that in reaction against the over-cerebral concentration of much Western and White theology, liberation theology in general, and Black theology in particular, have concentrated on the historical,

---

[31] Thandeka, *Learning to be White. Money, Race, and God in America* (New York: The Continuum Publishing Company, 1999), p. 12
[32] H. Kleinschmidt (ed.), *White Liberation. A Collection of Essays*: Special Programme for Christian Action in Society (Johannesburg: Spro-cas 2, 1972)
[33] Andrew Davey, 'Confronting a Beast: The Church of England and the British National Party', *International Journal of Public Theology* 5 (2011), pp. 435-457
[34] Paul Gilroy *After Empire: Melancholia or Convivial Culture?* (Abingdon: Routledge, 2004)
[35] Tony Benn (ed.), *Writings on the Wall: Radical and Socialist Anthology, 1215-1984* (London: Faber & Faber, 1984)
[36] Cornel West, *Democracy Matters: Winning the Fight against Imperialism* (New York: Penguin, 2004), pp. 145-172
[37] Fred Sanders, *Embracing the Trinity: Life with God in the Gospel* (Nottingham: IVP, 2010), p. 168

empirical figure of Jesus, and taken his liberatory praxis as the model for our own.

Perhaps, to further a Trinitarian emphasis to the wider 'Theologies of Liberation', we can take two lines. Firstly, the interior, social relations, of the Trinity are a model for the relationship within God's people, of sameness with difference, and contain, therefore, a hint of what may be helpful for White-Black relations. Secondly, it is important to recover a Black Holy Spirit, a counter-balance to the Black Christ. This has the added advantage of perhaps forging a connection with the BME Pentecostal churches. As Anthony Reddie has noted, Black theology has often failed to incorporate a specific emphasis on the Holy Spirit in its reflections, and he has, therefore, produced work on reinterpreting the doctrine of the Spirit, to redress Black theology's over-emphasis on Christology.[38]

Restoring the idea of the liberating Spirit does not, however, mean the eclipse of the Black Christ, since it is he who announced the presence of the Spirit in his own ministry, in his 'Nazareth Manifesto' (Lk. 4.18-19). It was this same Jesus who went on to operate in the power of the Spirit in his spirit-filled encounters with the forces of imperial domination and demonization (Lk. 8.30).[39] Hence, the Black Spirit inaugurates the way, a first step, towards a fully-Trinitarian theology of liberation.

As regards White churches, and White Christians, such a pneumatological theme may, moreover, help to build bridges with two diametrically-opposed constituencies. Firstly, with radical, social activists, within White churches. For them, this may also contribute to their spiritual renewal, away from arid initiatives, which have often become, in effect, secular. Devoid of any spiritual aspect, and therefore, enervating and exhausting, compulsive activism frequently furthers the tendency to burn-out among community workers and political radicals. For them, refreshing through a politically-engaged practice of prayer and contemplation, as described by Thomas Merton and Kenneth Leech,[40] could provide genuine spiritual renewal. Secondly, a Spirit-emphasis may encourage connections between the Pentecostal stream of BME churches, and the charismatic churches of the White highlands, and thereby, confront their frequent privatised, individualised distortion of the gospel.

Here, however, we must not just regard Black Christians merely as a resource for the renewal of White churches, as if they only exist for the benefit which White people can derive from them. This has the danger of producing a parasitic, neo-colonial renewal movement. It is possible, after all, to steal

---

[38] Anthony G. Reddie, *SCM Core Text: Black Theology* (London: SCM Press, 2012), pp. 114-140
[39] Ched Myers, *Binding the Strongman: A Political Reading of Mark's Story of Jesus* (New York: Orbis Books, 1988)
[40] Thomas Merton, *Contemplation in a World of Action* (London: George Allen & Unwin, 1971); Kenneth Leech, *The Eye of the Storm. Spiritual Resources for the Pursuit of Justice* (Darton Longman & Todd, 1992)

culture as well as countries. For example, it is commonplace to hear talk of how migrants have saved the British churches, as in London. This is to treat them, however, as if they only exist to save us, without any worth in their own right, along their own historical and theological trajectories.

White Christians need to attend to what the Spirit is saying to them. One of those will be that we must join the liberation movement of the Spirit that has begun elsewhere. We need to accept and rejoice in the decentring of our subjectivity inherent in that movement, and to do so, with all the peoples of the earth who form the empirical body of Christ. This is the apologetic work called for from a reconstructive, White theology.

Part Three: Post-Apology

The Journey: The Research Process
Graham Sparkes

When in 1986 the United Church of Canada made an 'Apology to First Nations', the 'All Native Circle Conference'[1] responded to this by receiving and acknowledging the apology, but not accepting it. Why? Because in the indigenous, native tradition, an apology has to be lived out if it is a real apology. Until it is lived out, it remains unfinished business.[2] Reconciliation requires a process of justice-making before it can be said to be complete. The making of an apology is only the first stage.

When in November 2007 the Council of the Baptist Union of Great Britain (BUGB) passed a resolution making apology for participation in the horror of slavery, Council acknowledged with humility that 'we are only at the start of a journey'. It then went on to declare:

> We commit ourselves, in a true spirit of repentance, to take what we have learned from God in the Council and to share it widely in our Baptist community and beyond, looking for gospel ways by which we can turn the words and feelings we have expressed today into concrete actions and contribute to the prophetic work of God's coming Kingdom.[3]

In other words, the fine words expressed in the 'Apology' could only be a first step. The task of reconciliation required much more of us as a community of Baptist Christians if that Apology was to have real meaning and to find proper acceptance.

It is this conviction that led the 'Faith and Unity Department' of BUGB, with the guidance of its Racial Justice Working Group (RJWG), to begin what became known as the 'Journey'. The 'Journey' had as its overall vision the building of a culturally inclusive way of living as Baptists – one that reflected our cultural diversity, where BME members would be a participatory presence at all levels, and above all, where they would know that they belonged. The 'Journey' was about pursuing racial justice within a context where the legacy of discrimination and racism continued to exist, and even at times, to prosper. The more detailed aims reflected this vision, expressing the

---

[1] For further details on this body see the following link: http://allnativecircleconference.com/
[2] See J. Bergen, *Ecclesial Repentance*, (Edinburgh: T&T Clark, 2011), p244
[3] Baptist Union of Great Britain, Council Resolution, November 2007. The full text can be found at: http://www.baptist.org.uk/Articles/366545/Faith_and_Society.aspx

need to support and resource churches, colleges, associations, and the central resource for BUGB to embrace and live out what it means to become a culturally, inclusive family.[4]

There is no doubt that both vision and aims were bold in their scope. Challenging structures and transforming patterns of living are not tasks to be undertaken lightly! At the time, however, there was a strong sense of conviction that nothing less was good enough! This journey towards reconciliation had to be all-embracing and it needed to address every aspect of our life together as Baptists in the search for truth and justice.

How was all this to be achieved? It quickly became evident that we had to begin by doing some very detailed research in order to establish a base from which to work. BUGB is a large and complex organisation. The Baptist Union is a mixture of very different communities and groupings, with a strong sense of interrelatedness, while often having a structural independence from each other. This unity and interdependence displays both strong institutional elements, and at the same time, a fluid commitment to being a movement.

To understand the existing awareness of issues of racial justice and to be able to respond effectively to current experience and practice required the kind of research that took seriously the multifaceted nature of BUGB. In a sense, we needed to hold up a mirror to the life of BUGB, to enable it to see itself much more clearly, and to reveal the kind of evidence that would support future action.

The RJWG decided on a methodology that involved two complementary approaches. One involved quantitative research and consisted of a questionnaire sent to all churches within BUGB. The questionnaire asked a range of questions designed to establish factual information regarding ethnic diversity within congregations, and more significantly, their participation in the worship and leadership of their churches. The other method used involved qualitative research, and consisted of a series of semi-structured interviews with representatives of the key institutions and groupings, within BUGB. It was this qualitative research that was to provide vital insight and strategic direction for 'The Journey,' and by the end of 2008, with the support of BUGB Council, preparations were made.

It is worth noting two features that were to be fundamental to the qualitative research. First, this was to be a listening process. The lived experience of the RJWG had taught us that giving expression to issues of racial justice could, and did, provoke defensive reactions from some within BUGB and outright resistance from others. For example, earlier offers of training in racial justice awareness had been met by a less than universal welcome.
The debate and discussion leading up to the 'Apology' itself had revealed deep-seated fears and tensions. So if the 'Journey' was to fulfil our vision we knew that we needed to begin, not by just giving voice to a set of tasks that needed to be done, but by allowing and enabling the different perspectives and

---

[4] See report prepared for Council, October 2008

experiences held within BUGB to be heard. We constructed a set of questions that would allow us to listen carefully and thoughtfully, that would as far as possible, give space and time for interviewees to be able to share openly and honestly.

Second, this was to be a discerning process. This was to be a way by which, with the help of one another, we would seek to discern what the Spirit was saying to BUGB. Interestingly, in preparing BUGB for this research process the RJWG offered a tentative vision of what the future might look like once the 'Journey' was complete. It spoke, for example, of having all the resources needed to build culturally diverse churches and association, of a central resource that was shaped by such diversity, and of colleges that drew on insights from many different cultures.

This was far from being prescriptive and certainly offered no pre-planned agenda. Indeed, one might suggest it did little more than paint a picture of what the Kingdom of God might look like! I believe this was an attempt to help everyone to see the research as discernment, as a way by which we listened to the voice of the Spirit and sought to discover what it might mean to build the Kingdom of God on earth.

These underlying features were supported by additional, careful preparation that included drafting the questions and issues to be addressed. Additionally, we also identified people whom we should interview, deciding how best the interviews would be managed, and carrying out a pilot exercise in order to test and refine both questions and process. The list of proposed interviewees included half of BUGB associations, the majority of its colleges, departments within the central resource at Didcot, representatives of the council, executive committees and the presidency, together with key members and groupings from the BME communities within BUGB. In other words, the qualitative research was to engage, primarily, with the institutional life of BUGB.

Just a few years earlier, the UK Government had published what had become known as the 'Macpherson Report': an enquiry into the police handling of the death of Stephen Lawrence.[5] Both the report and its aftermath had been on our agenda within the 'Faith and Unity' Department at BUGB, and particularly, the attention it gave to the need to address 'institutional racism'. Without doubt this was part of the background that shaped our own research process. In the light of the apology we wanted to give proper attention to the ways in which the legacy of slavery continued to be present within the institutional life of the church, in this country, including amongst Baptists in our Union. We wanted the process of listening and discernment, to address our structural life, not just that of our individual congregations.

The research began in 2009 and continued through much of 2010. Alongside the qualitative interviews, the questionnaires were also distributed to all churches. The interview team consisted of three people – Wale Hudson-

---

[5] W. Macpherson, *The Stephen Lawrence Inquiry*, presented to Parliament by the Secretary of State for the Home Department, February 1999

Roberts (BUGB Racial Justice Coordinator) and Rosemarie Davidson-Gotobed (first Racial Justice co-ordinator for the London Baptist Association) led the interviews, and I was present, mainly to record what was said and shared. As far as possible, we kept to the same team throughout, to ensure that our findings were as consistent as possible.

What was significant about being involved in such an intensive listening process? It is worth noting at the outset that there were over 1,500 completed questionnaires representing about three quarters of all BUGB churches, and of those invited to participate in the interviews, there were none who refused. I believe that this was an indication of the seriousness with which BUGB had embraced the 'Journey'. Most of the interviews lasted in excess of two hours and a majority involved at least two or three people. There was no indication of resentment or antagonism towards those of us demanding this level involvement. The importance of the 'Apology' had been widely recognised and the case for the 'Journey' had been successfully made.

At the same time it was, I imagine, a longer and more demanding process than any of us had anticipated when we began. While we could have conducted fewer interviews and been more selective in our listening, we chose to engage as widely as possible, with the result that we amassed almost 40 hours of recorded material from visits made over several months. We discovered that listening is demanding! Factual information (such as statistical data on numbers of BME staff, students and committee members) was easily collected. The substance of the interviews, however, was to discover levels of awareness, explore experiences of cultural diversity, reflect on the inclusivity of patterns of ministerial formation, and hear how issues of racial justice are addressed.

Words spoken can hide meaning as well as reveal it, and so the discernment required us to continually probe what was shared, in order to understand as deeply as possible. Time and care was needed, throughout, both in listening and then later in interpreting. An important realisation that emerged as the interviewing progressed was the variety of experiences being shared. We listened as both colleges and associations illustrated their very different contexts, and we attempted to distinguish that which was held in common and that which was unique to each circumstance. There were many examples.

- Geographical location meant that certain associations had little contact with BME communities and so had to consider what awareness of cultural diversity and racial justice issues looked like for their churches. For others the BME communities consisted primarily of adherents to other faiths, and so this presented particular challenges to churches seeking to engage in mission. For the South Wales Baptist Association, the relationship between Welsh and English was an important issue in addressing issues of cultural diversity!
- The difficulties faced by Baptist BME students at the colleges and ministers in the churches were disturbingly similar as institutions

struggled to provide the kind of support needed. Yet the responses that had been developed for dealing with complaints of racist attitudes and actions varied considerably and the attempts to offer appropriate guidance and support lacked consistency. The absence of BME representation within the structures was often a factor.
- The London Baptist Association and Spurgeon's College stood out as exceptions with both having levels of diversity unknown anywhere else. Thus, 45% of churches had majority BME congregations, and the college described itself as having a critical mass of BME students that enabled key issues to receive proper attention. At the same time, it was interesting to note that the challenge of ensuring proportionate representation within the institutional structures remained the same.

Through the listening we learned that there was a sense in which a range of strategies were needed that responded to the varying contexts in which BUGB existed and ministered. No one fixed programme would resonate with all constituencies within the Union. Agendas had to be developed that would respond to particular circumstances.

A concluding reflection is that the listening process left those of us involved with a mixed sense of hope and fear. There was hope due to the evident willingness to embrace the 'Journey' that has been noted previously, and in the resulting report that went to Council it was stated that there was 'wide agreement that the "Apology" acted as a turning point in the consciousness of many British Baptists'.[6]

The case for change had been recognised. Indeed, there was emerging evidence of the steps that were already being taken to build culturally inclusive communities within BUGB, and these offered tangible signs of what could be achieved. Alongside this, however, was a fear that our listening and discerning had uncovered a mixture of helplessness and inertia due to a number of inter-related factors.

Many throughout the structural institutions of BUGB were clearly weighed down by the demands and expectations being placed upon them. So, an agenda promoting cultural diversity and racial justice was regarded as just one more burden, however necessary and important as it may have been viewed. In addition, the complexity of addressing the tasks was acknowledged and recognised by many who were part of the listening process. Questions were articulated such as: How do we formulate an appropriate response when the clashes between different cultures feel insoluble? Where are the resources that can help us address identified concerns? How do we find the confidence needed to navigate structural change? Perhaps, most fundamental of all, people were asking whether real change was possible when the 'Journey' was raising such complex concerns.

---

[6] See report prepared for Council, October 2010

As those engaged in listening and discerning, we lived with these responses, recognising that they were often half-hidden, and sought to make them part of the task of interpretation, as the data came to be analysed.

The task of assessing and interpreting the wealth of evidence collected, and then seeking to draw out concluding recommendations, involved three stages. The first was a draft analysis that sought to summarize both quantitative and qualitative data, prepared by Richard Kidd, a member of the RJWG and an experienced researcher. This was subsequently developed into a full report outlining the main findings, which was presented to BUGB Council for discussion in November 2010. The aim was to continue to ensure proper ownership of the process by Council and to enable members to make a response prior to having to agree to way forward.

The final stage required the 'Faith and Unity' Department take the analysis and findings arising from the listening process, together with the comments and reflections offered by Council, as a result of their discussion and to propose a series of six recommendations that subsequently came to Council for approval in March 2011.[7]

These six recommendations sought to give primary attention to the research findings that had emerged from the listening and discernment process. This was vital for the integrity of the process. Attention was also given, however, to the context in which the 'Journey' had developed, the societal context in which BUGB engaged in ministry and mission, and the future demands of implementation. Thus, it is worth recognising how these various dimensions found expression.

The overall aim of the 'Journey' had spoken of building inclusive communities free of racism, and in keeping with the Baptist emphasis on the local gathered church, the first recommendation concentrated on church congregations and promoted the development of multiculturalism. The word 'multiculturalism' needed to be carefully defined and defended, not least, because it had become a contentious term within UK politics.

This was particularly case in the hands of those who wanted integration and assimilation of other cultures into some kind of British culture. The term was rooted in specific theological convictions. These convictions are ones that articulate a deep commitment to develop communities that genuinely value and respect diversity, that are open to enrichment through worship and sharing, and that seek to be multicultural.

Within several of the resolutions there was a deliberate attempt to build upon the past, both to affirm initiatives already taken, and to strengthen their direction and purpose. For example, the third recommendation called for the organisation of multicultural events to be extended in scope and location, having uncovered evidence, within the research, of their value to BUGB in the past. And as well as strengthening initiatives that had already proven their worth, there was a strong emphasis on the continuing provision of resources

---

[7] See report prepared for Council, February 2011

and training (particularly present in recommendations one, two, five and six), something that had always been a key part of the work of the RJWG and BUGB Racial Justice Adviser.

This reflected the clear struggles expressed by many interviewed in terms of knowing how to address the issues that had emerged as a result of the 'Apology' and the 'Journey.' This was important given the sense many expressed of being overwhelmed by the task. The recommendations sought to reassure, by voicing the hope of a collaborative programme of implementation that would offer genuine support and help, rather than simply making yet more demands.

As has been suggested, the process of listening was designed to hold up a mirror to BUGB in order that the steps needed to build diverse and inclusive communities could be discerned. It might well be argued that this approach has significant dangers. First, there is the risk articulated by Kenneth Leech that 'Diversity' can be seen as an end in itself, while inequality and oppression remain unchallenged.'[8] The complexity of structures that have become infected with racism, together with the challenge of overturning these in the name of justice, could easily be avoided, in our desire to create community. Second, there is the problem that the White person cannot be trusted!

Those of us who are White too often fail to recognise our Whiteness, to acknowledge the domination and privilege that accompanies us, and how this controls, for example, our reading of the Bible.[9] The research had concentrated on listening to White people simply because they were the dominant presence in interviews, but this brought with it the possibility of self-deception, and potential blindness to reality.

The work of those conducting the interviews, together with the careful reflecting and analysis provided by the RJWG, did much to off-set these dangers. Their work is evident, particularly, in recommendations four, five and six. Perhaps these were the most demanding, for they addressed directly, both institutional failures and structural inadequacies, and gave a voice to the young within BME communities who were the potential leaders of the future. They took hold of the research outcomes that focussed on the key issues of power and authority. It was recognised that there was need for a radical overhaul of Council and the committees present within BUGB and its constituent parts. This was imperative in order to move towards just and equal patterns of representation. The recommendations called for the implementation of policies that would confront the legacy of racism.

The research process, rooted in listening and discerning, was a crucial stage in the 'Journey'. It took over three years and was carried out with

---

[8] Kenneth Leech, *Race* (London: Church Publishing, 2005)
[9] This is discussed by John M. Campbell in his essay entitled 'Necessary Remembrance: Towards a White British Biblical Hermeneutic in the Aftermath of the Mass Enslavement of Africans'. In A.G. Reddie (ed.) *Black Theology, Slavery and Contemporary Christianity*, (Farnham: Ashgate, 2010), pp.109-128

considerable care and rigour. It was an attempt to recognise that 'the structure of racism and other social sins promotes collective blindness' and often 'entails entrenched structural barriers to its recognition.'[10] It sought to uncover something of the truth and remove some of the obstacles to change. But, of course, producing recommendations for change is one thing. Implementation of those recommendations is quite another!

---

[10] J. Bergen, *Ecclesial Repentance* (Edinburgh: T&T Clark, 2011), p.271

Reflections on the Implementation of the Journey
Gale Richards

In the bicentenary year to celebrate the historic relationship between Jamaican and British Baptists, BUGB produced a souvenir booklet entitled *Jamaican and British Baptists Together, Souvenir booklet (2014).*[1] I noted in the booklet that in the wake of 'The Apology' in November 2007, there was a growing recognition that BUGB needed to seek to address the racial prejudice and discrimination that individuals were still experiencing in British churches and societies. This led to the BUGB Council commissioning BUGB Racial Justice Group to research the nature and scale of the racism and discrimination being experienced in local Baptist churches, Regional Associations, colleges, central offices and structures that make up the union.

It was in March 2011, that BUGB Racial Justice Group[2] reported back to BUGB Council with its research findings. This report included six recommendations that, if followed, could help ensure that BUGB intentionally seeks to celebrate and embrace the rich cultural diversity found in multi-ethnic Britain. These recommendations were endorsed by the BUGB Council and have become known as the 'Journey' recommendations. By June 2014, the BUGB Racial Justice Group summarized these recommendations as follows:

- Building multicultural congregations.
- Developing the leadership skills of Black and minority ethnic (BME) youth.
- Training of ministers and church members for culturally inclusive ministry and mission.
- Multicultural events that strengthen the participation of Black and minority ethnic individuals and celebrate the cultural diversity within our Union.
- Establishing culturally inclusive Union structures (including Baptist House[3]).

With the endorsement of these recommendations, and as the BUGB Racial Justice Group together with the Racial Justice Coordinator began to contemplate an appropriate approach to implementing these

---

[1] See: *Jamaican and British Baptists Together, Souvenir booklet* (2014), p17. Extracts of this document can be found in the appendices.

[2] The name of this group has changed over the years. At one point it was known as the Racial Justice Working Group, but this was changed to the latter name that is presently in use.

[3] Baptist House is the headquarters of BUGB and BMS World Mission. It is located in Didcot, in Oxfordshire.

recommendations, the 'Futures Process'[4] was initiated, by the BUGB Council at its end of year meeting in 2011. The 'Futures Process' was said to be in response to 'an increasingly likely and significant budget deficit in the face of an unprecedented and prolonged recession.' However, what quickly became apparent was that this was being taken as an opportunity to deeply reflect on what the key priorities should be for BUGB in the years ahead.

In light of these developments, the focus of BUGB Racial Justice Group and the Racial Justice Coordinator had to turn to ensuring that the newly endorsed recommendations of the 'Journey' remained a key priority as the 'Futures Process' took place. As part of this 'Futures Process' BUGB members were asked to consider four key questions:

- How is the local church best served by the wider Baptist community so that the mission of God is furthered?
- What principles should guide this journey?
- What must we do together as Baptists?
- What could we / should we stop doing together as Baptists?

BUGB Racial Justice Group and the Racial Justice Coordinator met with members of the Futures Steering Group in March 2012, to state the case for why the principles of the 'Journey' recommendations had to be seen as a key priority moving forward. It was argued there were clear gospel imperatives for doing so, for the good of BUGB and the wider society.

2012 was to prove a key year for stating this case. The case was strengthened by a number of important interventions from the floor at the British Baptist Assembly from members of the London Baptist Association, particularly, from the perspective of a Black woman as a minister (Revd Charmaine Howard), and a young Black man, as a youth pastor (Daniel Shillingford).

May 2012 also marked the month when BUGB hosted a Jamaica Baptist Union (JBU) delegation. The delegation of four (Revd Karl Johnson, Revd Karl Henlin, Revd Merlyn Hyde-Riley and Revd Dr Glenroy Lalor), offered some powerful insights from their perspectives into the importance of different cultural expressions of the gospel. The Baptist family in the UK resonated to the incisive contributions from the JBU delegation as they blessed a number of our local Baptist churches, Regional Associations, colleges, central offices and structures, with their thought-provoking reflections. The JBU delegation used their contextual experiences to reflect on differing approaches to ministry and mission for the 21st century and effective ways of growing leaders of all ages and backgrounds.

The case was further stated at the BU Council of November 2012, which included presentations from BUGB 'Faith and Unity' Executive, as well as

---

[4] See: *The Story behind our renewed culture* - baptist.org.uk: http://www.baptist.org.uk/Groups/258896/The_story_behind.aspx Accessed 21 August 2015

members of the London Baptist Association (including contributions from Revd Charmaine Howard, and Regional ministers Revd Kumar Rajagopalan and Revd David Shosanya).

It was at this BUGB Council in November 2012, that Council members were moved to pass a resolution, which committed BUGB to seeking to have an interim target of at least 20% Black and minority ethnic individuals in the various roles that make up central offices and structures of the Union. In the later BUGB Council of March 2013, a resolution was also passed that provided for the moderators of BUGB three Justice Groups (Racial Justice, Gender Justice, and Disability Justice) plus the moderator of BUGB Young Leaders Forum to sit on the Nominations Committee. The Nominations Committee, which plays a key role in making recommendations for key strategic appointments, includes the Moderator of the BU Council and the Moderator of BUGB Trustees.

The passing of these resolutions arguably contributed to increased levels of ethnic diversity, present in areas such as the BUGB Council, Baptist Steering Group, the planning teams for key events like Baptist Assembly and on the tutorial and research staff teams of the various Baptist colleges. These changes all represented an outworking of the 'Journey' recommendation of 'Establishing culturally inclusive Union structures (including Baptist House)'. These structural changes meant, as a Union, BUGB began to hear about more diverse expressions of the gospel, which have the potential to enrich our shared Baptist life, and potentially, better equip individuals for mission and ministry, in multiethnic and multicultural Britain.

As I reflect on the progress that has been made on the implementation of all of the recommendations of the 'Journey', since its establishment, it is clear that at the heart of the progress is the reoccurring theme of members of the JBU working together with members of BUGB. It is to this reoccurring theme that I intend to address the next tranche of my remarks.

The recommendation to build multicultural congregations
In addition to BUGB hosting a JBU delegation in Britain in May 2012, to which mention has already been made, a BUGB delegation was hosted in Jamaica by the JBU in October 2012. British representatives, including myself, the Revd Wale Hudson-Roberts, the Revd Dr Larry Kreitzer and the Revd Davina Roberts all attended. This was followed by a further JBU delegation that was hosted in Britain by BUGB in October 2014, when the Revds Karl Johnson and Karl Henlin spent time in the UK. I would say that the key element to emerge from these exchange delegations was the greater necessity for more theological reflection in British Baptist congregations on the relationship between ethnicity and identity in Christ, and the relationship between ethnicity and the different life experiences for individuals in Britain. These forms of reflection will give rise to greater transparency on the ways in which prejudices grounded in ethnic identities and the cultures associated with them, impact on mission and ministry in the UK. It is from such critically informed theological reflections that truly multicultural congregations can be

built. BUGB Racial Justice group, in 2011, defined the term 'Multicultural' as:

> The word 'multicultural' is being used as a way of talking about diverse and distinct cultures living together and learning to interact with one another. It is not about each culture living separately, so creating self-contained ghettos. It is about valuing diversity, and recognising and respecting the contributions that can be made by different cultures to each other. It is not about each culture claiming a right to be accepted uncritically. It is about all cultures engaging in critical dialogue with each other, so that all can contribute to the building of community and a cohesive society.[5]

BUGB Racial Justice Group and the Racial Justice Coordinator were thus delighted that in October 2014, and August 2015, two key resources commissioned around the time of the JBU delegation visit to Britain in 2012, were published by British Baptists. These resources provided a means for churches to begin to enable the kind of theological reflection that JBU delegation members were highlighting as being needed during their trips to Britain.

The first of these resources was *Text and Story: Prophets for their time and ours*[6] commissioned by the Sam Sharpe Project and written by me. The resource comprised of a series of study notes to encourage adults and young people to reflect on the stories of 5 Black Baptist leaders who became prophetic leaders speaking out on behalf of the oppressed. The resource highlighted the scriptural texts that inspired these leaders, and then considers how adults and young people today might raise their own prophetic voices to build a more just and inclusive society.

The second of these resources was the *Multiethnic Church* resource, comprising of a six-week course for small groups in churches, commissioned by BUGB Racial Justice Group and written by Revd Malcolm Patten. This resource was created to help develop healthy, inclusive churches, which reflect the richness and diversity of the Kingdom of God.

Whilst the emergence of these results was undoubtedly an achievement, it remains as to be seen how many congregations will consider and or actually make use of them.

The recommendation to develop the leadership skills of Black and minority ethnic youth

The arrival of the JBU delegation in October 2014 provided an opportune moment for an event to facilitate the outworking of this recommendation. The event itself was the brainchild of Anthony Reddie and was organised under the heading of 'Legacy: Learning from the past, embracing the future.' As the

---

[5] Definition of 'multicultural' submitted by BUGB Racial Justice Group at the BUGB Council in March 2011, that was unanimously approved.

[6] See Gale Richards, *Text and Story: Prophets for their time and ours* (Oxford: Regents Park College, 2015)

moderator of BUGB Racial Justice Group, I organised the event in partnership with the Ascension Trust[7], which is well known for its initiatives such as 'Street Pastors', as well as its annual youth residential programme called 'Urban Youth Mission.' A group of people of Baptist heritage and from other denominations gathered at Highgate Baptist Church, in Birmingham, for the event. The aim of the event was to provide an opportunity for Christian young adults aged 18-30, to meet with and learn from Christian leaders in a range of fields. It was an opportunity for young adults to learn from those who have gone ahead and to embrace the possibilities of the journey before them.

The Revd Lynn Green (General Secretary BUGB) and Revd Karl Henlin (from the JBU) encouraged the young adults to learn from the Bicentenary story that was being celebrated that year, as they considered how God might be calling them now to be leaders. This was followed by four 5-minute presentations from guest speakers, who spoke on the impact that they have made as Black women and men, in the fields of leadership development, education, theology, and politics and integration. Their presentations enabled the young people to gain an understanding of what the speaker had accomplished in their field and why this was significant. Additional points of learning included gaining a sense of what had been the key to enabling the speaker to advance in their respective field.

After each presentation there were facilitated Table Top conversations amongst the predominantly Black 18-30 year olds present. The conversations enabled these young Christian adults to reflect on the speakers' stories, in the light of their own experiences, dreams and ambitions.

Revd Karl Henlin closed the evening with a rousing challenge for the young adults present to take every opportunity to fulfil the call on their lives, as leaders of their generation. He praised and prayed for young people like Jamiko Yapp and Christina Howell (from the JBU), who were at that time currently taking part in BMS World Mission's gap year 'Action Team' programme (with White and Black British Baptists). He felt that they would all learn much from their six months overseas, which, in turn, would prepare them for better knowing and undertaking God's plans for their lives.

The JBU participants left their mark on both the BMS World Mission's gap year 'Action Team' participants and the programme.[8] The Revd Karl Henlin, in particular, made a great impact on the hearts and minds of the young adults from the Ascension Trust Urban Youth Mission initiative that attended the event. The Ascension trust plays a key role in identifying and nurturing the leadership potential in BME youth from Baptist churches and beyond.

These efforts and initiatives represent progress to be celebrated, however, the bigger challenge remains for young adults and young people to

---

[7] The Ascension Trust is a leading Christian Charity that undertakes social justice related work in many parts of the UK, particularly in large urban conurbations. Further details can be found in the following link: http://www.ascensiontrust.org.uk/

[8] These activities took place within the Bicentenary Year in 2014.

be given voice and space within the life of their churches, and for their leadership gifts to be actually both acknowledged and utilized. The reality is that there is much work to be done to bring together the generations within our churches (i.e. where all generations are present, recognising that the 18-30 age group is missing in so many of our churches). [9]

The recommendation to train ministers and church members for culturally inclusive ministry and mission

The JBU 2012 delegation visit to Britain helped to inspire the writing of a Baptist College module descriptor by BUGB Racial Justice group entitled *Multicultural church*. This descriptor was introduced into the curriculum of British Baptist Colleges, in order to resource those training to be nationally recognised Baptist lay pastors and lay preachers, from September 2013.[10] The module aims to help learners gain an understanding of what racism is and its origins in the history of the modern world, plus the nature and extent of racial injustice currently experienced in the UK. Additional aims include effective ways of raising awareness of issues of racial justice and effective ways to challenge racial injustice in the local church and wider society.

The introduction of this module complemented the mandatory 'Racial Justice Awareness' training sessions that all Baptists in training for ordained ministry (as opposed to lay ministry) have had to undertake for some years now. Incidentally, this requirement was in place even before the 'Journey' recommendations were approved. However, facilitators of this compulsory training have reported not always finding students to be willing participants in these courses. Some have questioned whether such training is necessary, using arguments akin to a belief that we live in a 'post-racial society,'[11] where matters of racism and discrimination are considered to be a thing of the past. I and other co-facilitators have found some of the students to be oblivious or even unsympathetic (at least at the beginning of the training

---

[9] I was BUGB Racial Justice Group member that sat on BUGB 'Encouraging Young Missionary Disciples' group that in conjunction with 'Arise Ministries' produced the *Today not Tomorrow* resource (see: todaynottomorrow.org.uk), to help churches move to a more intergenerational model to bring generations together. This is essential in order to develop and release the leadership potential of young people and young adults of all ethnic backgrounds.
BUGB Younger Leaders Forum also held an event in October 2012 (and produced a report/videos) in relation to the missing 18-30 generation within churches
[10] The module descriptor was adopted at the September 2013 Baptist Training Partnership meeting, at which I was present.
[11] A concept of post-racial society seems to have come into recent mass public consciousness around the time of the initial election of Barack Obama as President of the USA. See: David O. Sears and Michael Tesler, *Obama's Race: The 2008 Election and the Dream of a Post-Racial America* (Chicago: University of Chicago Press, 2010).

sessions[12]), when evidence to the contrary is given that asserts, we are not living in a 'post-racial society.'

In the case of the *Multicultural Church* module, this of course is not compulsory, and so even where Baptist colleges have offered this module (not all have as yet), students have been able to choose whether they wanted to study it or not and so a significant number may well choose not to do so.

The recommendation for multicultural events that strengthen the participation of Black and minority ethnic individuals and celebrate the cultural diversity within our Union

BUGB Racial Justice Group had been used to holding an annual multicultural event 'The Gathering' for many years, usually in London. The JBU visit in 2012 led to a series of 'The Gathering' events across the different regions of BUGB, where members of the JBU delegation addressed local Baptists. Such was the success of these gatherings (increased attendance levels), the idea of having themed gatherings across the regions, thereafter, emerged. Consequently, in 2013, such regional gatherings took place under the heading of *Have a Dream tour*, marking the 50th anniversary of Martin Luther King's famous speech, and in 2014, under the heading of the Jamaican and British Baptist *Bicentenary* celebrations.

These events have been a great cause for celebration, but the reality remains that only a small fraction of Baptists have ever been to such gatherings, out of the many thousands that make up BUGB.

Concluding remarks

These brief reflections I have offered on the implementation and outworking of the 'Journey' recommendations following the 'Apology' has shown the significance of British and Jamaican Baptists working together. This mutuality and cooperative working, falls within the wider context of addressing issues of racial justice, as BUGB seeks to journey towards becoming a more culturally inclusive body, which challenge racism and discrimination within churches and the wider society.

We are, however, still very much in the early stages of this journey. I have already alluded to the limitations of what has thus far been achieved. Further, whilst the historic passing of the aforementioned resolutions by the BU Council (in November 2012 and March 2013) may have contributed to increased levels of ethnic diversity present (in areas such as the BU Council, the Baptist Steering Group, the planning teams for key events like Baptist Assembly, and on the tutorial and research staff teams of Baptist colleges[13]), the real challenge remains, with these individuals now in post, how do we ensure that they are sufficiently resourced and supported to deal effectively

---

[12] I have co-facilitated Racial Justice Awareness training in different forms in 3 different Baptist Colleges from 2012 onwards

[13] It should be noted that Black representation at staff level in Baptist Colleges in Britain has decreased since this essay was first drafted.

with the racism and discrimination a number of them do/may encounter.

Furthermore, how might they be supported in helping to 'raise up' others who are also both called and competent (of all ages and backgrounds) to be able to stand alongside them, whilst serving their terms? Who will come after them, once they have served their terms? Who will continue to be the prophetic voices and presence in this journey? A journey, I pray, British Baptists will continue to walk with Jamaican Baptists, in order to further this enduring and enriching partnership. This journey is one that will help bring forth justice and reconciliation to many more people, in both the life of the church and the wider society. It was always hoped the 'Apology' would ultimately help birth this form of prophetic change. The future is yet to be written and we pray it will accomplish this hope.

Standpoint Theory as a Tool to Understand Baptist Resistance to Owning the Apology and as a Tool to Own and En-flesh the Apology

Sivakumar Rajagopalan

Introduction

Those who were present to endorse, with unanimity, the Baptist Union (BU) Council's apology for the Transatlantic Slave Trade agreed that this was a *kairos* moment within the life of the Union. A key part of the moment and the apology itself was the final paragraph:

> We commit ourselves, in a true spirit of repentance, to take what we have learned from God in the Council and to share it widely in our Baptist community and beyond, looking for gospel ways by which we can turn the words and feelings we have expressed today into concrete actions and contribute to the prophetic work of God's coming Kingdom.

Within the London Baptist Association (LBA) this was acted upon in two ways:

1. The matter was discussed at the annual ministers' conference held in February, in 2008. At this gathering a survey was conducted, and the results can be viewed on the LBA website.[1]
2. In May 2008 at an event at the Docklands Museum those who had been present at the BU Council came to retell their respective stories of what had been said and how people were moved to make the apology. The proceedings were recorded and a DVD resource with an accompanying Bible study was produced to help churches understand why an apology had been issued. It is entitled: *The Baptist Union Council apology for the transatlantic slave trade.*

Both before and after the apology, the appropriateness of making an apology has been questioned. Such sentiments were reflected at the above-mentioned events and in the resources. Within the DVD, two men of Caribbean heritage offer contrasting perspectives:

> Well I think the government owe us a big apology in a sense, you get me, because they are the one who is, who have done it...so it's fair for them to come and say, 'I am sorry'.[2]

---

[1] See http://www.londonbaptist.org.uk/images/stories/documents/racial_justice/apology_survey.136.pdf

[2] BU & LBA DVD Resource: The Baptist Union Council apology for the transatlantic slave trade, *Introduction & Scope of British slave trade*

The government of the day, cannot apologise for what they had no hand in.[3]

Within this resource numerous Baptist ministers raise concerns from a biblical perspective. Following the apology I had a number of one-to-one meetings with White Baptist ministers who voiced considerable opposition to the apology. Often, their objections centred on the interpretation of particular biblical texts and the belief that only the perpetrators of the crimes of the transatlantic slave trade have the right to offer an apology.

Whilst the apology has been issued, resources produced, and extensive and excellent work undertaken through the 'Journey' programme, the commitment cited above has not been followed through in a manner that has led to ownership at either grassroots or institutional level, to bring about genuine change. Why is this the case?

The purpose of this essay is to explore how 'Standpoint Theory' offers a helpful perspective on why Baptist identity militates against accepting the need to issue an apology. It also seeks to illustrate how this theory, in conjunction with intersectionality, may also enable Baptists to meaningfully offer and en-flesh the apology.[4]

Origins and Definition of Standpoint Theory
Standpoint theory has its origins in 'Karl Marx's exegesis of class relations in capitalism' and 'in the 1970s some feminist social thinkers' adopted it.[5] These thinkers 'began to examine how inequalities between men and women influence knowledge production' and they '[stress] that knowledge is always socially situated. In societies stratified by gender and other categories, such as race and class, one's social positions shape what one can know.'[6]

> American feminist theorist Sandra Harding coined the term *standpoint theory* to categorize epistemologies that emphasize women's knowledge. She argued that it is easy for those at the top of social hierarchies to lose sight of real human relations and the true nature of social reality and thus miss critical questions about the social and natural world in their academic pursuits. In contrast, people at the bottom of social hierarchies have a unique standpoint that is a better starting point for scholarship. Although such people are often ignored, their marginalized positions actually make it easier for them to define important research questions and explain social and natural problems.[7]

Speaking from an African-American woman's perspective Collins states,

---

[3] ibid.
[4] Collins, Patricia Hill, *Fighting Words – Black Women & the Search for Justice*, pp.205
[5] Cockburn, Cynthia, "Standpoint Theory" in *Marxism and Feminism* ed. Mojab and Shahzrad, p331 & 333
[6] Borland, Elizabeth, Standpoint Theory http://www.britannica.com/topic/standpoint-theory (Accessed 23rd December 2015)
[7] ibid.

Standpoint theory posits a distinctive relationship among a group's position in hierarchical power relations, the experiences attached to differential positionality, and the standpoint that a group constructs in interpreting these experiences.[8]

In essence one's position within power structures determines what one knows, what one seeks to know, how one seeks to understand and make sense of one's location. For those who are marginalised and oppressed such knowledge also enables them to develop strategies to overcome the injustice that they encounter.

Roots of Baptist Identity

In 1612 Thomas Helwys planted the first Baptist church in England. In his work *A Short Declaration of the Misery of Iniquity*, he argues for religious liberty, saying, 'For men's religion to God is between God and themselves. The king shall not answer for it.'[9] Helwys was imprisoned for his views and died in Newgate prison.[10]

Baptists were considered heretics and persecuted by the state and its various apparatus. 'Most non-Baptists in the seventeenth and eighteenth centuries considered the Baptists "genes" to be genetic defects, ones that had to be eliminated from the body of Christ lest they be "inherited" by others.'[11] Therefore, they were persecuted and harried by both 'civil magistrates and ecclesiastical leaders' who 'used the power of the secular government to harass, fine, and imprison Baptists.'[12] However, neither imprisonment nor death silenced them since, 'other Baptists were ready to take their place and continue to preach the Baptist faith and understanding.'[13] King James I did not consider it right to persecute or execute people for their religious beliefs, but that efforts should be made to change their beliefs 'by the persuasive doctrines and examples of ministers'; hence Helwys' imprisonment rather than execution.[14]

---

[8] Collins, Patricia Hill, *Fighting Words – Black Women & The Search for Justice*, pp.193-4
[9] Peck, Tony, *Thomas Helwys – Unlikely Prophet of Universal Religious Freedom*, p2. Paper from Baptist World Alliance Annual Gathering, Santiago, Chile, July 2012, quoting from Richard Groves (ed.) *A Short Declaration of the Mystery of Iniquity, Thomas Helwys (ca.1550-ca1612)*, p53
[10] Further details on Thomas Helwys can be found in the following link: https://en.wikipedia.org/wiki/Thomas_Helwys
[11] Durso, Keith E., *No Armor for the Back: Baptist Prison Writings, 1600s - 1700s* p.22
[12] Durso, *No Armor*, p.22
[13] Durso, *No Armor*, p23
[14] Durso, *No Armor*, p23

Relevance of Standpoint Theory & Intersectionality for British Baptist Identity

Individual and group identity does not flow out of one but multiple categories, which overlap and intersect with one another. Collins states: 'Whereas race-only or gender only perspectives classify African-American women as a subgroup of either African-American or women, intersections of race, class, and gender, among others, creates more fluid and malleable boundaries around the category "African-American women".'[15]

Cassidy and Mikulich drawing on Collins work state:

> Seeing race, class and gender...as interlocking but not interchangeable opens up possibilities of both/and rather than an either/or stance 'in which all groups possess varying amounts of penalty and privilege in one historically created system.'[16]

They cite Collins statement, 'Depending on the context, an individual may be an oppressor, a member of an oppressed group, or simultaneously oppressor and oppressed.'[17] From a personal perspective as a former Brahmin caste Hindu, I am aware of the innumerable penalties and racist oppression that I face by virtue of being Black within a White society and church. However, I am saddened by the reality of privilege that I experience as a former Brahmin caste individual *even* within some South Indian and Sri Lankan congregations in London.

Employing intersectionality to interrogate British Baptist identity from its origins to today, the majority of British Baptists are *also* White, and whilst today the majority are middle-class, during the slave-trading era the majority were working class. The most difficult aspect within 'race' discourse is for White people to recognise that they are White: 'despite their comfort with identifying themselves as women, many White women in the United States have difficulty seeing themselves as already part of Whites as a group.'[18] This is equally true among White men and women within the British Baptist context. Whiteness, *irrespective of class*, has conferred upon White people vast amounts of unearned power and privilege, and in the context of this essay two specific aspects need to be owned by White British Baptists.[19]

---

[15] Collins, *Fighting Words*, p205
[16] Cassidy, L.M., & Mikulich, A, (ed.) *Interrupting White Privilege: Catholic Theologians Break the Silence,* p3 citing from Collins, *Fighting Words,* p225
[17] Cassidy & Mikulich, (ed.), *Interrupting*, p3 citing Collins, *Fighting Words*, p225
[18] Collins, *Fighting Words*, p208
[19] McIntosh, Peggy, 'White Privilege: Unpacking the Invisible Knapsack, is a very insightful essay on unearned white privilege'.
http://www.cirtl.net/files/PartI_CreatingAwareness_WhitePrivilegeUnpackingtheInvisibleKnapsack.pdf Accessed 28th January 2016

Mind-set

David Goldenberg concludes his exploration in *The Curse of Ham* with the following key assertions:

- 'I found no indication of a negative sentiment towards Blacks in the Bible. ...skin color is never mentioned in descriptions of biblical Kushites. Color did not matter.'[20]
- 'In short, no negative evaluation of real Blacks were found either in biblical or postbiblical sources. Race did not matter.'[21]

Goldenberg goes on to state that the 'Black slave trade' led to an 'association of Black with slave' and a subsequent change in exegesis, furthered by an erroneous 'etymology of Ham as "dark, brown, black" ', and these factors contributed to 'the gradual introduction of blackness into the retelling of the biblical story, which was originally colorless'.[22] Most importantly Goldenberg cites Kim Hall who 'showed how the colors black and white "become...the conduit through which the English began to formulate the notions of 'self' and 'other'"'[23] Furthermore, he cites Smedley who draws attention to how in the English language the word race itself 'was transformed...from a mere classificatory term...into a folk idea.'[24]

These mindset developments are clearly expressed by Neill who notes that by 1600, 'Europeans are beginning to think that their civilization is the only civilization in the world that is worthy of the name, and to develop the strange complex of the superior people.'[25]

Therefore, western theology is sadly still considered to be normative and universal by Westerners, and the Majority World[26] made a monumental exegetical error, which has inculcated our minds, and continues to have sinful consequences with respect to 'race' within the body of Christ.

Historical events throughout the 18th and 19th century, within Britain and abroad, including such events as the 1851 Great Exhibition, added to the British a sense of superiority, including racial superiority, which survives in the contemporary era. Nothing epitomises these sentiments better than the song 'Rule Britannia'. Whilst the reference 'never to be slaves' originates from a desire to never be slaves of the Roman Empire,[27] they were ready to enslave

---

[20] Goldenberg, David M., *The Curse of Ham – Race and Slavery in Early Judaism, Christianity and Islam*, p195
[21] Goldenberg, *The Curse*, p196
[22] Goldenberg, *The Curse*, pp196-7
[23] Goldenberg, *The Curse*, p199 citing Hall, Kim, *Things of Darkness*, p4
[24] Goldenberg, *The Curse*, p199 citing Smedley, Audrey, *Race in North America: Origen and Evolution of a Worldview*, pp6-7
[25] Neill, Stephen, *A History of Christian Missions*, p150
[26] Throughout this paper those who are often referred to as Black and Minority Ethnic (BME), are referred to as the Majority World, hereafter abbreviated MW.
[27] The song was written and popularised in the 1740s at the height of British involvement in the transatlantic slave trade.

Black Africans, whilst ensuring that they would never be slaves themselves.[28] That it is still sung with great passion and enthusiasm at the last night of the proms, which gives evidence to a continuing mindset of racism, power, privilege and prejudice.

> Rule Britannia!
> Britannia rule the waves
> Britons never, never, never shall be slaves.

Baptists cannot claim either for their forebears or themselves that they are ring-fenced from such nationalistic pride and condescending disdain for other nations. Despite Baptists opposition to the slave trade,

> ...throughout the British Empire - in Canada, Australia, and southern Africa - when Baptist settler communities tried to bring the gospel to the indigenous neighbors...it was their assumption that the original inhabitants were at a lower level of civilization, and so needed to be brought out of savagery as well as out of paganism.[29]

After the First Indian War of Independence in 1857[30] 'The *savagery* of the British revenge...is striking. Entire villages were burned down; mutineers were smeared in pig fat before execution, tied to the muzzles of cannon and blown to pieces.'[31] The absence of ring fencing of Baptists to such sentiments is demonstrated by the 'Prince of Preachers': 'Charles Spurgeon...thrilled an audience of 25,000 at the Crystal Palace in London when he told them that it was time for holy war on the Indians.'[32] Both then and now, savagery is not the exclusive preserve of the majority world, but such truths are often forgotten by sanctimonious western 'Christian' nations.

In late 2015 and early 2016 students at Oxford University launched a campaign to remove the statue of Cecil Rhodes from Oriel College.[33] Rhodes' mindset was one of absolute belief in the superiority of the British 'race': 'I contend that we are the finest race in the world and that the more of the world we inhabit the better it is for the human race.'[34] I contend that this mindset is not limited to an eccentric, old-fashioned colonialist, but survives within the psyche of the White British population, including Baptists.

Having preached on racial justice at a church, an elderly gentleman from East London recounted to me a childhood incident with a mixture of pride

---

[28] http://www.historic-uk.com/HistoryUK/HistoryofBritain/Rule-Britannia/ Accessed 5th February 2016
[29] Bebbington, *Baptists*, pp.143
[30] Referred to by the British as the Indian Mutiny.
[31] Paxman, Jeremy, *Empire – What Ruling the World Did To The British*, p95. Italics added
[32] Paxman, *Empire*, pp.95-6
[33] http://www.theguardian.com/education/2015/dec/22/oxford-students-campaign-cecil-rhodes-statue-oriel-college Accessed 28th January 2016
[34] Paxman, *Empire*, pp.156

and sense of loss; his mother had opened an atlas and said to him: 'See ev'ry fin that's pink son?, that's all awrs, all awrs!' Such attitudes are widespread: Soyinka recounts how in Germany, in November 2009, after a lecture he had given describing the numerous crimes that Islam and Christianity had committed on African soil, a young man said to him: 'Africans, you must admit, are inherently inferior. You must be, or other races would not have enslaved you for centuries. Your enslavers saw you for what you were, so you cannot blame them.'[35] Soyinka comments: 'I heard not one voice but many, from across Europe and other continents.'[36]

Racism's effect on White people 'is what…Harvard psychologist Maureen Walker has termed "internalized dominance" – the inbred assumption among whites that superiority over people of color is our birthright.'[37] Drawing on the work of Larkin and Walker, Katz explains: 'This attitude infects all interactions with people of color and influences our immediate reaction to their competence, talents and achievements.'[38] This attitude deeply affects how those from the majority world regard themselves and how they behave among White people and I am aware of how it affects my behaviour. The LBA Apology Survey cited previously notes the current mindset issues within Baptist church life among White people and the majority world, a sample of which are listed below:

- Black inferior, White superior; Black passive, White confident/active; Black lack confidence to lead.
- White people are not staying in the church or not prepared to be led by a minority [i.e. MW] pastor/leader.[39]
- Deference to White folk. Deference to White pastors.
- White people have a superior attitude without being aware of it.
- Reticence of Black members to value their own ministers.[40]

---

[35] Soyinka, Wole, *Of Africa*, p.xii
[36] Soyinka, *Of Africa*, p.xii
[37] Katz, Judith H., *White Awareness – Handbook for Anti-Racism Training*, p11
[38] Katz, *White Awareness*, p11 citing Larkin, W., &Walker, M., *Internalized dominance and workplace dynamics* [Workshop handout]. Washington DC: National Multicultural Institute.
[39] This was still true in 2015, and I cannot think there will be any substantial change by the time this publication is released. See Rajagopalan, S., "Migration Matters" in *Encountering London - London Baptists in the 21st Century* pp.52 (Ed. Bowers, Kapolyo & Olofinjana)
[40] http://www.londonbaptist.org.uk/images/stories/documents/racial_justice/apology_survey.136.pdf, pp8-9 Accessed 28th January 2016

One's mindset is pivotal to all aspects of life and the slave trade and imperialism have bequeathed White people with an outlook which has 'proved dominant and powerful in every way' over Black people.[41]

Steps to Realising the Apology

This section draws primarily on the World Council of Churches paper entitled 'Being church and overcoming racism: It's time for transformative justice' (hereafter abbreviated WCC)[42]. The paper's relevance for British Baptists is that the principles outlined are rooted in the following lived experiences:

- "The United Church of Canada: apologies to the First Nations Peoples (the original people of Canada, the Indigenous Peoples)
- The Lutheran Church of Norway: apologies to the Roma People
- The United Methodist Church in the United State: apologies to Native Americans (Indigenous Peoples), and apologies for acts of racism that prompted the creation of separate Black denominations

The fourth experience relates to South Africa. It does not highlight a particular church, but aims at presenting some of the challenges that the churches face on racism." (WCC)

WCC cite pp.23-49 of *Justice and Reconciliation* with respect to the three stages outlined below. I also draw on personal reflection/preaching from Isaiah 59 and engagement with the Dalit[43] quest for justice and equality.

Truth-Telling

Isaiah 59: 3, 4a, 4b, 13, 14 and 15 refer to lies, lack of integrity and the absence of truth. WCC emphasises the centrality of truth-telling. As Regional minister for Racial Justice my clarion call has been for all to speak the truth, even those who espouse racist thoughts and views, as only the truth sets us free to move forward. Since truth-telling inevitably leads to 'anger, pain and suffering', the dominant group often seek to avoid it.[44]

Glen Marshall, Co-Principal at Northern Baptist College, speaking at the London Baptist Association's annual conference in February 2016, shared how in the 'Introduction to Mission Studies' module, he invites those from the majority world to share their stories of coming to Britain, while the White

---

[41] Kapolyo, J, 'Theology and Culture – An African Perspective' in *Encountering London – London Baptists in the 21st Century*, p70 (ed. Bowers, Kapolyo & Olofinjana)

[42] https://www.oikoumene.org/en/resources/documents/central-committee/2002/being-church-and-overcoming-racism Accessed 5th February 2016

[43] Dalits are the most marginalized and oppressed community in India, where they have faced appalling treatment for several millennia and continue to do so. Sadly such prejudice and discrimination also occurs within the church.

[44] WCC

British are required to listen without interrupting for 30 minutes. He states that the initial reluctance of those from the majority world quickly dissipates, whilst the White British 'are OK to begin with but gradually they tend to get more and more frustrated as they want to "defend" British culture and "correct" what their fellow students are saying.'[45]

The key feature of the November 2007 Baptist Council was hearing the stories of those who had suffered racism within wider society and within Baptist life. Phil Jump, Regional Minister and Team Leader of Northwest Baptist Association, recounts:

> I had reservations...and was struggling to know why as Baptists we needed to make this apology...Through Council...one of the things that really affected me was hearing stories of brothers and sisters in Christ, and I began to realise that actually our relationship as a family today, needed some appropriate act...[46]

In my engagement with Dalit believers in India and Britain I have been deeply moved by their stories of prejudice and discrimination within wider society and the church. I have always curbed my impulse either to defend my Brahmin heritage or correct my [mis]/perception of their [mis]/perception. I have done this because such things are negligible when compared to the monumental injustices their forebears have faced for several millennia, which they continue to face today.

At every level of Baptist life, from local church, through association and Baptist Union General Secretariat, the painful stories of prejudice and discrimination need to be told and are ones to which we need to listen. Michael Jagessar's report to the LBA Board of Directors regarding diversity and inclusion notes: 'The entire discussion on exclusion often gets locked around the protection of the feelings of the dominant group.' Here I implore my White Baptist sisters and brothers to curb their instinct to defend themselves and bind up their hurt feelings. Parker advocates that such stories should be told and placed alongside those of the majority world stories.[47] I disagree because when the powerful and privileged, White British Baptists/Indian Brahmin heritage Christians, articulate their 'corrective' stories, we invariably negate and silence majority world/Dalit & other caste stories. This is not to say that the powerful and privileged should never share their stories, but that they do so in a mutually agreed manner with those who are less powerful and privileged,[48] very mindful of the significant differences in any prejudice and discrimination they have faced.[49] Also, I implore my majority world sisters and brothers to

---

[45] Cited with permission from the Rev. Glen Marshall.
[46] BU Apology DVD Resource: *Stories from Council & Response to the Apology*
[47] Parker, Russ, *Healing Wounded History – reconciling peoples and healing places*, p52
[48] Law, *The Wolf*, p66-7 & 79-88
[49] White women often equate the prejudice and discrimination they have encountered with what majority world people have faced. This is not the case and is a product of their continual, un-deconstructed White privilege. See Rajagopalan, K., 'What is the

truthfully speak their stories, without censoring their emotions, for fear of hurting 'the feelings' of our White brethren. This is essential for the next step.

Lamentation and Repentance
'Facing the truth is not an easy task for individuals or communities. Lament and learning how to lament...has helped people...move forward beyond denial and guilt.' (WCC). As Baptists we are activists, and the various tasks undertaken after the apology, by others and me, with good intentions, evidences this truth. Before we act, however, through lament we must first '...process the truth of what happened at the level of the heart. It is a faithful and biblical response.' (WCC). The absence of lament necessitates the need to repeat the stories of pain and hurt that majority world people have encountered because our White compatriots either deny or minimise our hurts, often by quickly jumping in with their stories. We have not made progress towards true justice because to date White British Baptists have not admitted the truth regarding their racism.
Isaiah 59: 14 reads:

> So justice is driven back,
> and righteousness stands at a distance;
> truth has stumbled in the streets,
> honesty cannot enter.

Only when the truth is owned, can justice be done. After all, our judicial system is based on establishing the truth, in order that just action can be taken.

How do we enter into lament? The WCC states: 'Protestant churches do not commonly use lament.' I cannot recall any context where I have learnt how to lament. In *The Wolf Shall Dwell with the Lamb,* Law draws attention to the Cycle of Gospel Living, which may be a useful tool for lament.[50]

Law states: 'Teaching a white group to bear the cross is totally appropriate in a multicultural setting.'[51] In relation to majority world people, White British Baptists' entry point is as the powerful needing to give up power, choose the cross, and experience death and powerlessness. Having heard the majority world share their stories, White British Baptists should lament at the cross, expressing their anguish and despair for how their sins and those of their forebears have caused hurt and pain to their majority world Baptist brothers and sisters in Christ.

Defining Divide? False Post-Racial Dogma and the Biblical Affirmation of Race' in *Black Theology, Vol. 13 No. 2,* August 2015 pp166-188

[50] Law, E., *The Wolf Shall Dwell with the Lamb – A Spirituality for Leadership in a Multicultural Community*, p74. To view the diagram, go to:
http://dailyofficeanchorsociety.com/tag/eric-law/ (Accessed 6th February 2016)
[51] Law, E., *The Wolf*, p56

Parker draws attention to another dimension from Rhiannon Lloyd's work among Hutus and Tutsis after the Rwandan genocide to take steps towards reconciliation. He says that vital to her work is her recollection of:

> ...how God disarmed [Lloyd a Welsh woman] of her own resentment towards the English...when some English Christians repented on behalf of their forebear for what they had done towards her own people. This helped her to connect with the sins of white Europeans against Africans and she soon found herself repenting for their actions.[52]

Law states that one's context determines one's location with respect to power and one can either enter the cycle as the powerful or the powerless: 'In a multicultural world, we might find ourselves shifting back and forth between being powerful and powerless depending on the context in which we relate to others.'[53] Therefore, whilst in the majority of contexts White middle class Baptists' entry point may be as the powerful, perhaps in relationship to Anglicans they enter as the powerless. Would an Anglican apology to Baptists better enable them to lament and genuinely apologise and do justice to majority world Baptists in Britain? Possibly!

However, my Indian compatriots and I have never received an apology for the injustice of colonial rule from either the British government or British Baptists. This does not prevent me taking responsibility for my own and my community's evil against Dalit and other marginalised castes; we could offer an apology and make restitution.

WCC refer to the United Church of Canada having to lament and grieve for the horrific stories associated with residential schools. The same is true with respect to the experience of past and present prejudice and discrimination against majority world Baptists from White British Baptists. Therefore 'it is right [for them] to be overwhelmed - lament is an expression of feelings which are not neat and tidy - grieving is part of healing.' (WCC)
Only having taken these steps of lament and moving towards the cross and experiencing the pain of the other in our hearts can we then move towards genuine repentance. In each context, questions must be asked regarding what are we 'turning away from'? And to what are we turning? (WCC)

Given that individuals and communities can, depending on context, enter the Cycle of Gospel Living either as powerful or powerless agents, this underscores the need for a greater awareness of the importance of intersectionality.

---

[52] Parker, R., *Healing*, pp73-4
[53] Law, *The Wolf*, p57

Seeking the Spirit
The Spirit's presence is essential for truth-telling, namely, having the capacity to hear the truth and to lament. However, the Spirit's presence is critical as we seek to move forward, because now we must ask: 'How can we go on? Where do we turn? We turn to God...this is the stage where, instead of acting, we need to wait upon God. Instead of talking, we need to listen.' (WCC)

The Spirit must be sought with respect to doing justice. In reflecting and preaching on Isaiah 59, I have drawn attention to the fact that it is costly to act justly; the cross is the ultimate example of this truth. Slave trading nations will not make an unequivocal apology for their action for fear that it will strengthen calls for reparation and doing justice, which may be costly in monetary terms.

Within the Baptist community, following truth-telling and lament, when we seek to do justice, we must be immersed in the Spirit because those who 'have suffered the injustice of racism themselves should be the primary actors to define ***what justice means and how do they see that justice could be achieved.***' (WCC)[54] Furthermore it is only through the Spirit that those with power and privilege will permit, '***Justice [to] redress the imbalance of relationships and the imbalances of power***' and only the Spirit can engender a commitment to becoming part of 'a community of transformative justice, [where] the ones ***who have suffered the injustice* are the ones who *have the credibility and legitimacy to say when*** racial-ethnic-gender-environmental ***justice has been achieved.***' (WCC)[55]

Without doubt, the aforementioned mentioned steps, with respect to justice, will be the most problematic for White British Baptists who hold power and privilege. Whilst the whole community must embrace those steps that will make for justice, the Baptist establishment has to take the courageous step of allowing majority world Baptists to define what justice will look like, how it will be achieved and when it has been achieved.
Isaiah 59: 8 states

> The way of peace they do not know;
>   there is no justice in their paths.
> They have turned them into crooked roads;
>   no one who walks along them will know peace.

The slogan, 'No justice, no peace' in various contexts underlines this biblical truth. When, by the Spirit's leading, painful and difficult truths are spoken, those who need to lament must do so. When the recipients of injustice define the shape of justice, and are permitted to state when it has been achieved, then through the Spirit's empowering we can act justly, redress power imbalances and begin the journey towards peace.
No truth, no justice.

---

[54] Bold italicization is in the WCC text.
[55] As above.

No justice, no peace.

Personal Reflection
In bringing these matters to the attention of my White British Baptist sisters and brothers I am very aware of my own need to act justly towards Dalit believers. In the summer of 2007, before my sabbatical, I wrote in the *Baptist Times* that God had taught me that I would always be encountering my caste prejudice. That I must be prepared to be broken again and again, and I must never seek to be the Dalit's saviour, but must empower them from the margins.

I am still learning these lessons but an incident in September 2007 encapsulates these lessons. I visited Rev. V. Devasahayam, Bishop of Madras, who is a Dalit. During the course of our conversation, I offered an unequivocal and heartfelt apology to him and his community for the unimaginable oppression that mine had inflicted on his. I cannot remember his immediate response. As the conversation continued I became aware of my irritation at his 'inadequate' response. At least he could have given a warm acknowledgment; better still, he could have told me what a humble and pious individual I was.

Every evening I recorded the events of the day and that evening the Holy Spirit brought to my mind Bishop Devasahayam's response, which I had heard, yet not heard: 'Many from your community have said what you have said, but they have never taken any steps to reduce their power and privilege.' I was shattered. My desire to be their saviour was exposed, and within that my prejudice, as I harboured the sense of being owed his gratitude and acknowledgment. My journey continues.

Conclusion
Standpoint theory gives a window on Baptist identity as a marginalised and oppressed community, which sees itself as a victim in need of apology from the Anglican establishment. This may well be a helpful step in deepening Christian unity. Furthermore, Baptist opposition to the slave trade and slavery adds to their sense of incredulity that they should apologise for such deeds committed by others.

Intersectionality helps to locate British Baptists within a specific ethnicity and class stratification during the slave trade era: White working class, whose labour within the slave plantation industry enabled them to accrue financial benefits, class uplift and a mindset and self-belief that places their progeny of the 20th and 21st century at a considerable advantage over majority world Baptists. As direct beneficiaries of the transatlantic slave trade, they have an obligation to apologise and act in ways to redress their unearned power and privilege.

Given that ten years have passed since the apology, with limited progress,[56] what must be done? The WCC paper '*Being Church and overcoming racism:*

---

[56] See Rajagopalan, K., 'What is the Defining Divide? False Post-Racial Dogma and the Biblical Affirmation of Race' in *Black Theology, Vol. 13 No. 2,* August 2015 pp166-188

it's time for transformative justice' offers an excellent plan of action to actualise the apology, because it locates everything in terms of our relationship to God. We would do well to set aside time to fast and pray and seek the Lord's face in order to take a meaningful step forward with respect to this issue.

Following Revd Billy Kim's sermon at Baptist Assembly in May 2004, there was a palpable sense among those gathered that the Lord was calling us to repentance. The BU Council apology in 2007 may have been a first tentative step towards such repentance, but we are yet to follow through on it as a denomination. The Lord's call to repentance remains: when will we respond?

'Sisters with Voices'
A study of the experiences and challenges faced by Black women in London Baptist Association Church ministry settings[1]

Michele Mahon

Introduction

> All my work, my life, everything I do is about survival, not just bare, awful, plodding survival, but survival with grace and faith. While one may encounter many defeats, one must not be defeated
>
> Maya Angelou[2]

In 2006, Kate Colman became the first Black woman to be appointed as President of the Baptist Union of Great Britain. Many ministers welcomed her appointment and in London several Baptist church members, many of them Black women, reported being excited that someone who 'looks like them' could occupy such an esteemed position. She provided a public example, which inspired hope and affirmation for others. Kate Coleman was one of the foremost thinkers in the area of what can be termed British Womanist Theology, as she has reflected on what it means to be a Black female Christian minister within the Baptist context.

Although currently her personal views have changed, her writing has made an impact on the British Theological landscape, in this area. She was also the first Black woman to become an accredited minister within the Baptist Union. She states 'My church didn't believe in women in leadership. And neither did I...within two years I was leading the same church. In a sense that became the tone of my life in terms of pioneering, breaking barriers and making shifts'[3]. The researcher's experiences as a Baptist Youth Specialist resonate somewhat with Kate's reflections and other Black female ministers within the Baptist family have reported similar struggles. This study aims to amplify these women's voices, raise awareness of this as an issue of justice, and contribute towards positive change in this important area.

The research area presented here is firmly rooted within the field of Liberation Theology, which insists on God's preferential option for the poor for the sake

---

[1] A longer version of this essay can be found in *Black Theology: An International Journal* Vol.13, Issue 3, 2015, pp.273-296

[2] McPherson, Dolly A., *Order Out of Chaos: The Autobiographical Works of Maya Angelou*, (New York: Peter Lang, 1990), p.10

[3] Coleman, K., *'60 seconds with...Kate Coleman'*, (*Idea*, Evangelical Alliance: London, 2013) http://www.eauk.org/idea/60-seconds-with-kate-coleman.cfm last accessed 8/06/14

of emancipation.[4] This work utilises other theological discourses that give the marginalised a voice: these include Feminist Theology, which takes its starting point from woman's experience and rejects patriarchy.[5] It also incorporates the insights of Black Theology, which aims to 'do theology in the light of the concreteness of human oppression as expressed in colour, and to interpret for the oppressed the meaning of God's liberation in their community'.[6] In addition to the aforementioned disciplines, there is also Womanist Theology, which among other things, is an 'intense critique relative to the multiple dimensions of Black women's lives, individually and collectively'[7].

Presentation of Research Findings
In this section the researcher will outline the responses received from the online questionnaire sent to all currently listed female ministers in the London Baptist Association. The survey asked participants for information about their age, ethnicity and theological training, seeking to ascertain their leadership journey, among other things, and took on average 20 minutes to complete.

Statistics
Forty-two women of various ethnicities were approached with the online survey. Nine of these women responded. Of these, three are African, three White English, one White and Black Caribbean and one Caribbean. There was one person of another background, which represents a twenty one percent response rate. The age ranges of these women were mainly between 45-65, accounting for six respondents, whilst the remaining three were below 44. All these women serve within multiracial communities in London and its suburbs. These settings vary widely with different classes, ages and needs represented. Three respondents specialise in youth ministry whilst the others work with the wider congregation and community. These characteristics are illustrated in the statistical charts below:

---

[4] Pope Saint John Paul II, *Ecclesia in America*, http://www.vatican.va/holy_father/john_paul_ii/apost_exhortations/documents/hf_jp-ii_exh_22011999_ecclesia-in-america_en.html, last accessed 09/06/14
[5] Watson, N.K., *Feminist Theology*, (Grand Rapids: Eerdmans Publishing, 2003), pp.2-3
[6] Cone, J.H., *A Black Theology of Liberation*, (Maryknoll, New York:Orbis, 2010), p.5
[7] Cannon, K.G., Townes, E.M., and Sims, A.D. (eds.), *Womanist Theological Ethics: A Reader*, (Louisville, Kentucky: Westminster, John Knox Press, 2011), p.14

Figure 1

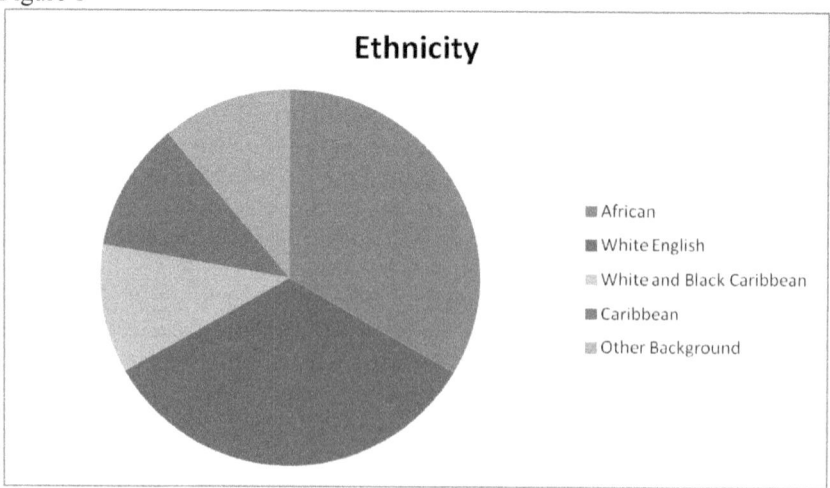

Figure 2

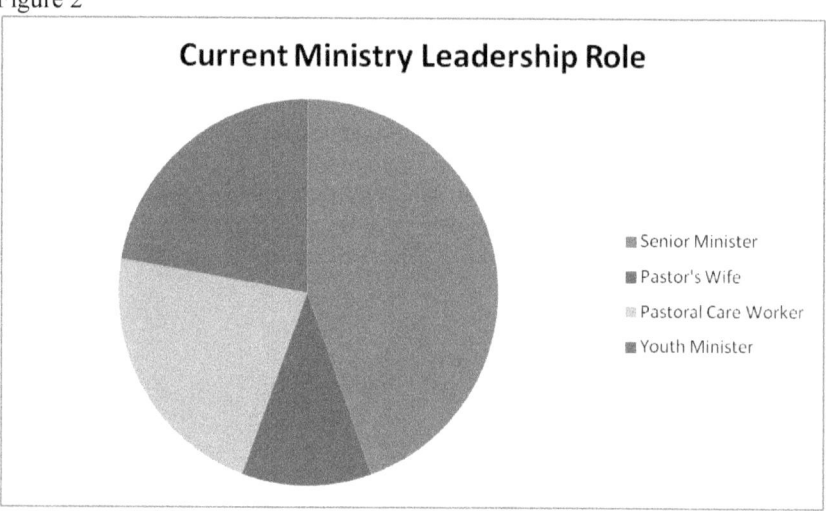

Figure 3

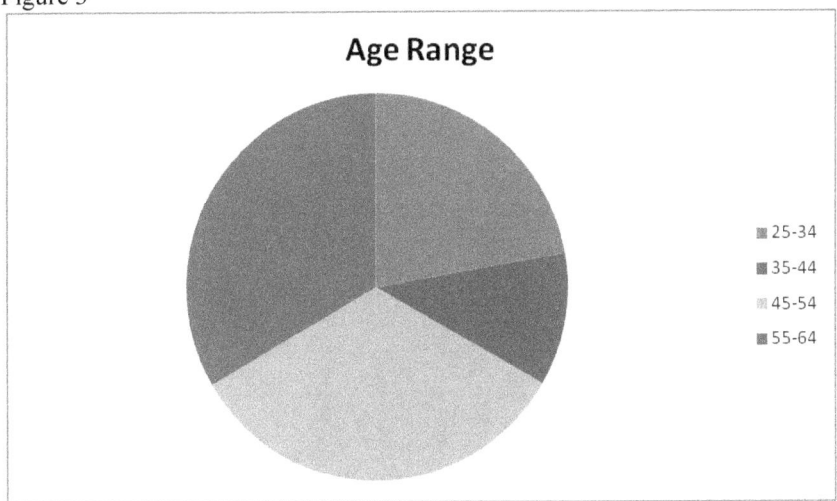

Figure 4

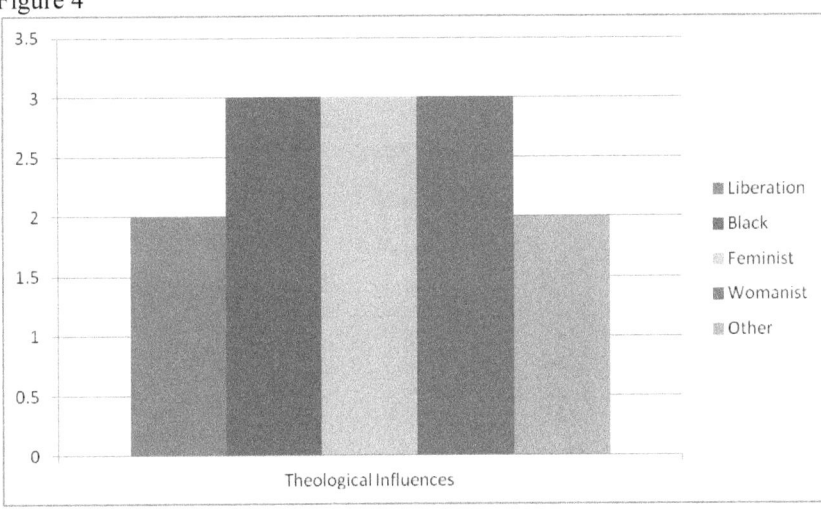

Figure 5

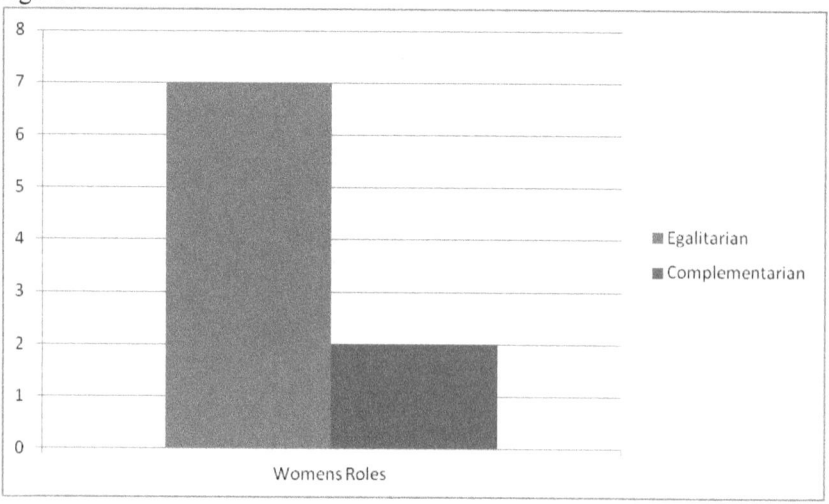

Figure 6

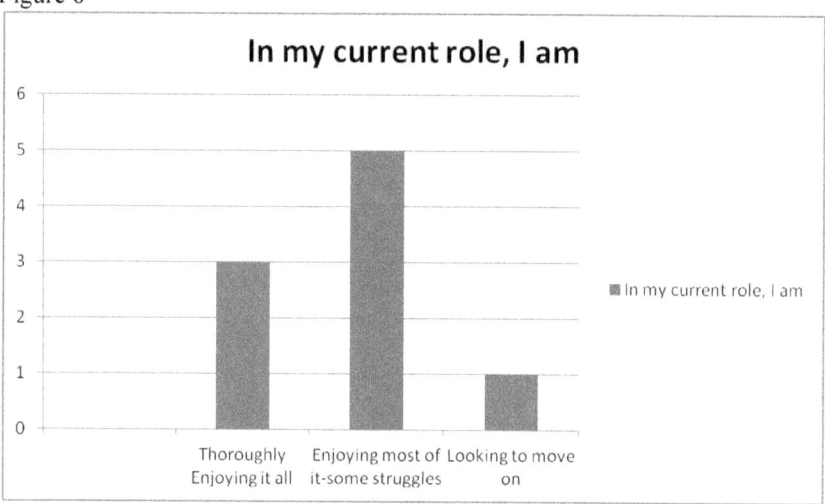

A common trend in response to the question asked about their church ministry setting is that these women serve in thriving multi-ethnic communities affected by immigration, connected by location and proximity, common interests, and a pervading missiological motivation, undergirded by love for God and neighbour. Though this snapshot cannot be the whole story, the interplay between ethnicity, faith and location is illustrated by Garnet and Harris, who state 'Journeys undertaken by migrants for whom religious identity is important have always carried literal, metaphorical, ideological and metaphysical meaning, which are highly contextualised and often materialized in time and space'.[8]

No single ethnic identity seems to have been identified as having an overwhelming influence on this community life. Rather, a rich ethnic diversity is displayed, which concurs with the picture presented by the Census information as mentioned in the analytic background, earlier in the study. These church communities are an accurate reflection of the people represented across London. Obviously, this growing diversity is not a new phenomenon, and it is likely that people's attitudes towards influxes of diverse cultural groups have changed from that of outright hostility,[9] to tolerance and even welcome.

Most of the questionnaire respondents are happy in their roles, which is a welcome reflection. Three respondents are thoroughly enjoying all parts of their role, whilst five stated they are enjoying most of it, though there are struggles in some areas. One is looking to move on due to personal reasons, as illustrated in Figure 6. Rediger shows us that job satisfaction amongst ministers is often low[10], and Rose points out that ministers often find it difficult to express this dissatisfaction.[11] Taking these responses at face value would lead one to a belief that, in general, women ministers are happy in their work within the church.

An overwhelming trend in the data (seven out of nine) points towards the egalitarian theological position regarding women in ministry as shown in Figure 5, believing that gender alone does not preclude women from any form of ministry. Two believe there are particular roles based on gender in which women are able to function, these tend not to include the pastorate,[12] but may apply to women's ministry, children's and youth work and one to one or small group ministry.[13] These reflections illustrate the shift in focus for some, concerning gender relations, as identified earlier in this study - from biology – a woman's ability to have children - to skills, class and functionality in the roles a woman can perform.

Ministry formation
The majority of respondents displayed a gradual awakening of dormant gifts and talents, illustrating a fascinating journey, upon which they have embarked

---

[8] Garnet, J. and Harris, A., *Rescripting Religion in the City: Migration and Religious Identity in the Modern Metropolis*, (Farnham: Ashgate, 2013), p.70
[9] Garnet, J. and Harris, A., *Rescripting Religion in the City*, pp.109-215
[10] Rediger, G.L., *Clergy Killers: Guidance for Pastors and Congregations Under Attack*, (Louisville, Kentucky: Westminster John Knox Press: 1996), p.15
[11] Rose, M., *Forecasting job satisfaction: What occupational profiling tells us* - Working paper 2 of the Bath University Work Centrality, Work Careers and Households Project, (Bath, UK: University of Bath Economic and Social Research Council, 1999), p.30
[12] Grudem, W., and Piper, J., *Recovering Biblical Manhood & Womanhood: A Response to Evangelical Feminism,* (Illinois: Crossway, 2006) Kindle
[13] James, S., *God's Design for Women*, (Darlington: Evangelical Press, 2002), p.137

in seeking to discover their calling. Daly refers to this as a process of self-actualization, and states it is very rare to come for it to materialise in concrete ways.[14] Henderson states:

> ...when I scanned the horizon for people doing the work of progressive faith-based leadership, women were most in evidence. There are men doing this work to be sure, but fundamentally it is women who are there at the grassroots level making the difference. It is time for us to see and celebrate that...Momentum is building.[15]

Theology
Four of the respondents are not in favour of emphasising any particular theological stance. As highlighted in Figure 4, most of them are familiar and in agreement with Liberation Theology (5 respondents) and Feminist Theology (4 respondents), whilst Black Theology and Womanist Theology have not been considered by most of the participants, with 2 stating they are familiar with the former and 1 person stating knowledge of the latter. One stated she is profoundly influenced by 'Open Evangelicalism', another emphasising the fact that we are essentially a missional community, and yet another emphasised the importance of Christ-centeredness.

In terms of institutional, theological training, seven respondents have engaged in this mode of study. For many, this is usually an entry way into church ministry, or seen as a way of enhancing the individual's skills and abilities, as what is learned is often applied directly to the ministry setting. Related to this, another noticeable trend in the data is the lack of current training. Like many ministers, once initial theological training is completed there is not a great deal of further training that is undertaken to update and refresh knowledge and practice. The concept of lifelong learning is yet to be pervasive in ministerial life,[16] and women ministers are not dissimilar to other ministers, in this respect. As intimated previously in the study, a level of theological reflection, which can take many forms, is required in order for any oppressed community to identify what constitutes liberation for them in tandem with the gospel of Jesus Christ.[17]

These women are not currently undertaking theological training and although most of them have been trained in some capacity, ongoing training does not seem to be a priority. Most are mainly getting on with the task at hand and some even do not see the need for ongoing theological training. However, others see such training opportunities as important, but there may be barriers

---

[14] Daly, M., *Pure Lust*, (London: Women's Press, 2001), p.78
[15] Henderson, K. R., *God's Troublemakers: How Women of Faith are Changing the World*, (New York: Continuum, 2006), p.15
[16] Harris, P., 'Lifelong Learning for Ministry: Mapping the Current Situation and the Future Potential among Clergy in the Church of Ireland in Northern Ireland', (Practical Theology, ISSN 1756-073X, 12/2010, Volume 3, Issue 1, 2010), pp. 81 – 92
[17] Cone, J., *God of the Oppressed*, p.11

such as time, location of the training venues and perhaps lack of information about what is available.

Journeys
There are many similarities in what people identified as their high points, mainly around ministry formation and affirmation of their calling into ministry - having their God-given gifts recognised and affirmed. In terms of serving, positive responses from their church community to their ministry understandably gave a boost to these women's' self-esteem and further confirmed their fruitfulness in ministry. Low points on their leadership journey include the judgemental attitude of church communities, especially during the 'Settlement' process – the process whereby churches select a new leader, where gender and ethnicity seem to have a disproportionate bearing on peoples' choice of leader, rather than prayerful discernment.

It was illustrated, previously, that not many of the participants in Adcock's study of Baptist women leaders were encouraged by their churches or senior leaders to pursue their ministry calling.[18] However, the research participants in this study seem to have had different experiences. Mentors are a key factor in providing much needed encouragement during ministry formation. Pervading sexist attitudes make it difficult, but not impossible, to effectively carry out their day to day ministry.

Significantly, none of the Black female ministers mention racism as a barrier to effective ministry. Parental expectation to engage in certain professions such as teaching or medicine are a common source of conflict in African families, and one respondent mentions this as a low point in her leadership journey.

There seems to be considerable emphasis on community gathering or relationship building having the potential to nurture and encourage Black women in ministry. Interestingly, one respondent felt her White English ethnicity made her more disadvantaged than a Black female minister, although she did not go on to elaborate why she felt this is the case.

Many of the respondents feel the key to progress for women like them is involvement with and of community, nurturing friendships and mentoring relationships, recognition of their input and achievements, and training to help people discover and use their gifts. Another interesting suggestion is the use of Positive Action', similar to the idea of 'Affirmative Action', which has been historically implemented in the US. Another useful suggestion is the call for further research into this area to expose racism and sexism within the church, combined with activism to end these blights on communities across London. It has to be pointed out that the respondents did not specifically name racism or sexism as barriers to effective ministry; however, this could be due to limitations in the research method.

---

[18] Adcock, R., *Women In Ministry'*, p.42

Key Findings

Women ministers of all ethnicities are working out their callings and using their gifts in various ways and in numerous circumstances. Eight out of nine respondents are enjoying their ministry roles as can be observed in Figure 6. It would appear that these women have been able to sustain a happy existence, having garnered a sense of what Daly describes as the 'Actualised Self'[19]. This actualised self is a form of subjectivity that celebrates who women are, for their uniqueness and their crucial contribution to the life of the church. This contrasts with Rendle's observation that 'More than one study offers evidence that clergy, especially female clergy, feel isolated and ill-supported by their denominations. Professional ministry within congregations is often presented as an amazingly difficult and overly demanding task.' [20]

These women have had to find their own way through in terms of recognising and nurturing their gifts and talents for service in God's kingdom. Although they have received encouragement from the Christian community, family and leaders, it has been noted that local church women's ministries could be an avenue for women's leadership skills and gifts to be discovered, nurtured and strengthened in order to serve the whole church[21].

There is no community of women who serve to encourage, support and equip budding female ministers within the London Baptist church tradition. In the past a national conference was organised on a yearly basis for ordained female ministers to learn together and encourage one another, however, this initiative ceased with the intention for local and regional groups to take up this role, but that has yet to concretely materialise in London.

Prejudices exist in churches, which hinder women from serving within the church. Although the number is rising, it would appear that Black women ministers in the London Baptist Association are few, and they hold relatively minor positions in local Churches and at regional level. There are historical reasons for this, including the fact that women continue to be voiceless in a world where patriarchy is prevalent, and the church is, unfortunately, a place where these negative world views seem to thrive.

Women seem to limit themselves in some areas when it comes to the extent to which they feel able to serve within the church. There are numerous fragmentations of the female self, which patriarchy has taught women to internalise. The resulting lack of solidarity, which is sometimes found among

---

[19] Daly, M., *Gyn/Ecology: The Metaethics of Radical Feminism*, (Boston: Beacon Press, 1990), p.26

[20] Rendle, G.R., 'Reclaiming professional jurisdiction: The re-emergence of the theological task of ministry', (*Theology Today*, 2002), 59.3

[21] Alvarado, A.G., *My Sister's Keeper: A Strategic Leadership Coaching Model for the Identity Formation of Women in Leadership at Total Grace Christian Centre in Metropolitan Atlanta, Georgia*, (Ann Arbor, MI,: Pro Quest LLC: 2008), p.19

women, has a destructive characteristic that undoubtedly has crippling effects on individual women and the collective whole.[22]

It has been interesting to note that questions have arisen as to whether women are discriminated against because of their gender or because of their ethnicity. Though it is hard to prove either case, definitively, to say that discrimination is purely gender based and not ethnicity based would be to say that racism does not exist for these women. Some (those who have experienced it and those who stand with them) more than others know that this is certainly not the case. There is a necessity for abandonment of the notion that 'Whiteness' is normative and central to Christian reality, yet this process of abandonment is not a simple task because the organisational structures within the world's major churches are inextricably bound up with 'Whiteness'[23].

There has been some confusion over what qualifies a person to state that they are a minister. A ministerial position, a theological qualification, a title or ordination? Rendle presents one definition as a situation 'where people make an intentional and voluntary choice to attend to the authority and interpretive role of the ordained person.'[24] For the purposes of this study the researcher has left it for participants to define what this role is, in an attempt to observe their understanding of what constitutes being a minister.

As expected, some participants sought clarification, in some cases stating that they do not feel eligible to complete the survey because they are not a minister, even though in one instance the respondent works full time for the church overseeing small, pastoral groups. She said 'I work full time for the church but I am not a Rev. I am part of a team and my role is caring for people and overseeing the 30 small groups that are part of our church. I don't do any preaching and haven't had theological training so I don't think I should be filling in your survey'. Time was spent reassuring them (all listed as current, serving ministers by the London Baptist Association) that they are eligible, according to the above definition and as recognised by the London Baptist Association. They may serve in the church or on the streets, but what makes them a minister is partly the fact that they have dedicated themselves to serving within the church context for their participation in God's mission in multiple ways. Rendle states

> Ministry involves locating oneself within the history of a faith tradition; learning the theological and hermeneutical tools as well as the spiritual disciplines necessary to explore and guide oneself and others fruitfully in a faith search connected to that tradition; wrestling with self-awareness and personal maturity to allow one to use oneself to reflect God's presence.[25]

---

[22] Daly, M., *Pure Lust*, p.136-138
[23] Leech, K., *Race*, (Church Publishing Incorporated: New York, 2005), p.99
[24] Rendle, G.R., 'Reclaiming professional jurisdiction: The re-emergence of the theological task of ministry', (Theology Today, 59.3 2002), p.22
[25] Rendle, G.R., *Reclaiming professional jurisdiction*, p.24

Going further, Anderson highlights God's personal word and action on the cosmos and in peoples' lives as a precedent to any ministry. [26] Porter specifically emphasizes multiple ministry leadership styles women are known to utilize, including Midwife, Choreographer, Weaver and Intercessor in what she calls 'Transformative leadership' that may not be easily identifiable at first glance.[27] If more women are able to recognize and celebrate our difference and uniqueness, both individually and as a community, greater levels of emancipation will inevitably result. Rizal, mentioned previously in this study, echoes this assertion.[28]

Seven out of the nine respondents believe that women can function in any role regardless of their gender. They subscribe to the Egalitarian perspective on the whole. Sullins maintains that 'congregations are quite welcoming of women priests in subordinate positions'[29] and thus, when these women engage in activities usually performed by men, conflict may arise. Challenging these patriarchal stereotypes needs to be balanced with careful listening, however, so that consensus can be attained: 'Unlike their counterparts in organizations and institutions based on employment relationships or civil authority, the professional minister succeeds more by developing consensus as the means for leadership - a role requiring listening as much as, or more than, directing'.[30]

Recommendations
With regards to the above findings, the researcher calls for the creation of forums and community groups where female ministers, including those of common ethnicity, can gather to decipher cultural codes.[31] These are mutually valued principles and norms that characterise a particular group of people, in order to share knowledge, experiences and learning. The purpose of this is in order to build social capital, social cohesion, and to facilitate positive change through mutual support and activism, within our churches and communities. If these forums existed, perhaps people would not feel so isolated and would gain greater encouragement for the journey ahead. They could engage in the Womanist principle of Theological audiation, seeking to learn from each other.

---

[26] Anderson, R. S., *The Soul of Ministry: Forming Leader's for God's People*, (Louisville, Kentucky: Westminster John Knox Press, 1997) p.6
[27] Porter, J., *Leading Ladies: Transformative Biblical Images for Women's Leadership*, (Philadelphia: Innsfree Press Inc., 2000), p.15
[28] Rizal, J., *The Subversive (El Filibusterismo)*, L.M. Guerro, trans. (Bloomington, IN.: Indiana University Press: 1962), p.54
[29] Sullins, P., 'The Stained Glass Ceiling: Career Attainment for Women Clergy', (*Sociology of Religion Journal:* 61:3, 2000), p.253
[30] Rendle, G.R., Reclaiming professional jurisdiction, p.40
[31] hooks, b., *Feminist Theory: From Margin to Centre*, (London: Pluto Press, 2000), p.58

Networking could also occur, which could make serving in ministry easier, as people could share best practice.

These conversation and learning forums should have discourse with one another, an example of which could be a group of Black women sharing and learning from each other, interacting with another group of White women formed for the same purpose. These groups could be in dialogue with a similar group of Latin American women and so on. This would mean sharing each other's cultural codes, around the issue of theology and identity, 'in order to maintain gratitude and respect for other traditions that challenge us to continue to both recover and discover resources and sources that point to a reality beyond ourselves.'[32] This is a key principle of Womanist Theology. To more faithfully follow in Jesus footsteps, 'Liberation theologians want a community effort in theology building and practice, thus they desire more laymen participation in creating and doing theology'[33]. This facilitates agency and emancipation.

The researcher echoes Beckford's biblical call for repentance. 'Therefore, confess your sins to one another and pray for one another, that you may be healed.[34] The prayer of a righteous person has great power as it is working' James 5:16. The Baptist Union of Great Britain and the London Baptist Association need to repent for ignoring the lament of the suffering in our midst; for declining the bearing of one another's burden in favour of seemingly more pressing needs at national, regional and local level. Congregations who, as a collective, actively oppress or ignore the oppression of Black people, women and Black women in particular, are called upon to reject their evil ways and seek forgiveness and reconciliation from those who have been wronged. Going further, these individuals and groups are called upon to add their voice to God's voice[35] and the voice of the marginalised, in prayer and activism to eradicate racism, sexism and classism.

In keeping with Bevans findings and in active opposition to utilitarianism, steps should be taken to present the 'naked gospel' to marginalised individuals and groups.[36] This should be a stripped down account of the life of Jesus and other major biblical characters, which should share these accounts and allow them to be 'played back' by the individuals and groups. As the Holy Spirit brings fresh insights, greater depths of meaning can be experienced, and a more authentic application of our Christian heritage and principles, could be reached. This allows us to create an element of praxis

---

[32] Cannon, K.G., Townes, E.M., and Sims, A.D., *Womanist Theological Ethics: A Reader*, (Louisville, Kentucky: Westminster John Knox Press,, 2011), p.xv

[33] Turner, J.D., *An Introduction to Liberation Theology*, (Maryland: University Press of America, 1994), p.57

[34] Beckford, R., *Jesus is Dread*, p.153

[35] Scott, P., and Cavanaugh, W.T., *The Blackwell Companion to Political Theology*, (Oxford: Blackwell Publishing, 2004), p.288

[36] Bevans, S.B., *Models of Contextual Theology*, (Maryknoll, New York: Orbis, 2011), pp.68-69

in our theology, which makes our faith come alive, while staying true to our cultural identity. This process, while promoting what Feminist theologian Daly espoused in her notion of 'speculative theology', is an inductive method based on 'positive knowledge of God through creatures'.[37] Her arguments formed part of a collective growing pressure at that time for theological education to be made accessible for women.

Continual theological training and development, both within and outside Bible colleges, needs to be made more accessible to Black female ministers. Also, whilst undertaking theological studies, targeted support needs to be provided for these individuals so they can thrive in such academic environments, not flounder and underperform. It is apparent that education has emancipatory benefits;[38] this particular group stand to contribute massively, and simultaneously, profit greatly from the opportunities that theological training presents, if properly implemented.

Mentoring relationships for women, especially Black women in ministry are crucial and should be actively promoted and facilitated by church and ministry leaders. Staying with the theme of relationship building, these one to one pairings can go a long way towards smoothing out the difficult parts of the ministry journey. Rather than having to seek these mentors out individually, a 'mentor bank' should be formed, giving people the opportunity to make use of such a learning partnership in order to enable accountability and theological reflection that can lead to more authentic praxis.

Congregations would benefit from collective theological reflection on the role of women in the church. Using scripture, theological concepts and helpful church tradition, in a prayerful atmosphere of respect, whilst taking the time to listen to one another with the help of a skilled facilitator, much could be gained from this type of discipleship. Williams notes the potential impact of Womanist theology and method if included in the interpretive circle of Christian theology and the liturgical life of the church.[39]

The researcher calls for the formation of a body similar to the 'Black Clergywomen' caucus of the United Methodist Church.[40] This should be supported by the Baptist Union of Great Britain and recognised and promoted at regional and local levels. This is clearly a matter of justice within the structures of the Baptist family, from local churches, through to the national level.

---

[37] Daly, M., *The Problem of Speculative Theology*, (Boston: Thomist Press, 1965), p.43
[38] Code, L., *Encyclopaedia of Feminist Theories*, (London: Routledge, 2002), p.86
[39] Williams, D., *Womanist Theology: Black Women's Voices, in Christianity and Crisis*, (Tennessee: University Tennessee Press, 1987), p 162
[40] Black Clergy Women of the United Methodist Church, (2014), http://Blackclergywomenumc.com/about-us/ Last accessed 17/06/14

Another recommendation is for all to support initiatives like 'I-am-possible',[41] which seeks to celebrate and showcase Black women who are community and business leaders, affirming their contribution to society. Schemes, such as this, coupled with nurturing community groups that concentrate on empowering young Black females like 'Black Girls Rock',[42] will ensure that less people will experience the debilitating effects of racism and sexism in the church and society. Feminist activism should be promoted to facilitate confidence-building, the seed-bed of creativity, and the fulfilment of potential for individuals and groups.[43]

Black female ministers should be invited to share their gifts with the wider body of Christ. They have a unique story to tell, one of courage and perseverance in the midst of difficulties, and hearing their stories will enable the church to confront the sins, which are so prevalent in her, namely, racism and sexism, to name but two.

Conclusion

Hagar, a Biblical figure commonly cited by Womanists, is the first person in scripture visited by a divine messenger. She is the only person in scripture who dares to name the deity. She is the first woman to hear the announcement that she will bear a child, a forerunner of Mary who will also hear an angel tell her that she will bear a child. Hagar is the only woman in the Bible who receives a promise of descendants from God. She is the first woman in scripture to cry for her dying child.[44]

Like Hagar in Genesis 16, some of these Black female ministers are voiceless, powerless and abused by the powerful. Their experiences are analogous to Sarai and Abraham's behaviour towards Hagar. Yet like Hagar, these women are still full of a growing hope for the future, just as Ishmael grew in the womb of Hagar, finding strength and encouragement from personal encounters with God.

This is very much similar to Hagar's wilderness experience. God's intervention is sometimes uncomfortable and difficult to understand. For example, God instructs Hagar to return to the abusive environment, promising future greatness for her and her descendants. Nevertheless, in spite of this seemingly strange intervention from God, Hagar encounters God, which elicits worship and praise of the God who sees and accompanies those on the margins.

Rather than rest in shallow dimensions of theodicy, which posit that all suffering is redemptive, it is important to express and come to grips with

---

[41] I-am-possible, celebrating the brilliance of British women of colour, (2011), http://www.i-am-possible.com/ last accessed 17/06/14

[42] BlackGirlsRock Inc., (2014), http://www.Blackgirlsrockinc.com/about-us/#.U6AH92fQf4g , last accessed 09/06/14

[43] Naples, N.A., and Bojar, K., *Teaching Feminist Activism: Strategies From the Field*, (New York: Routledge, 2013), p.289

[44] Trible, P., *Texts of Terror*, (Minneapolis: Fortress Press, 1984), p.28

the pain and suffering the Black woman endures.[45] The laments of the psalms give voice to an experience that is not dissimilar, with communal, personal, repentance and imprecatory dimensions.[46] The psalms enabled human beings to ask hard questions of a creative and omnipotent, yet loving and compassionate God, with a prevailing sense of hope as expressed in the spirituals. The spirituals captured the affliction of enslaved Africans in music and taught the Christian faith and its message of freedom to an exploited community.[47] They subsequently became a stepping stone to emancipation. 'The notion of lament and critical hopefulness is the most honest response to the presence of evil in the life experiences of Black people.'[48] So as a people it can be said 'My strength comes from God, who made heaven, and earth, and mountains... He guards you when you leave and when you return, he guards you now, he guards you always'. Psalm 121

---

[45] Pinn, B.A., *Why, Lord? Suffering and Evil in Black Theology*, (London: Bloomsbury Publishing, 1999), p.139
[46] Jinkins, M., *In the House of the Lord: Inhabiting the Psalms of Lament*, (Minnesota: Liturgical Press: The Order of St Benedict Inc., 1998), p.5
[47] Smith, Y.Y., *Reclaiming the Spirituals: New Possibilities for African-American Christian Education*, (Ohio: Pilgrim Press, 2004), p.71
[48] Reddie, A., *Working Against the Grain: Re-imagining Black Theology in the 21st Century*, (London: Acumen, 2008), p.177

Abolition, Diasporan Memory & the Curious Invisibility of Sam Sharpe from the Baptist Centenary Historiography
R. David Muir

Introduction
The phenomenon of the Jamaican rebellion, sometimes known as the Christmas rebellion in 1831, engenders a creative tension in the analysis and historical memory of Jamaican Diasporan consciousness. This arises for a number of reasons. First, however, I want to allude to three. Firstly, it forces us to retrace our steps in the sacred space of African displacement and dislocation, in a critical moment of time. Secondly, it compels us to seek a greater understanding of Diasporan movements of resistance that are consistent with universal and contextual understandings of freedom.

In terms of the former, we have the philosophical impulse of the Hegelian notion of the manifestation of 'Spirit' ('the Absolute') and the progress of freedom as the end product of all historical projects.[1] In terms of the latter, we have the urge for freedom and the priority of African agency, in their own liberation struggles. Thirdly, it helps us to renew our memory and the constant reformation of our matrix of consciousness and political judgements about what we bequeath to the next generation. It also challenges, of course, what we pass into the sociology of knowledge, which later becomes the interpretative 'norm'. History matters and its 'objectivity' and critical interpretation is a sensitive issue for people of African descent whose history and achievements are often negated, neglected and subjected to White mythologies, epistemology and power.[2]

Theologians recognize this as the 'hermeneutics of suspicion'. In a sense, all social, historical and theological interpretations are cognitive exercises in the hermeneutics of suspicion. Bob Marley's 'Redemption Song' not only conjures up intimations of this, but it explicitly invites individuals to 'emancipate yourself from mental slavery'. It also proceeds to echo the contours of what I mean by the primacy of agency by stating that 'none but ourselves can free our minds'.

During the 2007 Bicentenary commemorations in the UK, and in the many activities that took place, there were manifold opportunities for historical

---

[1] See G.W.F. Hegel, *Phenomenology of Spirit* (Oxford, Oxford University Press: 1977) (Translated by A.V. Miller, with Analysis of the Text and Foreword by J.N. Findlay); see also Francis Fukuyama, *The End of History and the Last Man*, (New York: Penguin Books: 1992), especially chapter 5 ('An Idea for a Universal History'), pp.55-70.
[2] See Robert Young, *White Mythologies: Writing History and the West*, (London: Routledge: 1990).

review and counter-renderings of abolitionist historiography and cinematography. Walden Media were quick off the mark with their film on Wilberforce.[3]

Contextualizing Abolition: moral repugnance and economic imperative
In setting the background for the rebellion led by Sam Sharpe in Jamaica in 1831, we need to situate it in the broader context of British colonial history without getting bogged down in the paralysis of historical details. However, we need to say that this is a historical period rich in irony and contradictions, but it is also fecund in biographical sacrifices and 'the general growth of philanthropic sentiment'.[4] Between the last quarter of the 18th century and first four decades of the 19th century, Britain and its Caribbean colonies experienced significant changes. An antislavery doctrine was forming and gained limited circulation by the 1760s. It was not until 1787, however, that a 'vigorous public movement'[5] was launched for the abolition of the slave trade from Africa, as the first step towards reforming and eventually eliminating slave labour in the Caribbean.

The British abolitionists' story and the part played by Wilberforce, Clarkson, Equiano and others are well told by Walden Media and others, so there is little value in rehearsing the details here.[6] Suffice it to say that in 1788 Parliament voted to regulate conditions on the slave ships. A bill for gradual abolition was passed by the House of Commons in 1792 but was rejected by the House of Lords. The Act to Abolish the Slave Trade finally came in 1807. In consequence of this, no significant deliveries of new African slaves reached the British 'West Indies', after 1808.

Among the moral calculations in the arguments for the abolition of the slave trade, was the idea that the slave masters would be more likely to take better care of their slaves if they knew that their source of cheap labour would be cut off. This did not happen. As a result of the continuing excess of slave deaths over births the British plantation export stagnated.

This, of course, raises a number of questions and conundrums as to whether the eventual success of the abolitionists was due to 'metropolitan repugnance against an increasingly flagrant moral evil' or because (as Williams argued) their cause served the national economic interests. To put it another way, the moral triumphalism and religious rectitude of the

---

[3] *Wilberforce* (Walden Media, released February 2007; certificate PG)
[4] See J.R. Ward, 'The British West Indies in the Age of Abolition' in P.J. Marshall (ed.), *The Oxford History of the British Empire, Vol. II: The Eighteenth Century* (Oxford, Oxford University Press: 2001), p.425.
[5] Ibid.
[6] See Stephen Farrell, Melanie Unwin and James Walvin (eds.), *The British Slave Trade: Abolition, Parliament and People* (Edinburgh, Edinburgh University Press: 2007). This excellent book, along with the accompanying Parliamentary Exhibition in Westminster Hall, (23 May -23 September, 2007) provided an excellent resource commemorating the bicentenary in 2007.

abolitionists and Wilberforce take a different interpretative slant when, as argued by David Richardson, the fundamental issue of 'the relative importance of economic factors in precipitating abolition,' is taken into account.[7] The question of why Africans were enslaved in such large numbers, and why the trade did not end earlier are, of course, important ones.

On the eve of the Bicentenary commemorations in the UK, no less a person than the Prime Minister, Tony Blair, raised some of these questions. In November 2006 Tony Blair wrote an article on slavery that appeared on the front page of *The New Nation* newspaper. In it, he acknowledged the horror, the scale and the duration of the transatlantic slave trade; he also expressed 'deep sorrow' that it ever happened and outlined how the British Government was responding to the current challenges of aid, trade and debt in the African Diaspora.[8]

Conundrums, the Church & Nonconformists thought
One of the conundrums of modern slavery intimated by the Prime Minister, and wrestled with by historians, is poignantly stated by Walvin: 'Quite why the Africans were recruited in such numbers *as slaves* has become a major historical conundrum.'[9] Was it to do with 'race', or was it fundamentally about 'labour' and the cheapness of African bodies at the height of British overseas and industrial development in the eighteenth century? Historians like Eric Williams opt for the latter explanation. In his classic, *Capitalism & Slavery*, he states:

> Here, then, is the origin of Negro slavery. The reason was economic, not racial; it had to do not with the colour of the labourer, but the cheapness of the labour. As compared with Indian or white labour, Negro slavery was eminently superior.[10]

Although the development of the plantation in the British colonies in the Caribbean, and the ideology of the plantocracy, brought in its wake theories to justify and rationalize African slavery (namely, racism), Williams maintains

---

[7] See David Richardson, 'The Ending of the British Slave Trade in 1807: The Economic Context', in Stephen Farrell, Melanie Unwin and James Walvin (eds.) *The British Slave Trade: Abolition, Parliament and People*, (Edinburgh: Edinburgh University Press: 2007), p.127.
[8] The Prime Minister's article was, undoubtedly, well received in many quarters. However, there were those who felt that Tony Blair should have, like the Church of England, used the opportunity to offer an 'apology' for the role Britain played in the Transatlantic Slave Trade in commemorating the bicentenary.
[9] James Walvin, *Black Ivory: Slavery in the British Empire* (Oxford, Blackwell Publishing, 2001) (Second edition; first published in 1992), p.viii. Another 'major conundrum' for Walvin is 'why did the British turn against their slave empire at the very point at which it seems to have been yielding such largesse to Britain?'
[10] Eric Williams, *Capitalism & Slavery* (London, André Deutsch: 1964) (first published in 1944) p.19.

that slavery 'was not born of racism: rather, racism was the consequence of slavery'.[11]

A transatlantic trade that lasted for nearly 400 years, saw over 30 million people violently removed from the African continent, provided the capital to finance[12] the Industrial Revolution in England and other parts of Europe and America, was more than just an 'economic phenomenon'. It was an institution supported by the state, financiers, and a powerful lobby of planters and politicians. There was also an 'intelligentsia' armed with specious and irrational philosophies and ideologies on 'race' in the age of reason and 'enlightenment'.[13]

Religion played a critical role in ending the slave trade and slavery. It also, paradoxically, played a role in its delay. This can be seen in the attitudes of the Church of England at the time and the Nonconformist missionary societies in the Caribbean. With its power, wealth and influence, the Church of England, argues Gratus, could have been an 'invaluable force on the side of abolition and emancipation had it chosen that course'[14]. However, its commitment to the 'sanctity of property' and its alignment with the West Indian merchants and the plantocracy acted as 'a brake on progress.'[15] The Church of England owned plantations in Barbados, with 300 slaves bequeathed to it by the wealthy slave owner, Christopher Codrington.

Nonconformist thinking, whether expressed by John Wesley or James Mursell Phillippo of the Baptist Missionary Society, sided with the slaves against the powerful plantation owners. In his *Thoughts Upon Slavery* John Wesley states:

> I absolutely deny all slave holding to be consistent with any degree of even natural justice...Give liberty to whom liberty is due, that is to every child of man, to every partaker of human nature. Let none serve you but by his own act and deed, by his own voluntary choice.

---

[11] Ibid. p.7

[12] Ibid. pp. 98-125. E.J. Hobsbawm makes the point that if a visitor had gone to Liverpool in 1750 he 'would doubtless have been impressed with the bustle of that fast-rising port, based, like Bristol and Glasgow, largely on the trade in slaves and colonial products - sugar, tea, tobacco, and increasingly cotton'. See his *Industry & Empire*, (Middlesex: Penguin Books, 1969), p24.

[13] In respect of the 'race' and the African, the 'Enlightenment' (1775) had its dark side as can be detected in the works of some its luminaries such as Kant, Hume and Hegel. In Kant's essay 'On the Different Races of Man' he comments on the thoughts of a Negro carpenter in the most irrational terms: 'And it might be that there were something in this which perhaps deserved to be considered; but in short, this fellow was quite black from head to foot, a clear proof that what he said was stupid.' See Emanuel Chukwudi Eze (ed.), *Race and the Enlightenment: A Reader*, (Oxford: Blackwell Publishers, 1997), p.57.

[14] See Jack Gratus, The *Great White Lie, Slavery, Emancipation, and Changing Racial Attitudes*, (London & New York), The Monthly Press Review:1973, pp.144-145

[15] Ibid.

In line with Wesley's sentiments on the incompatibility of Christianity with slavery, Burchell's close associate, William Knibb, gave one of the most moving antislavery speeches in 1833 at Spa Fields Chapel in London at the annual meeting of the Baptist Missionary Society. Knibb had first-hand experience of the brutality and dehumanisation of slavery as a Baptist missionary in Jamaica. In his speech he invoked the judgment of God and the responsibility of Christians to banish 'the evil of slavery' from the earth:

> God is the avenger of the oppressed, and the African shall not always be forgotten. I plead on behalf of the widows and orphans of those whose blood has been shed. I plead that the constancy of the Negro may be rewarded. I plead on behalf of my brethren in Jamaica, whose hopes are fixed on this meeting. I plead on behalf of their wives and their little ones. I call upon children by the cries of the infant slave, whom I saw flogged at Macclesfield Estate in Westmoreland. I call upon mothers, by the tender sympathy of their nature. I call upon parents by the blood-stained back of Catherine Williams, who, with a heroism which England has seldom known, preferred a dungeon to the surrender of her honour... If I fail in arousing your sympathies I will retire from this meeting, and call upon Him who hath made one blood all nations upon the face of the earth. And if I die without beholding the emancipation of my brethren and sisters in Christ, then, if prayer is permitted in heaven, I will fall at the feet of the Eternal, crying: Lord, open the eyes of Christians in England to see the evil of slavery and to banish it from the earth.[16]

The world in which Sam Sharpe conducted his Christmas 1831 slave rebellion in the parish of St. James in Jamaica was a world in moral and economic transition. It was a world of revolutionary possibilities. Whilst the existence of the slave was akin to the Hobbesian one of 'continual fear, and the danger of violent death' (not to mention the many for whom life was 'poor, nasty, brutish and short'[17]) it also had within, its contradictory 'politics of moral orders'.[18] This was a world where identities and subjectivities, were negotiated and contested through the ideology of the plantocracy, juxtaposed with revolutionary and humanizing potential. Equaino had written his bestselling autobiography[19] in the year of the French Revolution; America had waged a Revolutionary war against the British Crown, and the great Toussaint

---

[16] John Brown Myers, *The Centenary Volume of the Baptist Missionary Society: 1792-1892*, (London: The Baptist Missionary Society, 1892), (see *"The West Indies"* by Rev Jonathan East) pp.192-193.

[17] Thomas Hobbes, *Leviathan*, (Middlesex: Penguin Books, 1968) (first published in 1651), Part 1 Ch. Xiii.

[18] See Diane J. Austin-Broos *Jamaica Genesis: Religion and the Politics of Moral Orders* (Chicago and London: University of Chicago Press, 1997).

[19] Olaudah Equiano, *The Interesting Narrative of the Life of Olaudah Equiano. Or Gustavus Vassa, the African, Written by Himself* (originally published in 1789), edited and introduced by Vincent Carretta, (London: Penguin Books, 1995).

L'Ouverture had defeated the army of Napoleon, causing him to lose more than 50,000 soldiers (including 18 generals).

In his twenty two month attempt to regain the colony Napoleon suffered more causalities trying to retake this French colony (that later became the Republic of Haiti 1804) than he would at Waterloo. Sharpe was just a mere three year old slave boy at the time of this defining moment in Caribbean history, but he would later learn of the exploits of Toussaint the 'Gilded African' and how 'the hopes of slaves everywhere were embodied in this one territory where they had won freedom'.[20] Toussaint represented, as Hillary Beckles argues, 'the self-liberation ethos' of the slaves.[21]

If the 'Enlightenment' was principally about freedom from irrationality and emancipation from modes of tyranny,[22] and 'reason's right to shape reality',[23] then it was seen in the achievements of Toussaint and the people of this new republic. This quest for freedom was expressed well by William Wordsworth in his sonnet 'To Toussaint L'Ouverture' (1802):

> Though fallen thyself, never to rise again,
> Live and take comfort. Thou hast left behind
> Powers that will work for thee; air, earth and skies;
> There's not a breathing of the common wind
> That will forget thee; thou hast great allies;
> Thy friends are exultations, agonies
> And love, and man's unconquerable mind.[24]

Although it is beyond the scope of this short essay to explore this in any detail, it is worth saying that another slave rebellion had taken place in North America in the autumn of 1831 by another Baptist slave, namely, Nat Turner. In America, the slaves had eloquent theorists and political theologians in the form of David Walker and Robert Young to give succour to the cause of freedom. One hundred and thirty years before Malcolm X's 'by any means necessary'

---

[20] See Adam Hochschilds *Bury The Chains: The British Struggle to Abolish Slavery* (London: Macmillan, 2005), p.289.
[21] See his 'Caribbean Anti-Slavery: The Self-Liberation Ethos of Enslaved Blacks' in Hillary Beckles & Verene Shepherd (eds.) *Caribbean Slave Society & Economy: A Student Reader* (Kingston Ja.: Ian Randle Publishers Ltd, 1991), pp.363-372.
[22] See Jonathan Israel, *Enlightenment Contested: Philosophy, Modernity and the Emancipation of Man 1670-1752*, (Oxford: Oxford University Press, 2006).
[23] See Herbert Marcuse *Reason and Revolution: Hegel and the Rise of Social Theory* (London and Henley: Routledge & Kegan Paul, 1986), p.19.
[24] In his ballad 'A Morning Dream', kindred sentiments against oppression and slavery are expressed in verses by the poet William Wordsworth. Set to a popular tune, Cowper's ballad depicts the demon 'Oppression' vanquished ('the monster expir'd') and envisions a future without slavery in the British empire: "That Britannia, renown'd o'er the waves, For the hatred she ever has shown, To the black-sceptred rulers of slaves, Resolved to have none of her own." See William Hayley *The Works of William Cowper: His Life and Letters (*Vol. III), (London: Saunders and Otley, 1835), pp. 318-9.

slogan, Walker was advocating the moral legitimacy of slave insurrection through armed struggle. It was a rallying cry for freedom and the assertion of African manhood and womanhood. He was, according to Vincent Harding, the 'first writer to combine an attack on white racism and white economic exploitation in a deliberate and critical way'.[25]

In his famous seventy-six page pamphlet of September 1829 (*Appeal ...to the Coloured Citizens of the World But in Particular and very Expressly to those of the United States of America*) he argued:

> They want us for their slaves, and think nothing of murdering us in order to subject us to that wretched condition... Look upon your mother, wife and children, and answer God Almighty! And believe this, that it is no more harm for you to kill a man, who is trying to kill you, than it is for you to take a drink of water when an infidel, and, if he has common sense, ought not to be pittied.[26]

Where is Sam Sharpe in the Centenary volume of the Baptist Missionary Society?

This brings me to Sam Sharpe and his invisibility in the Centenary volume of the Baptist Missionary Society (1792-1892). I would like to now consider this briefly. The basic facts surrounding the rebellion led by Sam Sharpe are well known.[27] He lived a short life; less than half of the 'three score and ten years' allotted to man. Born in the first year of the nineteenth century and was executed in May 1832. He was a slave all his life, but as a Deacon at Montego Bay Baptist Church, he was allowed to become relatively well educated and, therefore, respected by the slave community as an itinerant preacher and a leader.

The decision by Sam (Daddy) Sharpe and the leadership of the Native Baptist Church in Jamaica in December 1831 to lead a non-violent form of resistance and protest by refusing to work without pay was, in essence, 'an attempt by the Native Baptist to organize themselves into a trade union arm of

---

[25] Vincent Harding, *There is a River: The Struggle for Freedom in America* (New York and London: Harcourt Brace Jovanovich Publishers, 1981) (especially chapter 4 "Symptoms of Liberty and Blackhead Signposts—David Walker and Nat Turner"), pp.75-100; Gayraud S. Wilmore, *Black Religion and Black Radicalism* (Garden City, New York: Doubleday, 1972). See also Herbert Marcuse *Reason and Revolution: Hegel and the Rise of Social Theory* (London and Henley: Routledge & Kegan Paul, 1986), p.19.

[26] Rousseau had argued similarly in his 'The Social Contract' (1762): "So long as a people is constrained to obey, and obeys, it does well; but as soon as it can shake of the yoke, and shakes it off, it does better; for since it regains its freedom by the same right as that which removed it, a people is either justified in taking back its freedom, or there is no justifying those who took it away." (Book 1 chapter ii.)

[27] See Delroy Reid-Salmon, *Burning for Freedom: A Theology of Black Atlantic Struggle for Liberation* (Kingston, Jamaica: Ian Randle Publishers, 2012). This book is a timely and excellent contribution to a reappraisal of the legacy of Sam Sharpe and his place in Caribbean historiography and memory.

the Native Baptist Church', essentially advocating and 'negotiating wages for enslaved people'.[28]

Eventually, this led what to what has been called the 'Native Baptist War'. In the aftermath of the revolt 600 African Jamaicans were killed by British forces and 14 White people lost their lives. According to Erskine, this revolt led by Sharpe 'signaled the beginning of the end of slavery in Jamaica'. Stating at his trial that he 'had rather die than be a slave', Erskine maintains that Sharpe and his 'freedom fighters interpreted the message of liberation through the hermeneutics of freedom'.[29]

Under the influence of Revd Thomas Burchell, we can surmise that he was imbued with 'nonconformist' tendencies and its biblical message of justice, spiritual equality, judgement of sin and unrighteousness. The editor of the Centenary volume, John Brown Myers, made no mention of Revd Thomas Burchell's Deacon who was left in charge of his friend's church while away on vacation in England. He talked about the 'social and political troubles of Jamaica' and the fact that the action of planters and 'some clergymen and the local press, led to the insurrection in 1831' on 'account of the slaves giving credence to a report that their freedom had been decreed' by the British Government. Myers was keen to point out the loss to church property, amounting to some £12,390. Even the Revd David Jonathan East in his regional report on the West Indies makes no mention of Sharpe. 'Unhappily', he states, 'occasion was given by an insurrection of the slave population, which broke out in the very district in which missionary labour had been most successful.'[30]

East is adamant in pointing out that the White Baptist missionaries knew nothing of the plans and intentions of the slaves until it was too late. Even then, they 'expostulated with the people, deprecating their intentions in the strongest terms, and exposing the delusion they were under that "free papers" from the Queen, giving them their liberty, were being withheld from them by their masters'.[31]

Both Knibb and Burchell were acquitted by the authorities in having any part in the revolt, either directly, or in their preaching and teaching. What, according to Bisnauth, is revealing is the way in which Knibb responds to questions during his interrogation about his teachings in respect of the 'temporal conditions' of the slaves and related matters. When asked 'What were the doctrines at all bearing on the temporal condition of the black population, which you inculcated?' Knibb replied:

> I never touched upon the subject in my life...Whenever I have had occasion to speak on that subject (freedom), I have explained that when freedom is

---

[28] See Noel Leo Erskine, *Plantation Church: How African American Religion was Born in Caribbean Slavery* (Oxford: Oxford University Press, 2014), p.93.
[29] Ibid, p.94.
[30] Op., cit. p. 191.
[31] Ibid, 191.

mentioned in the word of God, it referred to the soul and not to the body; that there were slaves at the times of the apostles as well as at present. [32]

Interestingly enough, in what East calls the 'battle of freedom,' it is Knibb, Burchell and Phillippo who are lionized as the three men who 'were evidently set apart by God' for their service to Jamaica, but not a word about Deacon Sharpe. Doubtless, we are forced to draw conclusions from this about the politics of the Baptist Church in regard to its centre-periphery nexus of socio-political values and communication in this period, and 'nonconformists' ideology. A counter narrative, and one which privileges and restores African agency in their own liberation, is given by Reid-Salmon when he argues that the Sam Sharpe Rebellion of 1831 'was a revelation of the will of God for the liberation of the enslaved and oppressed similar to the biblical story of the Exodus of the Hebrew people from Pharaoh's oppression in Egypt.'[33]

In their attitudes towards the slaves, the Nonconformists were not revolutionaries committed to armed resistance, but they did advocate justice and forms of equality for the slaves, radically dissimilar to the discourse of the Church of England. In a sense, it would not be unfair to say that the Nonconformists, like the English abolitionists' rejection of the slaves' 'revolutionary approach to freedom', shared the characteristics seen in the development of European colonial historiography. Although they wished to see the emancipation of the slaves they, nevertheless, saw the 'economic dependency and political subordination of blacks to whites' as both necessary and desirable for their own advancement, as well as for the continued growth of the Caribbean.

This was fundamental to the ideological tenets deeply embedded in abolitionist modus operandi. The racism implied in this perception of Black liberation, argues Beckles, was an 'entrenched feature of abolitionists' thought'. Additionally, the abolitionists' tendency to conceive of slaves as 'unfortunate children to be liberated from tyrannical parents' only served to deepen the racist perceptions of their audience that 'blacks seeking independence, economic autonomy and political power, were irresponsible, rash, ungrateful, in addition to being naïve'.[34]

The place of Sam Sharpe is critical in Baptist and Caribbean historiography, as well as wider Diasporan consciousness. In the 'unending dialogue between past and present' that is defined as history, we have a rich and didactic resource in resurrecting and reclaiming the place of Sam Sharpe in Caribbean theo-political iconography and memory. How does contemporary society 'restore to its public memory' momentous events of it past is a question asked by

---

[32] Dale Bisnauth, *History of Religions in the Caribbean* (Kingston, Jamaica: Kingston Publishers Limited, 1989), pp. 133-4.
[33] Delroy Reid-Salmon, op.cit.
[34] Beckles, op., cit. p.368.

Elizabeth Wallace.[35] In the case of Sam Sharpe, and the 1831 Slave Rebellion for freedom, Jamaican society has chosen to honour her nineteenth century prophet by conferring the Order of 'National Hero' upon him.

---

[35] See Elizabeth Kowaleski Wallace *The British Slave Trade & Public Memory* (New York: Columbia University Press, 2006), p.25.

Reparations: A call to fulfil the promise of education made by Baptists to the enslaved and their descendants through the 1835 Negro Education Grant
Doreen Morrison

In 2007 the Baptist Union of Great Britain used the two hundred year anniversary of the 'Abolition of the Transatlantic Slave Trade' to embark on a journey. This journey was one of seeking to better understand the truth of this trade. It was concerned with extending a hand of reconciliation to the descendants of those who were once enslaved, and seeking ways in which they could possibly make amends for their part in the enslavement of Africans in the Caribbean, by 'righting the wrongs' of racism and injustice.

We are now on that journey and a great many meetings, points of contact and sharing have taken place, resulting in greater understanding and appreciation for the legacy of slavery on a people and on the nations from which they had come. However, a meeting of Caricom[1] nations in St. Vincent in 2013 discussed the issues of legacy and raised the subject of reparations. Its conclusions were presented to the 'slave nations,' including Britain, in 2015. This has now become a cause for further consideration as to the part played by all Christian denominations in the negative legacy which remains today within the Caribbean, and in the lives of the descendants of slavery.

Using the Caricom's 10 point plan, which speaks to the subject of reparations, this essay will interrogate the issue of Education and the promises made by Baptist Missionaries through the 'Negro Education Grant' (NEG) of 1835 – 1845. It will discuss that which was agreed by both the enslaved and the missionaries, raising the argument that the missionaries failed in their goal of fulfilling their mandate of education to the enslaved and their descendants, ultimately being 'distracted' by a desire to evangelise Africa.

Caricom's Call for Reparations
In 2013 Caricom came together in St Vincent and unanimously agreed a ten-point plan proposed by the 'Caricom Reparations Commission' to 'achieve reparatory justice for the victims of genocide, slavery, slave trading and racial apartheid.'[2] This was issued in response to the injustices and legacy of the

---
[1] CARICOM is the acronym for the Caribbean Community. It is comprised of 15 countries. Further details can be found in the following link.
https://en.wikipedia.org/wiki/Caribbean_Community
[2] Caricom Nations Unanimously Approve 10 Point Plan for Slavery Reparations, 11 March 2014. Available from: https://www.leighday.co.uk/News/2014/March.2014. Downloaded 9 January 2016

enslavement of over 10 million Africans, which remains an ever present companion in the psyche of their descendants, to the present day.

Rather than document the whole 10 point plan, I shall deal only with point six, which concerns illiteracy eradication and was mandated to and accepted by the Church through the NEG of 1835. It states:

> At the end of the European colonial period in most parts of the Caribbean, the British in particular left the black and indigenous communities in a general state of illiteracy. Some 70 percent of blacks in British colonies were functionally illiterate in the 1960s when nation states began to appear.
> Jamaica, the largest such community, was home to the largest number of such citizens.[3]

The entire document argues that whilst the Caricom nations have, since Independence, suffered as a consequence of slavery and colonialism, those nations which practiced slavery were able to develop their economies in ways which would not have been possible without these crimes against the enslaved and their descendants.

Surely, you might say, 'The issue today is racism and injustice, as stated in the "Apology" and so any notion of reparations is choosing not to forget something for which this present generation cannot and should not logically be held responsible?' To go some way to answering this point, I believe that one has first to understand what 'reparations' mean. According to the *Oxford English Dictionary* the definition of reparations is, 'The act or an instance of making amends; a compensation; compensation for war damage paid by the defeated state.[4]

Reparations is, therefore, to 'make amends' or 'compensate for a wrong,' and this chapter will argue that there is a case to be heard, by Baptists in both Jamaica and Britain, for the promise of education that was made to the enslaved and all of their descendants. This promise was issued so that the descendents of the enslaved could take their rightful place, as equals in the world, able to determine their own futures.

However, before seeking to play our part in righting the wrong of history, we must first understand how and why the British Missionary Society (BMS) were given the reigns of leadership in the journey to Emancipation. So, we begin with the passing of the 'Abolition of the Transatlantic Slave Trade Act in 1807'.

The Abolition of the Transatlantic Slave Trade (1807)
It is a fact that during the period of enslavement, British colonies were allowed to establish their own laws through their own legislature, separate from that

---

[3] Ibid.
[4] Della Thompson (ed.) *The Compact English Dictionary* (Oxford: Oxford University Press, 1996).

which was handed down by the British Parliament. The enslaved in Jamaica were, therefore, subject to two 'masters', the British Government and the Jamaican Assembly, which was dominated by the plantocracy. Each legislature made laws governing the practise of slavery, and whereas, it would seem rational to assume that that which was passed by the British Government had precedence, this was not always the case. For instance, whilst British law did not recognise marriage, family structures, education or the religious practice of the enslaved, in Jamaica exceptions were made with many 'Christian' slave holders being allowed to carry out all these practices on their estates with the assent of the Legislature.

There was, therefore, no consistency as to how the enslaved were treated. Edicts from Westminster were often ignored, refused, or overridden by laws which the Jamaican Assembly put in place in order to circumvent what they considered to be objectionable laws 'handed down' by Westminster. This was the case concerning the Abolition of the Transatlantic Slave Trade Act of 1807, where such was the ire of the plantation owners that they quickly introduced legislation, which attacked the only visible 'instigators' and opposition to their 'rule' - the Ethiopian Baptist Society.

The Ethiopian Baptist Society was the first Baptist movement in Jamaica, led by the once enslaved African American George Liele, and his cohort of leaders from both America and Jamaica. Liele, on his arrival in Jamaica, not only established worshipping communities, but schools for the spiritual and social education of the enslaved, in order to empower them so that they would be able to determine their own futures, whether enslaved or free. We get an understanding of his own literacy skills and those of his members in his writings to Rippon in England:

> I have a few books, some good old authors and sermons, and one large Bible that was given me by a gentleman. A good many of our members can read.[5]

Liele was an educated African with a membership of 1,500 members, and therefore, clearly a force to be reckoned with because of his determination to right the wrongs of a people denied.

However, back to the 1807 Abolition Act. It was passed on 23rd February 1807 and was immediately followed by one of the greatest acts of repression against a powerless people, who were nevertheless determined to resist. In Britain, leading Baptists were pre-occupied by thoughts of abolition, playing their part in leading 'victory' celebrations in Britain:

> Rippon held a special service of thanksgiving at Carter Lane on 27 March to give people of colour an opportunity to spend 'a day of prayer and public thanksgiving to God...' The assembled congregation included some 4 – 500 Africans: 'such a

---

[5] Chatham County Ga Archives History…The First African Baptist Church, Chapter 2, 2-3 Available from www.usgwarchives.net/ga/chatham/history/other/gms373the1staf.txt

body of Africans,' Rippon recorded, 'never before assembled for religious worship in any part of Great Britain.'[6]

The Jamaican Assembly responded by putting in place additional clauses to the already draconian 'Consolidated Slave Act' of 1792. Their declared intent was to starve the enslaved of the 'oxygen' of their faith and education, which they feared would eventually lead them to their freedom. The amended law stated that:

> No Methodist missionary or other sectarian or preacher shall presume to instruct our slaves or receive them into their houses, chapels or conventicles of any sort or description, under the penalty of twenty pounds for every slave proved to have been there - imprisonment until the fine was paid...passed by the Assembly, November 11th 1807.[7]

The enslaved, therefore, found themselves in a battle for their faith and their education, but they were determined to succeed.

Armed only with their faith in God and a united spirit they held on to one promise, Psalm 68:31, 'Ethiopia shall soon stretch out her hands unto God,' believing that it was a promise that God wanted to fulfil for all the enslaved in their lifetime. We see demonstrations of their passion in the stories documented by the BMS, following their arrival from 1814.

Documented here are but a few examples of the faithfulness of a people desirous of having a better life, and refusing to give up on their means of getting there, though faced with tremendous persecution:

> Two persons were cruelly flogged by their masters for persisting in coming to chapel, and for praying to God.
> A man was cast into prison for praying too loud, between eight and nine o'clock p.m., in his own house.
> April 1808...The chapel doors had to be guarded by day, to admit only free persons into the house of prayer, and the poor slaves were sent back, some of them piteously exclaiming, "Massa, me no fe go to heaven now!" "Heigh! White man keep black man fra serving God!" "Nobody fe teach black man now![8]
> A free black man (Lewis) visited the neighbourhood; he talked to the slaves about Jesus, and afterwards baptized some of them... on one of his preaching excursions, he was seized by the opponents of the gospel and hung.[9]

---

[6] John H Y Briggs, 'Baptists and the Campaign to Abolish the Slave Trade'. *Baptist Quarterly Volume* 42, 271. Available from www.baptisthistory.org.uk/bhs_articles/BriggsJHY_Slaves.pdf

[7] John Clarke, *Memorials of Baptist Missionaries in Jamaica including A Sketch of the Labour of Early Religious Instructions in Jamaica* (London: Yates & Alexander, 1869), p.46.

[8] Ibid, pp.43 – 45.

[9] Combined quote taken from: Clark, Dendy & Phillippo. *The Voice of Jubilee*, p.37 and Mrs John James Smith, *William Knibb: Missionary in Jamaica A Memoir* (London: Alexander & Shepherd, 1896), 1.

So, here, we see a people who despite the fear of imprisonment, flogging and even death, sought to maintain their contact with the church, meeting for worship and education in the face of persecution. They endured and there was no obstacle too great and no distance too far for them to travel as they gained strength from a faith, which gave them a glimpse of heaven, and taught them to believe that freedom and a future was deservedly theirs. Even when their church was forced to go 'underground' soon after the abolition act, they were not deterred, buoyed by the support, which they received from Baptists in Britain and America, like Lady Gray of Portsmouth, who sent £5 to support the family of minister, Moses Baker.

Preparing For Freedom through the Baptist Missionary Society (BMS)
In 1822, at the age of approximately 72 years, Liele visited Britain for four years, to preach, meet with members of the Baptist Union and those interested in the plight of the enslaved in Jamaica. Given his age it is not inconceivable that he also used this opportunity, as the last of his leaders, to pass on the 'baton' of leadership to the BMS.

Having worked together for some 14 years, the Baptists of Jamaica had developed a level of confidence in the BMS, and especially Thomas Burchell, who of all of the BMS missionaries was their 'champion' at that time. This relationship was then further cemented in what became known as the Baptist War (1831 – 1832). The war began in 1831 when word got back to the plantocracy that on 15th April 1831, Fowell Buxton, a Member of Parliament had introduced a motion in the House of Commons aimed at the abolition of slavery. Determined to see that this would not occur, they promised their slaves that, 'Freedom was come from England, but that he would shoot every d-d black rascal before he should get it.'[10]

The plantocracy kept their promise, and many of us since 2007 will have attended the meetings and events surrounding the resistance movement begun by Sam Sharpe. This resulted in a people who were willing to sacrifice themselves for the freedom of their children and for generations of people whom they knew that they would never meet. About 540 people died as a result of this war; 14 White, 207 slaves in battle and between 310 and 340 executed for various offences to do with the insurrection, including the stealing of animals.[11] The majority of them were executed having confessed simply to being Baptists, and Old Virgil was typical of them:

> Old Virgil, of Windsor Lodge, a Baptist leader, was led out without trial and put to death. He inquired of Captain Hylton if he was to be hanged for praying to

---

[10] Ibid, p.112
[11] Doreen Morrison, *Slavery's Heroes: George Liele and the Ethiopian Baptist of Jamaica 1783 – 1865* (Florida: Liele Books, Create Space, 2014), p.147.

God? The savage man, full of enmity to religion answered "Yes." Then said the old Christian, "Hang me up at once that I may go to my Father."[12]

Plantation owners having killed many members of the Baptist society then turned their attention to the BMS missionaries who they determined must have inspired the 'rebellion,' as Black people were thought to be incapable of such ingenious planning. Up to that point BMS missionaries had followed their directive, 'Not to interfere with politics, but simply to preach the Gospel of Christ'. This changed, however, when thirteen chapels were burnt down, ministers restricted from preaching and prominent BMS missionaries, Burchell, Gardner, Knibb and Tinson were taken before the magistrates and charged with beginning the rebellion, and threatened with execution. This attack on the BMS was directed by the Colonial Church Union and led by Anglican 'Christians' who are best understood as being the Jamaican equivalent to the American Ku Klux Klan. They burnt down churches, executed women and children, and 'tarred and feathered' any who confessed to being Baptists, determined:

> To prevent hereafter a re-introduction of the Baptist sect into this parish and to recommend our Representatives to use their exertions in the Honourable House of Assembly, to expel them from the island.[13]

So by 1832 what developed was one movement of over 20,000 African Baptists, under the leadership of Thomas Burchell and William Knibb. Whilst Burchell had always demonstrated sympathy for the enslaved, it was Knibb who came to the fore at this time, and his change of mind was so dramatic that he gained the respect and the trust of the enslaved. As recently as 1831, Knibb had shown himself to be unsympathetic to the plight of the enslaved and been criticized for his sermon at Salter's Hill Chapel on 27th December 1831in which he condemned those who would withhold their labour, stating that:

> God commands you to be obedient to your master; if you do as he commands, you may expect his blessing, but if you do not, he will call you to an account for it at the Judgement day. If you refuse to work, and are punished, you will suffer justly; and every friend you have must and will turn his back upon you.[14]

This only served to inflame the situation, as the people in their anger, exchanged the following views concerning Knibb:

> Minister never said a word about freedom before; why does he come and talk to us about freedom now? The white people must have bribed him to it." The

---

[12] Clarke, *Memorials of Baptist Missionaries*, p.161
[13] Ibid, p.63
[14] The Baptist Missionaries, *A Narrative of Recent Events Connected with the Baptist Mission*, p.29

members of his own church, however, gave him credit; but one of them said to him at a later period, that "If minister had not been so urgent, he really should have believed, from the conversation of the planters and the slaves, that freedom was come."[15]

Yet, just three years after campaigning tirelessly for Emancipation in England, Knibb wrote home expressing how on his return to Jamaica:

> The people saw me as I stood on the deck of the boat. As I neared the shore I waved my hand, when they, being fully assured that it was their minister, ran from every part of the bay to the wharf. Some pushed off in a canoe...They took me up in their arms, they sang, they laughed, they wept, and I wept too. "Him come, him come, for true." "Who da come for we king, king Knibb. Him fight de battle, him win de crown."[16]

The selfless pursuit of emancipation, which he exhibited, endeared him to the people. It was no surprise that they confidently and freely delegated to him, Thomas Burchell and other BMS missionaries, the task of taking them on their final journey to Emancipation and freedom.

The question arises 'What has reparations to do with the BMS who seemingly sacrificed so much, and achieved such a great deal as advocates of emancipation'? It was many of their missionaries, including Rowe, Coultart, Tinson, Clark, Phillippo, Knibb and Burchell, who were often challenged to lay down their lives for those to whom they ministered.

I believe it would be foolhardy to think that these young missionaries, having overcome so much in this volatile situation, always made the right decisions. The role they played in the handling of the Negro Education Grant (NEG) is a direct case in point. Sadly in this regard, they and many of the missionaries of other denominations demonstrated their frailties, at a time when the enslaved needed them to be at their most selfless, insightful and visionary. It is a failure of judgment and moral integrity, which left a legacy of limited education amongst the majority, and one which prevails to the present day, as we shall now see.

The Negro Education Act (1835 – 1845)
On 14th May 1833, Mr Secretary Stanley rose to his feet in the House of Commons and led the house in an impassioned argument for the need to finally answer the issue of slavery and Emancipation. He stated that despite the cost to Britain's economic concerns both on land and at sea, there was a greater and more priceless consideration, which demanded that the Commons interfere and act now, and that was:

---

[15] John Howard Hinton, *Memoir of William Knibb: Missionary in Jamaica* (London: Houlston and Stoneman, 1847), p.118
[16] Ibid, p.194

The happiness of the descendants of those for whom I now propose to legislate – that generations yet unborn are to be affected for good or for evil by the course which this House may think proper to adopt.[17]

It was agreed, therefore, that those under 6 years of age would go free on the 1st August 1834, whilst those over 6 years old would be required to work as 'apprentices' for a further 4 years, if a house slave, and 6 years if a field labourer. Apprenticeship was, therefore, designed to prepare the enslaved for freedom, and in preparation for that, the 'Emancipation Act' was passed, which clearly defined its purpose as being, 'for the religious and moral education of the negro population to be emancipated.'[18]

The NEG was, therefore, established to assist in 'civilising' the Africans. It was a grant of £30,000, which was to be shared between Mauritius, the Cape and all the British Caribbean colonies, except Antigua who refused it, choosing instead to deliver immediate freedom to their enslaved population. However, such a seemingly great sum was really quite paltry in reality, being less than 1.2% of the £20 million 'compensation' paid to the plantation owners. Jamaica, the largest 'slave' owning island with 750,000 'slaves' was to receive £2,000, whilst other islands like British Guiana received £1, 950.

The plantation owners and legislature took no interest in the NEG in the early years, still grieving over the 'loss' of their slaves. They offered this money, instead, to another institution, which it believed could carry out its plan to provide the religious and moral education for those formerly enslaved. The Government, therefore, turned to the church. The purpose of such education was to provide transition for the populace, namely, a compliant, docile peasantry, 'trained' to be happy in servitude. This purpose was one shared by most people in Britain at that time, whether they were for or against abolition, and William Wilberforce, 'champion' of Emancipation even went as far as to declare that he himself did not want:

The slaves when they became free, or the working classes for that matter, to aspire "beyond their station in life" after they had received an education.[19]

Churches throughout the islands accepted the commission and mandate, to build school houses and to train Africans to be the teachers. Jamaica's annual grant of £2,000 was to be for the first six years of the grants existence, after which it was to be reduced by one fifth each year until its demise. The Government determined that 'match funding' would be the best way to take

---

[17] The Order of the Day for the House to resolve itself into a Committee to consider the subject of Slavery having been read, the House resolved itself on the Motion of Mr Secretary Stanley, into a Committee. Ministerial Proposition for the Emancipation of Slaves. HC Deb 14 May 1833,Vol. 17 cc1193-262
[18] Ibid.
[19] M K Bacchus, *Utilization, Misuse, and Development of Human Resources in the Early West Indian Colonies* (Ontario: Wilfrid Laurier University Press, 1990), p.269

the project forward. Missionary agencies were, therefore, called upon to pledge to provide one-third of the funds needed, and this would be matched by the NEG, providing the other two-thirds.

Most missionary organisations accepted this commission, almost immediately, except for the Baptists and Methodists who first demanded reparations for the churches that had been destroyed during the terror carried out by the Colonial Church Union. The Baptists, however, had additional theological concerns, which they had to consider. Namely, whether the BMS could accept monies on behalf of their independent Baptist missionaries. Whether each individual missionary should or could in fact accept the monies being offered by the Government. Should they choose, instead, compensation for the enslaved or advise them to accept monies for an education, which was designed to keep Africans subservient? Or, rather, should they encourage them to raise funds and be self-sufficient and self reliant?

The BMS agreed that as a denomination they would not take money from the Government, but would leave it to each individual missionary to make up his own mind. Burchell and Knibb initially accepted. They had both gone to England to argue the case for Emancipation. They had returned with a Parliamentary grant of £5,510 and £6,195 from Christian M.P.s, as 'compensation' for the chapels which had been destroyed and the debts that they had accrued. They also received a further £13,000 from members of the Church in Britain in order to establish schools.

In Jamaica the BMS missionaries discussed the issues amongst themselves and their congregation of enslaved Africans. Prominent in their thinking was not just education, but the link, which they had identified between the terms of compensation for slavery, and the evangelising of the then 'unploughed' harvest fields of Africa. I believe this latter concern, ultimately, became the distraction, which led to the failure of the NEG amongst Baptists.

Taking a lead in those initial discussions were Buxton, an Anglican, Sturge, a Quaker, and Knibb, who was of course, a Baptist. Sturge and Knibb argued that it would be beneficial for the freed slaves to be 'educated' to be hardworking, literate, self-supporting Christians who could take the lead in the Jamaica of the future. Knibb, therefore, having initially agreed to accept funds from the NEG, agreed at a meeting of the north-side missionaries in March 1837, against receiving any further assistance. We get an understanding of his reasoning in this impassioned plea which he made to his members:

> A fair scale of wages must be established, and you must be entirely independent! If you continue to receive those allowances, which have been given during slavery and apprenticeship, it will go abroad that you are not able to take care of yourselves, and that your employers are obliged to provide you with these allowances to keep from starvation. In such a case you will be nothing more than slaves. To be free, you must be independent. Receive your money from your work; come to market with money; purchase from whom you please; and be

accountable to no one but the Being above, who I trust will watch over and protect you.[20]

The enslaved having successfully resisted the plantocracy, gained their own emancipation, developed many varied skills in enslavement and having worked their own pieces of land in preparation for emancipation, found no difficulty in embracing this strategy.

So Baptists agreed to provide the education for future generations without turning to the Government for support, but it was to be a better level of education than that which was planned. This enabled freed Africans to one day take the lead in the nation, the church and most excitedly, the mission fields of Africa.

However, within three years of the grant beginning it was reported by the Colonial Office that many missionary organisations were found to be in difficulty. The identifiable problem was an over eagerness to receive the money, but an inability to purchase land on which to build the schools. This was exacerbated by poor leadership and perfunctory planning. Additional problems included little if no co-ordination between religious bodies, and what Charles Latrobe, the Government's Inspector of Schools described as a 'petty play on sectarian feeling,' with missionaries being 'small minded and jealous' of one another.[21]

Missionaries of all denominations worked independently of each other, often building their schools near to those of other denominations, believing that education would be a gateway to greater Christian conversion. Latrobe, who had once been a champion of Baptist missionaries, went as far as to state that each organisation had become a law unto themselves, and that:

> The strained relationships between denominations…resulted in confusion as to the objectives, evasion of financial accountability, and mismanagement of the grant could not be depended upon to give the slightest information to be depended upon concerning each other's proceedings or even to acknowledge the existence of rival schools.[22]

It became a 'scramble for souls' and the Baptists were by no means innocent in this regard, Phillippo expressing sectarian territorialism as he declared how they as Baptists might win this 'war':

---

[20] John Howard Hinton, *Memoir of William Knibb, Missionary to Jamaica* (London: Houlston and Stoneman, 1847), p.284.
[21] Patricia T Rooke, 'Evangelical Missionary Rivalry in the British West Indies: A Study in Religious Altruism and Economic Reality,' *The Baptist Quarterly*, Vol.39, No.8, October 1982, p. 343
[22] Ibid, 342 – 343.

> The whole land is before us and when once we take possession of it, which we as a denomination are doing in a most unexampled manner, the warfare to a great degree will be over.[23]

Such was the animosity demonstrated by the Church towards each other at this time that in 1839, Baptists and Methodists were observed openly brawling in the streets, to the amazement of all around them. Records state that such behaviour was replicated across the entire British Caribbean, to the shame of all missionaries, who called themselves followers of Jesus Christ.

Building Churches instead of Schools
In their zeal to evangelise and educate the children of the enslaved and those soon to be free, Baptists like all other denominations at that time, sought ingenious ways of 'killing two birds with one stone.' It is this factor, perhaps more than any other, which makes an argument for reparations, and the completing of the task promised and never fulfilled. The monies which should have been set aside for the erecting of the school buildings and to pay for teachers, soon became funds for evangelistic outreach, and so were often diverted to be used for the building of churches.

Missionaries of all denominations encouraged their colleagues to accept the NEG or write home to ask for funds to build schools, but with the clear intention of using any received monies to build churches. Those soliciting funds were encouraged not to state that the funds were to be used for any other purpose but to fund schools. One can still see the legacy of this in Jamaica today. St. Paul's Baptist church in Gibraltar is a fine example of how churches were built on top of schools. This building remained as a basic school until 2010, when the Gibraltar Basic School was built in its own right, a mere 150 years after it was originally intended.

Education Provision
In order to understand what took place in terms of the actual education provided, one has first to understand the racial climate of Jamaica at that time, as expressed by Knibb in a letter he wrote to England in 1839. In it he stated that:

> There are infamous laws existing in the island, which we must try to get abolished. One of them has been alluded to in the House of Commons, by the Under Secretary for colonies. It is to this effect:- 'All rogues, vagabonds, or other idle persons, found wandering from place to place or otherwise disorderly, may be apprehended by the constable, and taken before a magistrate, who is empowered to order him or her to be whipped on the naked back, not exceeding thirty-nine lashes.'...This act makes it lawful to send any coloured person who comes within the act to the workhouse, to be set to work for any time, not exceeding six months; but all white persons committed for the same offences are to be fed, lodged, and worked, separate and apart from the free negroes,

---

[23] Ibid, 343.

mulattoes, and slaves. This law makes the distinction of complexion the rule for the measurement of punishment. The white man, or the white female, who is taken up as a vagrant, is to be fed, lodged, and accommodated with comparative comfort; but the black man, or the black female, is to be subjected to the withering influence of cruelty, and to all the agonies that may be inflicted by the cart whip.[24]

The British, having abolished slavery, introduced racism into Jamaican society. This manifested itself in the lives of the missionaries. They took on the mandate to educate the indigenous population, but they did so, fearful of making themselves redundant, and through lenses which regarded Black people as inferior.

Teachers of all denominations were recorded as being most cruel in the treatment of their charges. One typical case documented by Tucker, describes as 'quaint,' a Baptist teacher's report regarding his charges:

What have you done with the boys of your school to keep them occupied while you are away? "Please, sir," he replied, "I went round with the cane, and gave them all a good thrashing."[25]

Generations of African Caribbean people, educated in Jamaica and living in Britain today, can attest to having been 'trained' by the cane, which many were taught to 'affectionately' refer to as 'Dr Do Me Good.'

Racist attitudes also prevailed in the establishing of schools, in that it was reported that missionaries and parents of 'coloured' (mulatto or mixed race) children, often demanded that their children should not be educated with Africans. According to one teacher African children were, 'Little negroes whose truly degraded habits (stealing, lying and swearing) exceed his own expectations.'[26]

In fact such were their anxieties that parents demanded that other schools or separate classes be established so that their children would not be educated with Africans. This unnecessary pressure on funds resulted in the establishing of three types schools; those for rich White children, those for rich Black children, and the 'inferior' education for the African masses.

Baptists were no different in their thinking in this respect. It was in fact Phillippo who had passionately led the drive for education amongst Baptists, who placed both types of schools in one and the same building, thereby, making the difference visible for all to see.

So, added to their racism, the missionaries introduced social stratification; they created a rigid class system in Jamaica, not too dissimilar from that practiced in England, with dire consequences for those who were

---

[24] Hinton, *Memoir of William Knibb,* 315 - 316
[25] Leonard Tucker, *Glorious Liberty: The story of a hundred years' work of the Jamaica Baptist mission,* (London: Baptist Missionary Society, 1914), p.120
[26] M.K. Bacchus, *Utilization, Misuse and Development of Human Resources in the Early West Indian Colonies* (Ontario: Wilfrid Laurier University Press, 1990), p.262.

poor Africans. The latter, were left to fulfil their destiny and become the agricultural workers they were expected to be, with no pretentious expectation that they would ever attend secondary school. They were taught agriculture and the three Rs, reading, writing and religion, with the Bible being the central text book. Only those with 'potential,' the middle classes, would be allowed the 'privilege' of attending secondary school, and be exposed to the sciences, mathematics, classical languages and grammar.

The class system had truly arrived in the heart of the Jamaican education system, which resulted in a majority population being consigned to receive a 'Bantu' style education, designed to keep them as 'servants.' This was a bitter pill to swallow for the majority population who had fought so hard and made innumerable sacrifices in order for education to be available for all on the island. Happy, then, was a British government and a Church whose views were knowingly summed up by George Dennis, Inspector of Schools in Guyana who stated that:

> If schools taught the black child "to read, write and cipher alone...he *(would)* be so puffed up with his acquirements as to forsake the occupation of his fathers."[27]

At the outset of the NEG the prospect of schooling filled the enslaved with such great enthusiasm that they participated in large numbers, as can be seen in four of the schools established by Knibb, Suffield, Wilberforce, Waldensia and Camberwell. These schools recorded a combined student roll of fifteen hundred students. However, as discrimination and injustice raised its ugly head, all schools saw their rolls falling away as it became obvious that the planned education for equality was never meant to come to fruition. Central to its failure were the missionaries.

Native Teachers
The native teachers were also to be disappointed. They had expected to be trained as teachers. They saw their opportunities also falling by the wayside as they soon learnt that if they had not been educated in 'middle class' secondary schools, then primary schools were to be their domain.

Yet in the midst of this, native teachers had a 'champion' in the colonial office who oversaw the establishing of the schools and teachers. As the grant neared its end, the government complained that each organisation (BMS,[28] LMS,[29] WMMS,[30] CMS,[31] Anglicans and Methodists) was failing

---

[27] Ruby King, *Education in the British Caribbean: The Legacy of the Nineteenth Century* (Mona: University of the West Indies Institute of Education, 1998)
[28] Baptist Missionary Society.
[29] London Missionary Society.
[30] Wesleyan Methodist Missionary Society.
[31] Church Missionary Society.

abysmally in its mandate to fulfil the training of native leaders. However, on being asked why even those men who had shown great promise were only partially trained, and put in charge of a school to 'do the best they could,'[32] the missionaries responded by making a number of excuses. They argued that due to the ignorance of the enslaved, the large numbers of children to be educated, and in many instances adults too, the quality of the teaching provided to trainee teachers had to be sacrificed in order to increase their numbers as quickly as possible. Phillippo (and other Baptists) even went as far as to argue privately that he believed that the training of Africans as teachers was a morally unrealistic expectation, declaring that:

> Because of the damage done to their personalities and values during slavery, it would take some time before their moral development could reach the "desirably superior order" required for "teachers of religion or of any other subjects for that matter... *(black teachers)* were lacking in moral and intellectual talent...were ostentatious, mystical, ambiguous, indirect and verbose.[33] "The time was 'not yet ripe' for the despised children of Ham to take over positions of Christian leadership."[34]

If this was the view of folk known to be 'friends' of the Africans then one can only imagine the views of others. Tensions, therefore, naturally arose on all fronts as great expectations were received with a great deal of disrespect, resulting in a diminishing respect for missionaries of all persuasions, including the Baptists, in whom, perhaps above all else, many had placed their confidence.

However, as dispiriting as this was, I shall now conclude this chapter, by arguing that the Baptist failure to fulfil its mandate concerning education arose because of a specific and yet often underappreciated, contributory factor. In addition to all the aforementioned contributory factors, the mandate concerning education ultimately failed because of their desire to 'evangelize' Africa. This led to a shift in the utilisation of their resources away from the education of the majority, in order to concentrate on an elite minority, namely, ministers and teachers, people just like themselves.

Africa Must Be Saved – A New Jamaican Mission Field
It would be true to say that by the time Emancipation came along, William Knibb and the other Baptist missionaries, who had led the people to freedom, had received the gratitude of the wider populace, just as if he were Moses leading them to the Promised Land. They trusted him to lead them through the Wilderness years as they began to form themselves into a society and a nation. However, unbeknown to them, central to missionary decision-making were

---

[32] Leonard Tucker, *Glorious Liberty: the story of a hundred years work of the Jamaica Baptist Mission* (London: the Baptist Missionary Society, 1914), p,120
[33] Bacchus, *Utilization, Misuse and Development*, p.308.
[34] Rooke, Evangelical Missionary Rivalry, p,350.

discussions on reparations, compensation, education and, most significantly, an African mission, which somehow all became united as one project, Buxton declaring that:

> I have a strong confidence that Africa *(will)* be opened to commerce, civilisation and Christianity: and then there will be need, indeed, of educated and religious black schoolmasters. The idea of compensation to Africa through the means of the West Indies is a great favourite with me and I think we shall see the day when all shall be called to pour a flood of light and truth upon miserable Africa.[35]

Knibb was one of the first Baptists to see the possibilities in 'free' Africans returning 'home' to take the good news of the gospel to Africa, raising the subject with the BMS, in 1832. However, despite the case that he made for Africa, the BMS encouraged him to concentrate on working with the peasants in Jamaica first. Knibb, however, was determined, and it is clear that his thoughts were for Africa, when in 1835 he established *The Baptist Herald and Friends of Africa* newspaper, designed to encourage interest in his African mission.

Knibb returned to the subject in 1840, when speaking at a meeting at Exeter Hall on 22nd May 1840, he talked of how, in freedom, the Baptist mission, with the selfless giving of African Christians, was proving itself to be self-sufficient and therefore ready for mission, stating that:

> When the apprenticeship came our chapels were in ruins, and our people were scattered; but such is their attachment to the house of God, and such their delight in his ordinances, that where only eleven small chapels stood, twenty large ones have been erected... I am happy to inform you that I need now only your prayers...since my return to Jamaica, we have erected three chapels, two school-houses, and a mission-house, connected with my own church, at a cost of about £18,000 currency, and we have paid it all.[36]

Impassioned statements of Africans ready to go to Africa were also shared, Knibb recalling how:

> I asked him when he would be ready to go, "Tomorrow," was his reply. I said to them, "Perhaps you would be made slaves if you were to go." What was their answer? "We have been made slaves for men, we can be made slaves for Christ." These are men that ought to go, and whether you send them or not, go they will...You tell us you have not the money. You have it, and, if you don't bestow it, God may take it away...Will you, my brethren in the ministry, deny me this one request, the introduction of the gospel into Africa?[37]

---

[35] 'Church of England Normal School', *The Training System Moral Training School and Normal Seminary.* Available from www.forgottenbooks.com Downloaded 19 January 2016.
[36] Hinton, *Memoir of William Knibb,* p.357.
[37] Ibid, p.363

Given these facts as presented, concerning the decline in education and the enthusiasm for a new mission in Africa, it is no surprise that the BMS changed its mind. They were encouraged to have learnt that Africans were willing to take the gospel to Africa, thereby, making it a more feasible proposition than having to train up 'foreign missionaries' as had been the case when the subject was first mooted.

So on the 3rd June 1840, just midway through the implementation of the NEG, the Committee agreed that Africa 'would be saved' through the missionary endeavours of African Jamaicans, confidently stating that:

> In compliance with the representations of our brethren in Jamaica, and following what we apprehend to be the clear indications of Providence, we determine, in reliance on the divine blessing, to commence a mission to Western Africa.[38]

So, led by Knibb, Burchell and Phillippo, the BMS committed itself to raising funds for a new work in Africa, and as a result, the Jamaica Baptist Mission was formed in 1842, separating itself from the financial support of the BMS. It is to be noted that in 1842, BMS missionary Dendy sent a letter to John Clark, stating that his membership at Salter's Hill Chapel contained at least 12 ethnic African groups, many of whom, had resumed speaking and learning their mother-tongue, and teaching it to others - perhaps in preparation for their mission to Africa.

United in their purposes, this cohort of missionaries turned their attention to establishing a college in Kingston for the training of missionaries and ministers, to undertake their mission to Africa. It was as result of this that Calabar College, led by Joshua Tinson, was established in April 1843. Funds were provided by the British Baptist Home Committee and this was the beginning of the development of a truly African, Jamaican middle class education system, namely, Calabar High School for Boys. The school was 'designed to educate the sons of Jamaica ministers, Church officers and members of good standing who…became fitted to be clerks and accountants, or for apprenticeship to one of the learned professions.'[39] The equivalent for girls was Westwood High School for Girls, where the best in womanhood in Jamaica was taught 'Bible…needlework, cooking, *(and)* house-management.'[40]

What this meant for the NEG and African Jamaicans was that the educational emphasis of the church had changed. No longer was the priority to provide education and teachers for the majority of Jamaicans. Rather, they now concentrated on preparations for the ploughing of a new harvest in Africa, through a small minority of educated elite African Jamaicans.

Such was their determination to educate the population for this great new work that even the government of the day got involved, giving Knibb the

---

[38] Ibid, p.366
[39] Tucker, *Glorious Liberty*, p.122
[40] Ibid, p.123

African 'slaves,' who had been freed from slave ships in Caribbean waters. As a consequence, the name 'Baptist' became synonymous with 'African,' building up an expectation in many Africans that one day soon they would all be repatriated to their motherland. This would mean leaving Jamaica to the vagaries of a defunct plantocracy. Tragically, drought, hurricane and the death of both Knibb and Burchell by 1846, saw this project come to an end, though it did successfully send African missionaries to the Gold Coast, in Ghana.

However, all this came at the expense of the financial support which had been planned for the schools in Jamaica. As funds declined dramatically, by the time that the NEG expired in 1845, the Colonial Office was justifiably able to accuse missionaries of all persuasions of misappropriating the funds which they had received. In ten years, funds had been used to either increase denominational territory rather than privileging education for the many, or to form the foundation of a new mission to Africa. Their mission was not aided by the petty denominational rivalries, which brought only shame to the European missionary movement in the Caribbean.

Conclusion

The Jamaican Baptist journey to justice began in 1783 when George Liele and his cohort of American and Jamaican leaders planted a seed in the minds of the enslaved. Liele planted the belief in a God that had not forgotten them and that if they held on to their faith in God, no matter the opposition, then they, like the children of Israel, would reach their Promised Land. So, in their hundreds and thousands they remained faithful in the face of much persecution, preserving the Christian faith for generations who were to follow them. Many of their descendants now live in Britain, the 'Windrush generation' whose arrival in Britain can truly also be said to have 'revived' a dying church.

Yet, it is clear that as much as they have contributed to Britain, we should all be reminded of the cost paid by their descendants. In return for their faithfulness, British Baptists, both here and in Jamaica, promised that if they were willing to contribute, that they would provide them with an education so that they could determine their own futures. This education was intended to enable them to take their rightful place as leaders in society and the wider world. This essay shows that, due to racism and the social stratification engineered by missionaries, who refused to see the majority of Africans as their equals, generations of people and their descendants have had their futures denied. Rather, they have been relegated to settle for an education which saw them as only being suited for agricultural work, and were, therefore, denied the opportunity of attending secondary school, and ultimately university.

The missionaries of the day accepted their role in this failure, as reports home from all quarters of the missionary world expressed concerns in regards to their failure. Their views can be summed up in the words of two organisations, the CMS and the readers of *The Evangelical Magazine and Missionary Chronicle*, who said of the work in Jamaica that

...all seek their own, and not the things of Jesus Christ and there remains yet very much land to be possessed, and nothing except the natural depravity of our own hearts, to prevent cordial union and co-operation between us.[41]

There are voices from the past and voices from the present crying out for justice and asking that this sad conclusion to such promising beginnings be rectified and not be the truth, which now defines us as Baptists, and as Christians. As the daughter of Jamaican parents, raised as Baptists in Gibraltar, and who were 'educated' to be agricultural workers, I know that I have them to thank for my present day successes. We all have brothers and sisters in Jesus Christ, in Jamaica, who should not have to travel on a boat to England, as my parents did in the 1950s, in order to seek educational opportunities for their children.

Caricom's challenge to governments to provide reparations, gives those of us who are on this 'journey to justice,' the opportunity to exercise some real 'Ubuntu'. This Ubuntu is one of recognising that 'I am because we are' and that the best of us can only be seen in how well we treat those of us who are suffering the most. We, as Baptists, can right a wrong and make amends for promises left unfulfilled. This can be accomplished by now seeking ways of working with the Jamaican government to fulfil the task of eradicating illiteracy. We can assist them to build the schools, and provide the teachers and resources, which the majority of the people so badly need, and which we as a denomination promised to provide through the Negro Education Grant of 1835.

---

[41] Patricia T Rooke, 'A Scramble for Souls: The Impact of the Negro Education Grant on Evangelical Missionaries in the British West Indies', *History of Education Quarterly*, V, pp.438 - 439

Part Four: The Future

Martin Luther King, Jr.
Dwight N. Hopkins

Martin Luther King, Jr. was a Black, southern Baptist preacher and one of the few Black Ph.D. graduates in systematic theology during his time.[1] How should we remember King? What parts of his legacy are helpful today?[2] What we want to learn from Dr. King today are some of the beliefs he held, particularly, at the end of his career, from 1966 to 1968. We have to remember that King had come a long way as he neared the end of his life. He had moved from Montgomery, throughout the South, eventually to Chicago, the North, plans for the 2nd march on Washington (called the Poor People's Campaign), and on to his final campaign in Memphis. Rev. Dr. King began to focus his ministry increasingly on the plight of the poor.

---

[1] See 'The Drum Major Instinct' in James M. Washington (ed.) *A Testament of Hope: The Essential Writings of Martin Luther King, Jr.*(San Francisco: Harper and Row, 1986), p. 267

[2] For a comprehensive assessment of the life, work and legacy of Martin Luther King Jr. see Keith D. Miller, *Voice of Deliverance: The Language of Martin Luther King, Jr. And Its Sources* (New York: The Free Press, 1992); Richard Lischer, *Martin Luther King Jr. And the Word that Moved America* (New York: Oxford University Press, 1995); Valentino Lassiter, *Martin Luther King in the African American Preaching Tradition* (Cleveland, Ohio: The Pilgrim Press, 2001); and Mervyn A. Warren, *King Came Preaching: The Pulpit Power of Dr. Martin Luther King Jr.* (Downers Grove, Illinois: 2001). See also Hanes Walton, Jr., *The Political Philosophy of Martin Luther King, Jr.* (Westport, Connecticut: Praeger, 1971); Kenneth L. Smith, and Ira G. Zepp, Jr., *Search for the Beloved Community: The Thinking of Martin Luther King, Jr.*(Valley Forge, PA.: Judson Press, 1974); and John J. Ansbro, *Martin Luther King, Jr.: The Making of a Mind* (Maryknoll, N.Y.: Orbis Books, 1982). Additional texts include William D. Watley, *Roots of Resistance: The Nonviolent Ethic of Martin Luther King, Jr.* (Valley Forge, PA.: Judson Press, 1985); David J. Garrow, *Bearing the Cross: Martin Luther King, Jr. And the Southern Christian Leadership Conference* (New York: Vintage Books, 1986); James H. Cone, *Martin, Malcolm & America: A Dream or a Nightmare* (Maryknoll, N.Y.: Orbis Books, 1991); Vincent Harding, *Martin Luther King, The Inconvenient Hero* (Maryknoll, N.Y.: Orbis Books, 1996), Lionel Lokos, *House Divided: The Life and Legacy of Martin Luther King* (New Rochelle, N.Y.: Arlington House, 1968), Coretta Scott King, *My Life With Martin King, Jr.* (New York: Holt, Rinehart and Winston, 1969); and The Rev. Martin Luther King, Sr., *Daddy King: An Autobiography* (New York: William Morrow and Company, 1980)

He came to this belief as a result of a number of factors. By 1966, King felt that he had set the stage for a new paradigm in race relations in the U.S. with the passage of the 1964 'Civil Rights Bill' and the 1965 'Voting Rights' Act. Encouraged by these apparent successes, he then attempted to take the old civil rights coalition from the South into the ghettoes of the North. His northern journey, however, proved to be much more brutal and strange than the familiar territory of the South. When he arrived in the north, the urban riots presented a new challenge to his faith, and his organizing skills.

At the same time, he began to experience resistance from some northern White liberals who were willing to support him as long as he led civil rights struggles in the South; but it was a different issue when King began to shift his desegregation campaigns to the North. And of course, he finally decided to go public with his opposition to the Vietnam War. As a result of these challenges, new directions and new possibilities opened up. In fact, King began to build a new coalition of conscience, which gave rise to a new movement explicitly aimed at supporting the plight and predicament of poor people.

Widening the agenda

King felt the time had finally come to advance the Civil Rights movement to a higher level, where the nation's poor, Black, and other minority communities and White people would take centre stage in a powerful, new, non-violent united front. A year before his death, King wrote:

> From issues of personal dignity [Black people] are now advancing to programs that impinge upon the basic system of social and economic control. At this level Negro programs go beyond race and deal with economic inequality.... In pursuit of these goals, the White poor become involved, and the potentiality emerges for a powerful alliance.[3]

Increasingly, King felt compelled to zero in on the margins of society, those without a voice to represent them nationally, those at the bottom of the nation. He became increasingly sure that his calling as a minister and as an international ambassador of peace started with the poor; even if it cost him his funding and the support from his liberal Black and White allies. In fact between 1966 and 1968, his preaching, lecturing, and speaking engagements, as well as organizing efforts, revolved around gaining structural power for what he called 'the little ones' among us. Back in 1968, King had already given us a definition of multiculturalism. Speaking two months before his death, he said:

> And when I say poor people, I'm not only talking about Black people... There are poor people... in the Puerto Rican community... Mexican American

---

[3]Martin Luther King, Jr., *Where Do We Go From Here: Chaos or Community?* (Boston, MA.: Beacon Press, 1967), p. 17

community... the Indian community... the Appalachian community. I'm talking about poor people's power, that is what is needed.[4]

We can see that for King multiculturalism is not only different races and ethnic groups coming together, it also includes what he calls 'poor people's power'. Even King's reading of the Bible and how he interpreted it became more influenced by this concern for the poor. For him, the Bible's story of how Jesus suffered before his death and the tales about how Jesus was crucified could no longer be left at a general level of salvation.

Given the fact that King saw himself as a Christian preacher, he felt that bearing the cross for himself, meant supporting people who suffer and are locked out. King challenged those with privilege to do the same thing. The nation could reach its highest potential when the haves began to share with the have-nots. This was not a lukewarm and empty moral challenge. For King, the earth's resources belonged to all peoples. So the rich had to give back to the lower classes in society. During the last few of years of his life, King commented on this when he preached:

> I choose to identify with the underprivileged. I choose to identify with the poor. I choose to give my life for those who have been left out of the sunlight of opportunity... This is the way I'm going. If it means dying for them, I'm going that way.[5]

Toward the end of his life, Dr. King interpreted his calling as a minister of the gospel of Jesus Christ in such a radical and prophetic way that he felt anointed to launch a new campaign against the federal government in Washington D.C., the symbol of the centre of the power in the U.S. He called this second march on Washington 'The Poor Peoples Campaign'. This great moral effort targeted the federal governmental power structure because the issue of poverty was not local but national. Those who decided on the fate of the nation's poor had to be forced to provide relief for those who lacked adequate resources to be human.

To understand King's life and death attitude of urgency toward eliminating poverty, we only have to compare the 1963 March on Washington, with his plans for the 1968 Poor Peoples Campaign (PPC). In contrast to the 1963 march, where people heard speeches and then left town the same day, King stated that the PPC would be radically different. Unlike the 1963 march, when aides to President JFK stood near the sound system prepared to pull the

---

[4]Martin Luther King, Jr., 'A Proper Sense of Priorities,' speech to Clergy and Laity Concerned about Vietnam, New York Ave. Church, Washington, D.C., 6 February 1968, p.4; found at the Martin Luther King, Jr. Center, Atlanta, Georgia.
[5]Martin Luther King, Jr. quoted in David Garrow, *Bearing the Cross: Martin Luther King, Jr., and the Southern Christian Leadership Conference* (New York: Vintage Books, 1986), p. 524.

plug on any speakers who criticized the Kennedy administration, the 1968 march would be controlled by the unemployed, working people, people of colour and other progressive supporters.

An advocate for the poor
For King, the 1968 march would 'dramatize the whole economic problem of the poor. He was now trying to deal with the economic problems through massive protest.' This new March on Washington would have thousands upon thousands of the poor of all colours descend on the nation's capital and stay there for months until the federal government passed meaningful legislation for the dispossessed. If this fundamental change did not take place, then poor people would be forced to take over governmental buildings and sit-in, in congressional offices. The PPC would usher in a new form of nonviolent militancy. King had this to say about this new campaign: 'This action may take on disruptive dimensions'.[6] The federal government would no longer function in its normal way unless it first addressed the needs of the poor. King continued to hammer home this point home when he said:

> We got to go to Washington... We've got to camp in. Put our tents in front of the White House... [The federal government] will have to come to terms with us, because the nation will not move.... There will be no rest, there will be no tranquility in this country until the nation comes to terms with our problem.[7]

We can see that it was no accident that at the time of his assassination, King's two major projects included support for the Black working class in Memphis, Tennessee and organizing an integrated movement of the poor to dislocate the normal functioning of the United States government.

The idea for the PPC was a result of King's deepening analysis of class relations in the United States, the difference between those who own wealth, and those who are poor. Earlier in his public career, he tried to aid 'the discouraged beggars in life's market place'. A year before his death, however, he saw the need to not only help the beggar but also reconstruct the causes forcing people to beg.

> We are called upon to help the discouraged beggars in life's market place. But one day we must come to see that an edifice which produces beggars needs restructuring... When you deal with this, you begin to ask the question, "Who

---

[6].Martin Luther King, Jr., 'We Still Believe in Black and White Together' in August Meier, Elliott Rudwick, and Francis L. Broderick (eds.) *Black Protest Thought in the Twentieth Century*, (Indianapolis, Indiana: Bobbs-Merrill Educational Publishing, 1980), pp.586-90.
[7].Martin Luther King, Jr., speech at a rally in Birmingham, Alabama, following a press conference in that same city, 11 November 1967, p. 3; found at the King Center.

owns the oil??"... "Who owns the iron ore?"... "why is it that people have to pay water bills in a world that is two-thirds water?"[8]

Here, King makes a distinction between income and wealth. Income is money someone pays you for working for them. Wealth, however, raises question such as: who owns the shopping malls, who owns the land in the city, who owns airline, television and radio industries? Where is the concentration of wealth in the U.S.?

So when King questioned who owned the major resources and the production and distribution of those resources, he questioned and condemned the capitalist system in the U.S. Then, he called on the voiceless in the society, the least, the last, and the lowest, to rise up and claim their God-given humanity, by carrying out a non-violent revolution against the system of capitalism. This is what he had to say during the last two years before his death:

> The dispossessed of this nation — the poor, both White and [Black] – live in a cruelly unjust society. They must organize a revolution against the injustice, not against the lives of the persons who are their fellow citizens, but against the structures through which the society is refusing to take means which have been called for, and which are at hand, to lift the load of poverty.[9]

Just as King's understanding of poverty began to broaden, so his views on race relations also began to develop, in new directions. He started to come to the conclusion that the Civil Rights Movement faced a far broader evil than the stubborn racism found in the southern U.S. In time, he began to appreciate the larger dimensions of racism. Instead of racism just being the bad habits of an individual or a group of people, he now connected racism to what he called, in his words, the White power structure. As King stated in 1967, a basic problem in Black life was the 'lack of power,' which made Black people 'subject to the ... White power structure.'[10]

This was a huge leap in his perspective on racism. Racism could not be ended by only changing the hearts of an individual or groups. This was still important, because King still kept his faith that there was hope for a new integrated society at, some point. He still believed that the moral arch of the universe moved toward justice. He still believed that ultimately, at some point in America, all races and ethnic groups could and would live together as sisters and brothers. It was just that he had a more sober understanding of the reality facing poor people in America. Along with changing hearts, the social,

---

13. Martin Luther King, Jr., 'The President's Address to the Tenth Anniversary Convention of the Southern Christian Leadership Conference, Atlanta, Georgia, August 16, 1967' Robert L. Scott and Wayne Brockriede (eds.) *The Rhetoric of Black Power*, (New York: Harper & Row, 1969), p.162.

9. Martin Luther King, Jr., *The Trumpet of Conscience* (New York: Harper & Row, 1967), pp.59-60.

10. 'The President's Address', p.156.

political, and economic system of the country, the structure of the country had to be completely revamped.

Systemic Analysis
Now having added the issue of power to his civil rights analysis, and his moral beliefs, King also developed further his earlier perspectives on love. Previously, he overemphasized the pricking of the moral conscience of racists by having Black people show their love when they were bleeding from the blows of racist attackers. Although King never gave up his belief that the Christian might have to sacrifice their bodies and their lives as an expression of love, a year before his death, he began to redefine love and connect it to power. In 1967 he wrote:

> There is nothing essentially wrong with power. The problem is that in America power is unequally distributed. This has led Negro Americans in the past to seek their goals through love and moral suasion devoid of power and White Americans to seek their goals through power devoid of love and conscience.[11]

In other words, from his reading of American history and his own experience in the Civil Rights Movement, King concluded that Black people had sought goals incorrectly, by only using an appeal to morality but not using power. White Americans had gained their goals through the use of power but without love or morality. To put it differently, he began to see that integration based on appeals of love and morality was without substance. In fact, it was immoral to call on poor folk and Black folk to love and suffer, while not organizing to also give them some power.

This power was not for individuals. It was power that came about from restructuring, non-violently, the American economic, political, and social system. So King pulls together love, power, and the transformation of material structures. It is hard to love someone when they have a monopoly or a disproportionate amount of power based on their skin colour and privileges. To be a Christian is to love someone by surrendering and sharing power. It would be hard to have a Christian community, where one group has the power to make decisions and the control over resources, while another group lacked equal power or the access to attain it.

When we look at King's final position, on Black and White social relations, we also see some interesting developments. Previously, he had waged a civil rights struggle for Black Americans who, he felt, had been locked out of the U.S. Constitution's 'promissory note.' In fact, he uses the phrase 'promissory note' in his famous 1963 'I Have A Dream' speech at the 1963 March on Washington. If we think back, we will remember that from the success of the Montgomery Bus Boycott in 1956, up until about late 1965, King had spoken glowingly and poetically about little Black children and little White children holding hands throughout the land. He not only meant children

---

[11].*Where We Do We Go From Here?*, p.37.

in terms of age group, he also meant all of humanity as children of God. In this early phase of King's civil rights career, he fought for integration of Black people, into public accommodations. For example, he asked the powers to be to allow Black children to visit amusement parks. Several things moved him, however, to look again at what would really be an authentic picture of racial integration in America.

First, was his rereading the Bible and appreciating, even more deeply, the Exodus theme of 'Let my people go' and how Pharaoh tried to prevent God's will or even attempted to co-opt this liberation movement. Similarly, the Gospel narratives became clear to him in Jesus' siding with the 'little people'. Second, were his hard fought lessons from the first 10 years of the civil rights movement. People had died, people had been maimed, people's houses and churches had been bombed; ordinary people had been laid off from work because of their civil rights activities.

Looking back on this phase of the struggle, King began to question what had really happened, and how did this add to or not add to the goal of integration. Third, was the new terrain and tactics of White supremacy he confronted in the North. King's northern campaign was heavily centred on Chicago. Unlike the southern experience, however, he found out that the mayor of Chicago maintained racism with a smile. The mayor would not set dogs on demonstrators and was even willing to meet with civil rights leaders. All the while, White supremacy did not budge.

In certain respects, many northern White liberals (and many of them had supported desegregation struggles in the south, as long as King stayed in the south), were more crafty and more skilled and refined than their southern counterparts. At the same time, physical violence and the intensity of the visceral hatred coming out of White ethnic communities in Chicago were a totally new experience for King.

In fact, King said that the northern experience in Chicago was some of the worst encounters of White supremacy he had seen, even when compared with all of his efforts in the south. Finally, when he walked the streets talking to Black folk who participated in northern urban riots, he began to appreciate why, for northern Black people, the integration campaigns in the south had not changed much of anything. Though there was still segregation in the north, many places did not have the obvious laws and public signs supporting segregation. In this sense, many northern Black people were already living in a desegregated environment. Racism, however, continued to be the dominant factor that defined northern social relations.

Rethinking Integration
Based on these experiences, King started to re-image the idea of integration, by linking it with power:

> Integration is more than something to be dealt with in aesthetic or romantic terms. I think in the past all too often we did it that way... and it ended up as merely adding color to a still predominantly White power structure. What is

necessary now is to see integration in political terms where there is a sharing of power.[12]

So King is clear on what is integration. He saw the reality of one group having a monopoly on power or a disproportionate amount of it in a community, so much so, that those lacking in power cannot be said to be integrated in a communitarian setting. Just adding bodies to a structure that has not changed is not integration. True integration cannot take place if the structure of power remains the same. No matter how many people are added, no fundamental shift has taken place. A good example would be the former apartheid South Africa where White people were a minority and there were plenty of Black people in the country, but the economic, educational, and social systems were left in the hands of a few.

So given this new appreciation of integration, King was no longer interested in leading Black people into any type of social relations, where they would still be at the bottom. In fact, he strongly denounced a false kind of integration into the capitalist system. Alternatively, he called for a new dream where new visions and new values helped to bring about a redistribution of power in these new social relations. During the last year of his life, King preached the following sermon where he proclaimed: 'Something is wrong with capitalism as it now stands in the United States.' Black people 'are not interested in being integrated into this value structure.' Why? Because 'power must be relocated, a radical redistribution of power must take place.'[13] So for King, true integration in social relations called for a political reinterpretation of Black-White relationships, one where there was a sharing of power.

King's calling from the spirit of freedom began to grasp him more deeply. His clarity on his ministry became even clearer. In addition, to connecting power to politics in America, King also linked power to culture. Eventually, he saw the shallowness of Black and White unity based on the negation of Black culture. In the earlier parts of the civil rights movement King never completely distanced himself from Black culture. He did emphasize that Black people were part of a universal human culture. Even when the Black power slogan hit the national scene in June of 1966, King wanted to suggest that the word Black be not used with the word power.

As his efforts to build his coalition of conscience continued to run up against the depths of racism in the north, coupled with the lack of progress for northern Black people, despite the southern civil rights gains, he began to appreciate the need for African Americans to have a firm sense of their identity. Speaking at a 1967 staff retreat of his organization, the Southern Christian Leadership Conference (SCLC), King stated the following:

> Where do we go from here? First, we must massively assert our dignity and worth [as Black people]. We must stand up amidst a system that still oppresses

---

[12].King in Garrow, p.608.
[13].Ibid, p. 581.

us and develop an unassailable and majestic sense of values. We must no longer be ashamed of being Black.[14]

Reaffirming Black identity and culture

Despite his years of leading an integrated Civil Rights movement with White people, despite his attempts to speak to the universal commonalities among all peoples, King began to conclude that Black folk were still oppressed based on their culture. Yes they were integrated with progressive Whites in the movement as they sought to integrate into the broader White American society. The 1964 bill had given them legal civil rights. The 1965 bill had given them the legal right to vote. Other legal decisions had struck down segregation in eating, housing, employment, and in other areas. These were important goals. How could a people have any sense of authentic self, however, if they integrated with White people and, at the same time, believed they were White?

Did Black folk have a history, a culture, a language? Did Black folk have any contribution that was unique to them and, at the same time, was a contribution to the larger American community? In a sense, King was confronted with progressive northern liberals who were not as crude in race relations as southern conservatives. Many of the northern liberals supported the civil rights cause, they supported integration. This was a form of integration, however, where it was all right for Black people and White people to hold hands and sing 'We Shall Over Come' as long as the norm for being a human being remained White. In this sense, too many White people accepted Black counterparts who were like Oreo cookies 'Black on the outside but White in the inside'.

So at this 1967 SCLC staff retreat, which takes place about a year to 18 months after King's start of his northern civil rights campaign, at this meeting of the national civil rights leadership, King lays out the future direction of the civil rights movement. In summing up where they have been and what is the very next phase in the struggle for justice, the very next task for Black people, was a massive assertion of Black dignity and worth, aggressively pushing Black culture. Black folk had to unashamedly and publicly declare their Blackness (in contrast to their being coloured people). They had to appreciate their history, culture, unique identity and their connection to Africa. Black folk could never be what God made them to be, and America could never reach its greatness if White history, culture, and identity, were the norms and the deciding factor in race relations.

King stated that the progress of Black freedom and race relations would come to a halt if Black people did not free their minds from the racist restrictions of White culture. So King's position was not simply a light argument just to be fashionable with the times. The spirit and souls of Black people were dying when predominantly White institutions made White

---

[14]. 'The President's Address', p.155.

experiences the dominant reality and norm for non-White and other minority peoples.

Unfortunately, many progressive liberals were willing to let Black and other minority peoples into predominantly White institutions, as long as people of colour accepted that White authority and knowledge, history and experiences, would be the norm and considered most valuable. At that 1967 staff retreat, King continued with the following: 'Any movement for the Negro's freedom that overlooks this necessity is only waiting to be buried. As long as the mind is enslaved, the body can never be free.'[15]

Our review of some of the ideas of Revd Dr King at the end of his life is just a glimpse of his contributions to America and, in fact, the world. What he shows us is the importance of having faith in something greater than ourselves. It means facing human fears and taking the road less travelled. It means heeding the vocation of witnessing outside of the box. As a Black Baptist preacher, the one who is set aside to proclaim 'Thus saith the Lord', this meant that King could always rely on God to carry him through.

There were many times when the road seemed unclear, but King persisted, because he believed that what he was doing was what Jesus would do. Namely, he was clothing the naked, feeding the hungry, visiting the prisoner, providing water for the thirsty, fighting for jobs for the unemployed, taking on the federal government and forcing it to heed the pains of the voiceless in America. He was challenging the unjust policies of the U.S. government as it fought wars abroad. His prophetic actions were directed at challenging those who would deny Black power, Black culture, and Black equality, not only for African Americans, but for all oppressed people of any colour across the globe.

King was truly a martyr. For example, though everyone supports King today, towards the end of his life, he was not as popular as we think. He was attacked, increasingly, and was critiqued by the White House, Congress, the U.S. military establishment, White funders, White liberals, other Black civil rights leaders, and the press.

In our present context, however, King's name now garners worldwide recognition. It shows that universal contributions to humankind can emerge from a Black Baptist clergyman from Georgia, in the USA.

---

[15].Ibid, p.155.

An Ongoing Apology
Richard L Kidd

I have some cards to lay on the table before I begin to tell my story. I am a White, male, middle-class Baptist minister, fortunate to have received a highly-privileged education. This is my testimony. It is testimony heavily littered with confession, but I am not unhappy about that; confession should be very much at home in a collection of writings inspired by the theme of 'apology' in the context of racism and racial injustice. Some readers will identify immediate resonances with their own life stories, but perhaps, even those who find minimal overlaps will find value through an additional insight into a world significantly different from their own.

We have little choice about the factors that shape our early lives but, as the years pass, we have to take ever more responsibility for who we are, and who we are becoming. With all the benefit of hindsight, I am now sorry that I did not make rather faster progress with some of the choices I made in the first half of my sixty-five year span. A classic baby-boomer, I was a first-born into a loving family that was typical of those who found themselves delighted to have survived a war, now able to settle down comfortably, with their new and hard-won securities. I grew up in an almost exclusively White neighbourhood and, as far as I can remember, there were no Black people at all in my primary school. In fact, I reached secondary school without, as memory serves me, ever speaking with a non-White child of my own or similar age.

Arriving at an Independent School in the private sector for my secondary education, nothing was likely to change; once again, I do not remember seeing even one Black person in its 1000-strong student community. The strangling links between Whiteness and educational privilege were everywhere evident throughout my schooling.

Sadly, my social and cultural isolation did not change even when I reached university. In an elite 1970s Cambridge college, there were no Black or Asian people in my year. There might have been an occasional continental European but, if so, they were only there because of their exceptional intelligence, and I was not sufficiently in their league for an opportunity of close friendship. I made it through, then, for worse rather than better, all the way into young adulthood without significant cross-cultural contact of any kind, certainly never enjoying the intimacy of a personal friendship. The Black and Asian people I had seen were nearly all bus drivers and street cleaners, or ran curry houses or kebab shops.

This was, of course, the stage at which I should have been making more decisive choices of my own to explore other dimensions of the multi-faceted world I inhabited. Once again, sadly, that is not a decision I made at that time. Instead, I made my way through yet more stages of privileged education into

Christian ministry and leadership in local Baptist churches, all located in predominantly White middle-class communities. It was not that I altogether lacked ideas about the wider world. In fact, I still comfortably adhere to many of them, through to the present day. My confession, however, is that they remained largely ideas, rather than committed forms of action, and for that I now would like to offer an apology. Many of my values had been shaped by a particular combination of private schooling and involvement with the Scout movement which, despite their shared tendencies to perpetuate the inheritance of Empire, nonetheless, grounded me with a set of values largely centred around respect for other human beings. These are values, which would lurk in my background, waiting for a time when eventually they could have their day and come more fully alive.

It was not until early middle-age, around the time that my ministry moved to focus on theological education, that something distinctly new began to happen. This was something which, with hindsight, I gladly credit entirely to the grace of God. One early marker along the way was the morning I delivered a public lecture on what in those days many people, me included, still called 'The Doctrine of Man'. Having concluded the session, I found myself firmly pinned to the wall by a group of angry women demanding that I justify repeatedly using the term 'Man' as if it were effective as an inclusive term. I might have left the room unscathed if it were not for one simple fact. They were right!

Then I found myself drawn into ministries with people with disabilities, especially learning disabilities, and soon I was arguing, in the face of strong and vocal prejudice, for their full and inclusive humanity. Around that same time, I also spent an afternoon with a group of gay Christian men who, at the end our time together, asked whether I would support them in their campaign for more equal social acceptance, in church and in the wider community. The truth was, I could think of no good reason to refuse them. So, on all these fronts, I was finding that my thinking increasingly demanded a parallel commitment to action. In the early 1980s, none of this was likely to make me popular amongst many of my Baptist ministerial colleagues. 'There he goes again,' was a message I seemed to be hearing, even if only by implication.

When, eventually, the opportunity for a new kind of cross-cultural experience finally arrived, the pump was already well primed for a time of far-reaching change. I had been invited to an international conference of Baptist teachers in Johannesburg, around the time when legalised apartheid in South Africa was finally coming to an end. It was not scheduled to be part of the official programme but, against the odds, and following the elusive promptings of grace, I found myself in the homes of pastors in some of the township communities around Johannesburg and Pretoria. Another confession: Initially, I found myself very fearful, not knowing at all what to expect, only to be amazed by the welcome I received and the friendship that was offered. It had taken nearly forty years to get me there, but for the first time I began to make real inter-cultural friendships.

These were friendships that were sufficiently secure for people actually to tell me first-hand what it was like to grow up as a Black person in apartheid South Africa. I was shamed by my own ignorance and by the poverty of my active engagement. It was in South Africa that I also had my own first experience of being the only White person in a crowd of several thousand Black Africans and discovered for myself, what it is like to be a minority of one, inescapably exposed to scrutiny by the colour of my skin. I returned to Britain shaken and knowing that I was badly in need of re-education, this time, an education that privilege could never buy. It was time to re-think many of my own priorities for life and ministry.

In the years that followed, much of my ministry has indeed unfolded around a focus of social justice. I offered such solidarity as men can to those small groups of Baptist women who were naming the truth about inequality in our Baptist denominational world. I became the Convenor of our national Baptist group championing causes relating to disability. I continued to work with and on behalf of gay friends, men and women. I began to take much more serious interest in the experience of people of other faith, especially Jews and Muslims, who have to find ways to survive as minorities in this land. I also began to make connections with those who were working to give voice to Black and Asian minorities in our majority, White Baptist Union.

It was, you might say, still a continuing story of privilege. I was repeatedly offered a voice in contexts where most Black and minority ethnic people were unlikely to ever be heard. That is structural racism at work and few institutions manage to cut free from it. It remains a cruel and vicious circle and I have tried my best to work within it, with integrity, although, not without a lasting sense of shame.

Now I must apologise to my readers that it has taken us so long to get to this point in my story, the point at which I can begin to talk more explicitly about the Baptist Union of Great Britain and its approach to racial justice. My excuse, if one is needed, is that I have felt it to be important to paint the wider context out of which my later involvement in racial justice has taken shape. It remains hugely important for me to see all my justice commitments as facets of a single whole. Once we are grasped by a strong conviction about the one global shared humanity, it would be ironic to major exclusively on one injustice, and simply to ignore all the others.

I always found it hard to understand how many Black Baptists who had lived through the destructive experience of apartheid remained reluctant to embrace the cause of equality for women in their post-apartheid land. I had been gripped by the concept of 'ubuntu' and it seemed to me that it demanded near universal application, but perhaps I am just being naive. I remain committed to a conviction that all humans, regardless of gender, race, ability, age, sexual-orientation, or whatever else we feel obliged to label, are equal under God and are recipients of grace and love in abundance.

This conviction, it seems to me, logically obligates all of us who make claim to Christian discipleship to respond similarly to every human that crosses our path. Please do not hear me wrongly at his point. For myself, I have only managed to make partial inroads into this new way of being; like most humans, my words are still too far ahead of my actions. All I can claim is that, with the help of grace, I am still working at it. Doubtless, I have clocked notable failures along the way, and have let numerous people down, but who hasn't? I remain committed, however, to aim for what I see as a priority gospel goal.

All of which finally brings me to my own involvement in the process by which the Baptist Union of Great Britain came ten years ago to endorse an Apology to the Baptist Union of Jamaica, in consequence of the appalling history of the trans-Atlantic slave trade. Time for confession again, this time, with a modicum of pride! The first draft of the Apology was in fact shaped on my own computer the night before the crucial vote in the Baptist Union Council. This was done so that I would be up and running to chair a small group who refined its final form of words ready for presentation. When I then came to stand at the front of the Council and explain our carefully crafted proposal, I was hearing once more in my head that all too familiar refrain, 'There he goes again!'

To my surprise and delight, however, speaker after speaker endorsed our chosen form of words, affirming that they did indeed express very clearly what had been unfolding through the discussions of the previous two days. The emergent resolution was accepted unanimously, and the 'Apology' was launched on its way.

In making a contribution to the final wording of the 'Apology', two things were uppermost in my own mind. First, I was adamant that human solidarity spans not only the geography of contemporary space, but also the history of extended time. There is nothing at all inappropriate, as many had argued, about an apology for the actions of our forebears, not least because we remain so tightly enmeshed in the consequences of their actions. We continue to reap the benefits of the gross injustices wrought in their time.

Second, I wanted us to name as clearly as we could, the challenges we must continue to face, if we want our apology to be more than mere words. There was the recognition that our actions would be under scrutiny, long into the future, way after our words had all but been forgotten. One promising arena for action takes me full-circle, back to the injustice of a privileged education. There has been hopeful talk of developing new ways to enhance theological education both in Jamaica and Britain, by sharing more of our resources, and encouraging greater opportunity for two-way learning. I do hope that this trajectory will be sustained.

Ten years on I am still saddened when I hear those who voice incredulity that today's community can usefully make an apology for the actions of a previous generation. I remain convinced that they are wrong. Even more seriously, however, I now find myself wanting to apologise all over again. This time, I want to apologise because, although there have been some actions that have followed from our earlier words, it seems to me that they remain woefully inadequate. There are still nettles to be grasped. There are still prices to be paid, if our words are to ring true. We still need to put more money, metaphorically, where our mouths are and we need to be more proactive in making it clear, beyond all reasonable doubt, that social justice belongs at the very centre of our gospel responsibilities. I am sorry that this remains not sufficiently the case, and I apologise for my own continuing complicity, with our in-action.

Nonetheless, it has been an inspiring journey, and I will be lastingly grateful for the privilege of being caught into such a timely and crucial, prophetic movement. When I ask myself how I came to be as involved as I was, I can only point, once again, to the prompting of God's grace. Strangely and wonderfully, sometimes God takes us and shakes us in ways we would never have expected, and I gladly testify that this is the case.

I found it to be a steep learning-curve and, pray God, the learning is not yet over. Since retirement from paid ministry, I find myself very much drawn into the work of Freeset in Kolkata. This is an organisation with Baptist roots that works to facilitate high quality employment for some of the vast numbers of women trapped in India's horrific sex trade, the roots of which, no doubt, also have trails reaching back into the inheritance of Empire and British rule. History has so many parallel tracks and traces, spreading widely across both time and space. For myself, I would like to think that I still have a little time and energy to give, and I remain committed to look for the ways that, under God, my remaining energies can best be put to work. These I offer, along with the testimony in this chapter, as part of my own ongoing apology.

Developing multi-ethnically minded leaders
Malcolm Patten

My daughter is just entering her teenage years as I write this chapter. As she is a descendant of both Jamaican and British Baptists this book is really about her. It is about the history of her spiritual ancestors, the good, the bad and the ugly incidents and experiences along the way. It is about her present experience as a young Baptist of shared-heritage, learning about and following Jesus, in and through the Baptist structures. This essay is about her future and what kind of Baptist church and Baptist union she will want continue to participate in, and to what extent will she see them as places where she feels at home and in which she feels she can participate, shape and challenge?

My contribution to this book reflects on my twenty or so years as a Baptist Pastor across four London churches, the result of this being that I am convinced that leadership is the key to develop growing, healthy multi-ethnic churches.

My story
In 1989 I left my modest regional town in the north-east of England and arrived in London to begin my ministerial training at a Baptist training college. I was immediately struck by the diversity of life in this great world city and was excited to be a part of it. So many people from so many parts of the world created an ambience in which I revelled. I soaked it up day and night. I spent three years in a student pastorate while at college and this raised for me a question that still challenges me today. Put simply, how do we move from being a congregation with many nationalities present, to become a missional church that is shaped, challenged and empowered by the experiences, insights and world-views of everyone present?

There are four reasons why this question mattered to me. The first was that we were a Baptist church and I had been raised with the conviction that one of the strengths of the Baptistic tradition was that we believed in the participation of all believers in the life of the church. It was obvious to me that not everyone was involved, but more to the point, those who were from minority ethnic backgrounds found it more difficult to be involved because of the cultural expectations amongst those who already held roles in church life. This was clearly an injustice that was not only holding individuals back but also the potential of the church as a whole. Gifts, talents and insights were being lost to the church as a result of this.

This leads to the second reason why this mattered to me. I feared that many people from differing ethnic backgrounds would simply try to accommodate themselves in order to become involved in church life. They would merely present themselves in such a way that the person (or people) in the position of patronage would want them to behave. How could I somehow develop a church environment where people could feel set free to express themselves in church life in such a way that it contributes critically and constructively to shape our corporate expression of church?

The third reason why this mattered to me was because there emerges in every church racist incidents, and the fear of the fall-out when racism is confronted brings paralysis to most British congregations. The consequence of this is that such incidents go unaddressed and resentment ensues. A way forward was needed that offered an incentive to address racism providing tangible benefits going forward for both victim and perpetrator alike.

A further question arising out of these three emerged, namely, how I could encourage a desire in the hearts of the congregation to see the church develop in this way. How could I develop the congregation to see themselves as the present manifestation of an eschatological vision found in the New Testament, people of every tongue, tribe and nation worshipping God together? How could I nurture an understanding that we are stronger as a church family together when we are a multi-ethnic family who love and honour one another?

As the years have passed and I am currently pastoring my fourth multi-ethnic church in London, I have become convinced that the key to unlocking the prejudices, and beginning to fulfil the multi-ethnic vision, lies in our ability to develop leaders who have a heart to develop the church multi-ethnically. So, consequently, I present this as the theme of my contribution to this book.

Why is leadership key?

Gordon Allport was an American social psychologist who became best known for his seminal work, *The Nature of Prejudice*.[1] The enduring legacy of his work was to show that increased contact between people of different ethnic and cultural groups served to reduce prejudice. Given his context in the United States in the 1950s, when the integration of Black and White people in schools and factories was still a contentious issue, this was a bold attempt to change the social climate of his time. Allport maintained that:

> Prejudice [...] may be reduced by equal status contact between majority and minority groups in the pursuit of common goals. The effect is greatly enhanced if this contact is sanctioned by institutional supports (i.e., by law, custom or local atmosphere), and provided it is of a sort that leads to the perception of common interests and common humanity between members of the two groups.[2]

In so doing he highlighted two factors that he thought were essential, and two factors that he thought would enhance the process. The two essential factors

---

[1] G.W. Allport, *The Nature of Prejudice* (New York: Basic Books, 1979) [25th Anniversary Edition])
[2] Allport, 1979, p 281.

were 'equal status contact' and 'the pursuit of common goals'. The two factors that would enhance the process were 'institutional support' and 'a perception of common interests and common humanity'.

It is worth noting, at this point, that the incident of the neglect of the Greek-speaking widows in Acts 6.1-7 could be a case study of Allport's observations:

> But as the believers rapidly multiplied, there were rumblings of discontent. The Greek-speaking believers complained about the Hebrew-speaking believers, saying that their widows were being discriminated against in the daily distribution of food. So the Twelve called a meeting of all the believers. They said, "We apostles should spend our time teaching the word of God, not running a food program. And so, brothers, select seven men who are well respected and are full of the Spirit and wisdom. We will give them this responsibility. Then we apostles can spend our time in prayer and teaching the word." Everyone liked this idea, and they chose the following: Stephen (a man full of faith and the Holy Spirit), Philip, Procorus, Nicanor, Timon, Parmenas, and Nicolas of Antioch (an earlier convert to the Jewish faith). These seven were presented to the apostles, who prayed for them as they laid their hands on them. So God's message continued to spread. The number of believers greatly increased in Jerusalem, and many of the Jewish priests were converted, too.[3]

If we analyse this scripture in the light of Allport's observation we can see that the 'complaint' was of discrimination in the daily distribution of food to widows and the 'need' was to ensure that all the widows (Greek-speaking and Hebrew-speaking) were fairly provided with their portion of food. The 'pursuit of common goals' and 'equal status contact' are virtues that were reflected in the desire to ensure all the widows received food equally.

The twelve apostles called a meeting to address this problem, appealed to the wider interests of the need to share the gospel, proposed a solution, gained common consent, implemented it and left everyone happy. In so doing, they had taken responsibility for the problem ('institutional support'), inspired a 'common interest' amongst all the believers (the unhindered spread of the gospel) and consequently, reduced the potential for prejudice and conflict. This incident in Acts 6 resonates with Allport's observations perfectly.

What is key, in both Allport's observations, and their effectiveness in the incident of the neglected widows, is the role of leadership. The factors that would reduce prejudice that arose from Allport's research require implementation by leaders or those who carry responsibility in an organisation or community.

Four leadership challenges
Allport's findings give rise to four challenges that potentially confront every church. First, is everyone treated equally in the church? Is there any reason

---

[3] Acts 6.1-7, (*New Living Translation*)

why a person would not be able to take up the most senior roles in church life provided their training, experience or gifting enabled them to do so? Is there any reason why people would be judged differently because of their ethnic background? This is a key question as there are many minority ethnic people in our congregations who would willingly accept a White British Pastor in their church, but the converse is not equally the case. There are many White British members of our congregations who celebrate diversity but would stop short of accepting a minority ethnic Pastor in their church. When appointments are being made at all levels of leadership in our churches, associations and unions, these questions need to be asked for prejudices and racist actions run deep and wide.

There was a time when we needed a new church administrator, a voluntary role, within our church. Although, it would be down to the Church Meeting to vote a new administrator into position, the leadership discussed what possibilities there were amongst the people of the church. Who could we encourage to consider this role in church's life? What became evident to me, very quickly, was that this leadership team, made up of White men, were only coming up with names of other White men to nominate for that position. So I suggested the name of Monica (not her real name). The reply was unanimous, 'Who is Monica?' Monica is a Black woman, originally from an island in the Caribbean, who had been a member of the church for over ten years. We left the issue for prayer and further consideration.

The next leadership team meeting came around and we spent a little time again considering possibilities for a new administrator. The same names were raised again, so I asked, 'What about Monica?' The reply this time was, 'Is she able to do the job?' My reply was that she was a committed Christian, had been a midwife for many years, was secretary of her allotment club, and worked in a voluntary role in administration for a local Christian charity. Also, I mentioned that she was retired and had some time on her hands. It seemed to me she was eminently equipped to undertake this role. We left it for further prayer and consideration.

When the next leadership team meeting came around, and the issue was raised again, the reply was different. 'We've been thinking, maybe, Monica would be a good choice'. Monica was duly nominated to the church, was voted in unanimously, and proved herself to be a very capable administrator. In fact, not only was she a capable administrator, instinctively, she also empowered others from a minority ethnic background to take up roles within the serving teams in church life.

Second, are there common goals? Allport noted that prejudice lowered when people of different ethnic backgrounds worked together on a common task. What this means for us in church life is that the most likely way to integrate people of different backgrounds is not by discussion, but by encouraging multi-ethnic teams, that is teams of people working together, on a common task. Whether those teams are flower arranging teams, welcoming teams, Sunday school teams, or Deacons, developing them all to become multi-ethnic, will encourage the lowering of prejudice, increase cross-cultural friendships and strengthen the network of people within that church.

An example of this is when I found myself wondering how I could possibly add new worship leaders to our all-White worship team. I was not sure how I should proceed. How could I find out whether someone was a good worship leader? Should I just give someone a go? What if they proved themselves not up to the task? It would then be difficult to say 'thank you but you are not what we need right now'.

As I stood at the back of the church one Sunday I asked the Lord to help me, and the Lord said, 'Look for the worshippers'. I looked around and I saw two women, one Nigerian and one Jamaican, who always come into church ready to worship God, wholeheartedly, come rain or shine. I began to give them opportunities to lead others in worship and they now lead regularly as part of our team. They naturally bring cultural twists to the way we normally order things, in terms of how they link the songs, the language they use, and of course, their spirituality finds its way into the mix of our weekly corporate worship.

As they begin to rub shoulders with the other worship leaders they begin to get to know them better, and as a result, deeper friendships emerge and mutual respect for one another grows. People who have been in the same church together for 10 years, and yet have never spoken, begin to drink tea together.

Third, is there institutional support? In other words, are the Pastor and church leaders declaring openly that this is a multi-ethnic church, encouraging the celebration of that and reflecting it in the church's publicity materials? Support from the top encourages those who are feeling like outsiders; such support gives succour to those who are wondering if there is space for them on the inside. It also challenges those who harbour prejudices and wish church life were returned to a previous era. It gives support to those within the congregation, with a passion for greater inter-ethnic reconciliation, to do their reconciling work.

I visited a large majority Black Baptist church twice over a number of years. The first time I went I was one of only two White people in a large congregation. All of those on the platform were Black and although I felt welcomed it was difficult to feel at home. The second time I went, a few years later, there were a greater number of White people in the congregation. More significantly, there was a White person in the music group, and the church's publicity showed White people mixed in with the Black people. It communicated to me that the leadership of this church wanted people like me to know that I was welcome there, there was a place for me in this body, and they actually wanted me there.

Finally, is there a sense of mutual benefit? In other words, will everyone feel the benefit of this church developing multi-ethnically? There are three ways that developing a multi-ethnically minded leadership will benefit a congregation. First, a multi-ethnically minded leadership will grasp the breadth and depth of scripture in a way that a mono-culturally minded leadership will not. There are resonances in scripture that only make sense when they connect with something one has personally experienced in one's own ethnic or cultural background.

A multi-ethnically minded leadership also serves to develop trust and authentic cross-cultural friendships, which reduces prejudice, and releases the inhibited expressions of all members of the congregation. It reflects a maturity when members of a leadership team are able to present different ways of doing things. This may find expression, for instance, in solving problems and understanding scripture openly, and then discussing this together in a critically, constructive way, with a view to everyone present learning and growing as a result. If there is no trust, and no friendship, there is no meaningful conversation. Third, a multi-ethnically minded leadership understands better the multi-ethnic community around the church, and this in turn, enhances its potential for mission and community outreach.

It is worth noting, here, how well these principles reflect Baptist values and theology. The participation of all believers in church life is natural territory for Baptists, and to develop multi-ethnically, is merely to become what we have always aspired to be. In my experience, developing the church multi-ethnically actually helps it return to these values, having often been dominated by the few in leadership for many years or even decades. Applying these same principles that have proved effective in the local church, to the wider Baptist structures, will continue to liberate us to discover new gifts, new depths of insight and re-invigorate our Baptist way of doing things.

Leadership in the wider structures
It seems to me that these principles for evolving multi-ethnic leadership and structure within the local church apply equally well to Baptist Associations, the wider Union, and other Baptist organisations. First, there is the need to ensure there is equal opportunity for all. We need to empower under-represented people groups, in appropriate ways, in order to remove any institutional barriers that may exist. Second, there has to be a commitment to ensure that all committees and task groups are multi-ethnic, both in their outlook and their members.

Third, we must continue to make it heard and seen from those in positions of influence and in publications that the Association, Union or organisation is, and delights to be, a multi-ethnic group of people. Fourth, there must be a commitment to work hard to ensure that the people feel the benefit of growing as a multi-ethnic group of people because of a better understanding of scripture, an increased wisdom and capacity to build vision and trouble-shoot, which will lead to a greater effectiveness in mission.
In a book entitled *The Difference* the author Scott Page uses mathematical principles to draw attention to the effectiveness of diverse teams of people.[4] On one occasion Page uses the example of the television quiz programme *Who*

---

[4] S. Page, *The Difference* (Woodstock: Princeton University Press, 2007), p 182.

wants to be a millionaire? to observe that there are different ways the contestant can improve his or her odds of finding out the correct answer. One of these ways is to 'phone a friend,' someone the contestant has pre-arranged to be ready at the end of the phone in order to help answer a question. Of course, sometimes the friend knows the correct answer. But often the friend does not, because he or she could not possibly be an expert on everything.

However, another option is to 'ask the audience,' at which point, everyone in the audience has to indicate out of a choice of answers, which one is correct. The audience is nearly always correct because of the breadth of knowledge across a wide and diverse group of people. Furthermore, even if no one person actually knows the correct answer, they can arrive at the correct answer because of the influence of the greater whole, in which the correct answer, is likely to reside. This means that the crowd as a whole can know something that no one individual actually knows for sure. This is the vision that is before us, to be wiser, more effective and more visionary because we draw on the talents and insights of the many, not the few.

However, there is also the potential to reach higher and wider as a family of Associations, the whole Union and other Baptist organisations. When we apply local church principles to the wider structures we are assuming that gifted people of differing ethnic backgrounds will be empowered from within. We may look within our Associations, the wider Union and Baptist organisations to see who has the potential to assume greater responsibility. The limitations of this approach have been illustrated above. It works if there are multi-ethnically minded leaders, who can see potential beyond long-held and well-embedded ideas of what such a person will look like, beyond the 'someone like me' mentality.

Let us take a step back and view our wider structures, from a global point of view, and envision the potential to develop real-time working collaborations between our wider, national Union and more local day to day operational matters. In this new dynamic, a challenging but potentially exciting cross fertilization begins to take place. This will cultivate the fruitfulness of a multi-ethnically minded leadership far more quickly and effectively than simply empowering from within. Secondments, internships, exchange programmes, Association/Parish twinning and joint theological research projects, will be the tools to begin to enable a new way of being and belonging together in the Kingdom of God.

Is there any reason why a Jamaican Pastor may not be able to spend a year as part of a UK Regional Team, in say the London Baptist Association or the Heart of England Association? Similarly, might not a British Pastor spend a year as part of one of the Jamaica Baptist Union ministries? Is there any reason why an Association in the UK could not twin with a Parish in Jamaica and enable exchange visits embracing holiday time? Surely this would be an invaluable opportunity to learn more in the context of structured participation in local church life and mission?

If such collaborative efforts were to prove fruitful would this not model a new way of partnering across nations? Is it a model that could be replicated with other nations, such as Nigeria, India and Poland, especially given that we have many members from these countries already present amongst our British churches? Within an atmosphere of mutual respect, humble truthfulness, and a willingness to step out in faith, there are potentially many benefits for the Kingdom of God, many friendships that could emerge, and a fellowship in the gospel that remains at present a distant dream.

Leaders and friends
The landmark 1910 World Missionary Conference caught the imagination of the churches in both the East and the West. Most of the 1,200 representatives were from North American and Northern Europe. However, seventeen of them were from the 'Global South' and that included Bishop V S Azariah from India. Notably, one of the best-remembered speeches of the entire 1910 Conference at Edinburgh was that of Bishop Azariah who appealed for friends. As a delegate of that historic conference, the Indian Bishop spoke on the theme of the 'Native Church and Foreign Mission'.
Bishop Azariah addressed the gathering saying,

> I do not plead for returning calls, handshakes, chairs, dinners and teas as such. I do on the other hand plead for all of them and more if they can be expressions of a friendly feeling, if these or anything else can be the outward proofs of a real willingness on the part of the foreign missionary to show that he is in the midst of the people to be to them not a lord and master but a brother and a friend… we ask for love. Give us friends.[5]

In a way that is no different in principle to the needs of the local church. Within the local church we need the space and opportunity to nurture friendships, reduce prejudice, and develop new ways of working. This is just as vital in the local church context as it is across nations. Jesus Christ is Lord, not merely of the local church, nor a national association of churches, but is Lord of the global church. The extent to which we may establish such fellowship between us is the extent to which Jesus' prayer may be fulfilled in our generation, 'I am in them and you are in me. May they experience such perfect unity that the world will know that you sent me and that you love them as much as you love me' (John 17.23).

Such a vision needs to be sown amongst our young people. If I have a dream, it is that our young people will take the lead in developing these new ways of collaborating together and developing friendships across the nations. It will be our young people, (my daughter included), who will overcome the struggles of the past and move through them to establish this new, multi-ethnic way of being the church; a new multi-ethnic way of being a network of Baptist

---

[5]www.christiantoday.co.in/article/bishop.vs.azariahs.appeal.for.friends.still.relevant/5

407.htm Accessed 30/11/15

churches. This will be a wiser church, a more authentic church, the manifestation, at least in part, of the eschatological realisation of the Kingdom of heaven.

The Passion of the New Generation: Where Next in the Struggle for Justice?
Rhea Russell Cartwright

On the 6th September 2015, I was sat on a plane after a long, unforgettable summer in Jamaica, and out of nowhere, something hit me right in the pit of my stomach. I tapped onto the moving map and could see we were flying directly over the North Atlantic; at this precise moment somewhere in between North America and West Africa. It then hit me that this journey was parallel to the route my grandparents had made decades before to start their new life in England. In the midst of reliving it with them, every leg of my journey home brought a new set of nerves ready to embrace once more a culture I had forgotten about, for a while.

This essay aims to discuss the passion of the next generation and to pinpoint where next in the struggle for justice for Black people in Britain, and in many cases, a continuation of such issues. This essay will also make reference to the 'Apology'[1], the 'Journey,'[2] and the relationship between BUGB, BMS World Mission and the JBU, in order to support and contextualise where such issues find relevance within the Baptist Church.

First, just to clarify the context of how the following terms will be used in this essay. 'Black' will be used to refer to the African Caribbean community in Britain with occasional references to our African American counterparts in the US. Equally, the term 'White' will be used to refer to the largest ethnic group in England and Wales, as of 2011, namely the White British community. The sections in *italic* are quoted snippets from popular culture taken anywhere from social media, to online newspaper videos that reflect or further enhance the case being made, throughout the essay.

The first point to address when discussing the struggle for justice for the next generation is the secular world in which we now live and in which we operate. The relationship between BUGB and the JBU provides an interesting angle from which to write given the 'Apology' and subsequently the 'Journey' on which the Baptist churches are embarking. However, this essay will have a strong focus on struggles contemporary to the time, and equally applicable to those outside of the church. Unfortunately, I do not have the capacity to discuss

---

[1] See the 'Apology' accessed via the Baptist Union website:
file:///C:/Users/user1/Downloads/The_Apology%20(1).pdf
The text of the 'Apology' can found in the appendices of this book.
[2] See the 'Journey' accessed via The Baptist Union website:
file:///C:/Users/user1/Downloads/TheJourneyReport%20(1).pdf
See also the text of the 'Journey' can be found in the appendices of this book.

all key issues for my generation in the fullness that they deserve, and I am aware of my own limitations that could flaw my perspective, to some extent.

The most problematic factor that faces the generation today is the way in which racism has been placed in specific periods of time and has allowed society to 'whitewash' over injustices happening today. It is seemingly uncomfortable for mainstream society to acknowledge that racism has not ceased but merely shifted. Moreover, this a time in which Black women are being refused from high-end London clubs for being 'too dark'. Then we have the 'I, too, am Oxford[3]' social media campaign launched by Oxford University's minority ethnic students that has arisen from a sense of communal disaffection at the constant negative portrayals of young Black males in the media.

These two examples illustrate the point that issues pertaining to 'race' and racism still need to be discussed within the UK context. The advantage we have in today's society is the growth of social media and the internet as a means of monitoring such blatant examples of injustice more closely.

Many believe that more damage arises from entertaining the concept of racism and enabling it to dominate in our discourse. It is easy to overlook the past and the damage that racism has caused. The past errors linger on and generational victims remain. Consequently, the real damage is not in the discourse about racism, rather, it is in the failure to enable future generations to better understand and support themselves socially and economically. So, unfortunately, racial discrimination will not simply disappear when we stop talking about it or by moving on from the past. This is the case because many White people have become embedded in a sense of privilege, hierarchy, and an unawareness of their own shortcomings.

This is the sin that impacts us all and requires processes to overcome it. This essay will look into two specific issues: 'Cultural appropriation' and 'Reparations' and the startling impact this can have on popular perception within and external to the African Caribbean community. The salient question is what cultural appropriation has done to this community and where does it leave us now? Whilst society might not want the discourse concerning racism to have any kind of prominence in the 21st century, the truth is, this view exposes a marked reluctance and an unwillingness to look more closely at ourselves.

The 'Journey' opens with the declaration on diversity, as 'the Lord's mark of creative ingenuity,' to which all Baptists would agree. It concludes with the need for all churches to strive to become multicultural in order to reflect our conviction that diversity is a gift from God. The 'Journey' puts forward six strong recommendations that will inevitably ensure a radical shift in our path to a more multicultural union. Prior to this, however, a discussion into some of the ongoing challenges posed by multiculturalism will be the starting point for this essay. As this is largely an issue that can be addressed

---

[3] See the following link for more details: - http://itooamoxford.tumblr.com/

for the wider British society, in addition to the church, it strikes me that this is a very relevant topic for forthcoming generations in the country.

One of the main challenges that a growing multicultural society such as Britain experiences, is the issue of cultural appropriation. Cultural appropriation has been defined by Nadra Kareem Nittle as

> Taking intellectual property, traditional knowledge, cultural expressions, or artefacts from someone else's culture without permission. It's most likely to be harmful when the source community is a minority group that has been oppressed or exploited in other ways or when the object of appropriation is particularly sensitive[4].

It could be argued that one such example is the 'Blackface case' in 2014 with the Britannia Coconutters[5] or the University of Birmingham's crackdown on fancy dress costumes.[6] Such cases have met with outrage and given rise to a backlash, as they have been termed cultural appropriation and seen by many as an 'obsession,'[7] and an attempt to look for wrong-doing, when it is clearly not present. There is a notion that minority groups are hyper-sensitive and that we are now living in an age where 'everyone gets offended,' for no plausible or sensible reason. Some also argue that such appropriation has been mistaken for efforts to embrace and appreciate the other's culture.

Cultural appropriation is a 'race' issue that emerged long before Britain became a multicultural nation, but has cleverly moved and has morphed with time. There are two key points that could make it problematic for the Baptist Union in embracing the concept of multiculturalism arising from the 'Journey'. The first being that cultural appropriation allows us to 'cherry pick' or appropriate the parts of a culture we want to exploit. As Nittle rightly reinforces:

> As such, a member of a dominant group can assume the traditional dress of a minority group for a Halloween party or a musical performance. Yet, they remain blissfully unaware of the roots of such dress and the challenges those who originated it have faced in Western society.[8]

---

[4] N.D. Nittle, 'What is Cultural Appropriation and Why Is It Wrong?' 2015. Accessed 12/12/2015: http://racerelations.about.com/od/diversitymatters/fl/What-Is-Cultural-Appropriation-and-Why-Is-It-Wrong.htm
[5] M. Holehouse, 'Racist? No our black-face dance is a proud tradition,' 2014 http://www.telegraph.co.uk/news/politics/labour/10777858/Racist-No-our-black-face-dance-is-a-proud-tradition.html Accessed 29/12/2015:
[6] C. Carter, 'University bans sombreros as 'racist' costume', 2013 Accessed 12/12/2015:
http://www.telegraph.co.uk/education/universityeducation/10427042/University-bans-sombreros-as-racist-costume.html
[7] Ibid
[8] N.D. Nittle, 'What is Cultural Appropriation and Why Is It Wrong?'

The second harmful aspect is that it feeds into our ability to put certain cultures and communities, and thus people, into a box. In the most delicate of situations, this feeds into paranoia, or a distrust of the other.

So where does this impact on BUGB's efforts to build a multicultural church? Firstly, if we turn our attention back to the 'Journey'[9] and we look at recommendation number five: 'Youth Leadership,' under the heading 'Gang culture' it states the following:

> 'The Racial Justice Committee have taken significant initiatives, particularly in working with the Ascension Trust on issues around gang culture'.

This signifies that the Baptist engagement in opposing gang culture is one that recognises that this has, undoubtedly, been a significant problem for the young, Black male community in Britain. For example, take the very widespread case of the killing of Mark Duggan, a young Black British male in 2011. The widely used image of Duggan that spread across all main media outlets at the time was quite evidently used to make him seem like an angry, intimidating gangster-figure. What then emerged was that this was, in fact, a cropped image the media had taken out of context. The full image showed him holding a heart at his daughter's grave.

The incident demonstrates the trouble we are up against, namely, being in a society that is intent on putting young Black, British males into a box of gang culture and associated with the more negative aspects of rap music. The danger of this scenario is that the aforementioned phenomenon of gang culture and rap music is what becomes perceived as cool and this is then associated with Blackness.

Unfortunately, this is a problem that cultural appropriation has done nothing to help rectify. Yes, the students at Birmingham University might have meant no harm in wearing sombreros and drawn on moustaches or engaging in the 'gangster' themed fancy dress nights; the underlying problem, however, was that the same outrage was not echoed for the Duggan case or his portrayal in the media.

The stereotype has gone too deep for us to change?
This is the true damage of cultural appropriation in that it enables us to distil Black culture that has distortedly been fed to us via mainstream media, and it then ignores the concerns that are at the very heart of the same community that helped to produce that culture, in the first instance. It is for these reasons that we should not believe we are entitled to cherry-pick elements that suit one's own privilege.

---

[9] The Journey accessed via The Baptist Union website:
file:///C:/Users/user1/Downloads/TheJourneyReport%20(1).pdf

For Baptists, this means when we reflect on the 'Journey', and where we are aiming to travel, we must first address ourselves at a very personal level. For the recommendations of the 'Journey' to be fully embraced for the coming generations,[10] we must first be very honest about where we are in our thinking, and what we have been exposed to via the mainstream media. How do the media affect our perceptions of the youth we come into contact with in everyday life?

So this essay is not attempting to question the need for the Baptist churches to become more diverse and multicultural. Rather, it is trying to create an awareness of this issue that has juxtaposed multiculturalism with negative media portrayal; the latter is fast becoming a struggle for justice, for the next generation. How do I grow and develop in a multicultural society without allowing my culture to be exploited? Where is the middle ground? Many say we now live in an age where everyone gets offended and quite often people pride themselves on racism being 'a thing of the past'.

The issue discussed above also requires us to return to one of the most potent lines in the 'Apology': 'our unwillingness to listen to the pain of our Black sisters and brothers, and our silence in the face of racism and injustice today.'[11] This requires one to listen, in order to have those difficult conversations around what it means to utilise another culture's dance, dress, music and language. It calls for us to be ambassadors to the communities in which we operate, and turn words and feelings into concrete action, as required by the 'Apology'.

In comparison to the first half of this essay, which has focussed on a social issue, we will now progress onto an economic case, with which the next generation will, undoubtedly, continue to battle.

When historic crimes have generational victims who should pay?

Although David Cameron's visit to Jamaica, in September 2015, was seen as a momentous first visit by a British Prime Minister in fourteen years, it was, nonetheless, a highly contentious one. When questioned on the case for reparations Cameron essentially called for us 'to move on'. Jamaica has been a leading player along with the other Caribbean states on the request for reparations from Britain, France and The Netherlands. Whilst abhorring slavery in all its forms the British Prime Minster managed to manoeuvre his way past calls to atone for and apologise formally for slavery. Despite the highly controversial nature of the topic and the fact that there has been a challenge to Jamaica not to make slavery a scapegoat for internal political failures, the injustice, nonetheless, is clear.

---

[10] In applying the 'Journey' to future generations, I am thinking of the work that needs to be undertaken, incorporating such elements as the training and the building of multicultural congregations and culturally inclusive structures.

[11] The Apology accessed via the Baptist Union website:
file:///C:/Users/user1/Downloads/The_Apology%20(1).pdf

Sir Hilary Beckles has highlighted the spill-over effects, as Jamaica, Britain's largest slave colony, as late as '...Independence in 1962, has struggled since with development and poverty alleviation.'[12] Different measures have been put in place since the seventies to alleviate illiteracy, and the challenge of reparations made by Beckles, was that Jamaica was owed 'an educational and human resource investment initiative.'[13] Given what the aforementioned has suggested, on the state of Jamaica in post-colonisation terms alone, one would argue that this translation into supporting economic racial justice, is long overdue.

Equally, what is often overlooked with reparations, in the heat of debating numbers and sums, is the request for a formal apology and recognition of an historic atrocity. This is something on which BUGB can take some pride. An apology from Britain would, in turn, have a considerable impact on the 'healing and rehabilitation of the Caribbean.'[14] Unfortunately, where Cameron seems to hit rough waters is when he mistakes reparations for a handout, and then monetarises this in terms of thinking of specific, grandiose figures. This can, in some ways, undermine the UK contribution towards development in the Caribbean. It can imply a quick fix response as opposed to engaging in a very deep rooted problem, to which he has also been targeted as having a personal connection.

This essay is attempting to highlight the significance of the psychological impact of the reparations debate on African Caribbean people and the need for the Baptist churches to continue to engage with wider society in the struggle for economic justice.

The struggle for the next generation will be to continue to engage in this discussion, even more so, because of the privileged position and special relationship between BUGB and the JBU. The case here has much to do with honouring the 'Apology' already made and acknowledging 'that we speak as those who have shared in and suffered from the legacy of slavery and its appalling consequences for God's world'.[15]

If we cannot understand reparations in its entirety and cannot see why modern day Britain should be engaging in this debate, acknowledging and repairing something that happened over a hundred years ago; then let us look closer to home. We discussed, previously, what generational victims looked like in Jamaica; in comparison, let us turn our attention to African Caribbean communities in the UK.

It is no secret that the communities from the Caribbean were met with hostility upon arriving in England throughout the 'Windrush' era of the 1950s and 60s.

---

[12] 'What Britain Owes The Caribbean for Slavery', 2015. Accessed 30/12/2015: http://www.jamaicaobserver.com/mobile/editorial/What-Britain-owes-the-Caribbean-for-slavery_19222161
[13] Ibid
[14] Ibid
[15] See The Apology accessed via the Baptist Union website: file:///C:/Users/user1/Downloads/The_Apology%20(1).pdf

Race and Community Conflict portrays a councillor in Birmingham's widely accepted viewpoint: How much longer have we Englishmen to tolerate the overt propaganda urging us to love the coloured immigrant who comes in peace and humility'[16]. Such overt racism has found its expression in other forms as well, such as the menial jobs and extremely poor living conditions to which Black people were exposed. The latter arose as a result of housing policies that impacted negatively on migrant communities, forcing many into expensive and low quality lodging houses.[17]

There is a popular notion that the Caribbean communities came to post-war England imbued with a deep sense of England's traditions of 'fair play'. They expected equal treatment and no colour discrimination. These hopes were said to have been universally destroyed after a few weeks in England. At the very least, this reality can convey, in part, the economic instability that the migrating communities of the Empire experienced upon arriving to the so called 'Mother Country'.

Again, the spill-over effects upon the following generations can still be highlighted in findings as recent as 2015, which have indicated: '41,000 16-24 year olds from black, Asian and minority ethnic communities are long-term unemployed - a 49% rise from 2010 according to an analysis of official figures by the House of Commons Library[18]. This was meanwhile coupled with a '2% fall among white young people.'[19]

The stereotype has gone too deep for people to work for a set wage.
On a different scale, the previous point mirrors injustices that are present in the US, with regards to Black communities in that context. An important issue addressed in Angela Davis' *Are Prisons Obsolete?*, is the role of the 'Prison Industrial Complex'. Davis draws attention to the need to seriously engage with social issues in the wider society, particularly those that stem from racism and the ever increasing range of capitalism, both of which set out to disadvantage the Black communities. The book also indicated, via Mary Ellen Curtin's study, in Alabama:

> ...that before the four hundred thousand black slaves in that state were set free, ninety-nine percent of prisoners in Alabama's penitentiaries were white. As a consequence of the shifts provoked...within a short period of time, the overwhelming majority of Alabama's convicts were blacks[20].

---

[16] See J. Rex, and R. Moore, 'Race Relations and Housing', *Race, Community and Conflict: A study of Sparkbrook*, (Oxford: Oxford University press, 1969), p.24
[17] Ibid, p.24
[18] M. Taylor, '50% rise in long-term unemployment for young ethnic minority people in the UK', 2015. Accessed 04/01/16:
http://www.theguardian.com/society/2015/mar/10/50-rise-in-long-term-unemployed-youngsters-from-uk-ethnic-minorities
[19] Ibid
[20] A. Davis, *Are Prisons Obsolete?*, (New York: Seven Stories Press, 2003), p.12

This fed into a popular post-slavery mentality that all African-Americans were 'inherently criminal'. Davis also highlights that during the later prison construction boom, official crime statistics were in fact falling. From all the aforementioned, we can at least infer that Black communities have been economically exploited in post slavery America. The situation in North America is undoubtedly very different to that of the UK, but what is just as relevant, is the issue of Black prisoners in Britain who disproportionately make up an average of 20% of the prison population; this is, arguably, also the a result of social conditions and their associated stigmas.

This point was made in order to demonstrate the different ways in which Black communities have been exposed to economic, racial and social catastrophes, since the abolition of slavery, and the necessity of finding alternative solutions, in addition to simply throwing money at the problem. To enhance this final point we can return to Davis, who also makes a very compelling case in her analysis of the 'tough-on-crime' mantra of the Reagan era in the US: She states 'the practice of mass incarceration during that period had little or no effect on official crime rates...Larger prison populations led not to safer communities.'[21] She continues arguing that the only significant expansion was in the corporate involvement and use of prison labour. With Davis in mind should Britain be really throwing twenty-five million pounds at a prison, as a means of responding to the reparations request from Jamaica?

Overall, can we really continue to justify the rhetoric that we have no connection with reparations? This is especially the case when there appears to be strong evidence that the events of the past have impacted Black people in a variety of ways that continue to socially and economically disadvantage Black communities in the Caribbean, and here at home in the UK?

In conclusion
It is said that the relationship between the JBU, BUGB and BMS has been 'forged through the epochs of slavery, colonialism and the Caribbean "Windrush" to the UK'[22]. This essay has sought to reflect on where modern day Britain finds itself; investing millions into the Caribbean, but unwilling to engage in the reparations discussion. Embracing a multicultural society, but overlooking core issues at the heart of the Black communities in the country. Above all, this essay has sought to shed further light on how multi-faceted is racism in the 21st century.

Initially, this essay was going to conclude with the struggle for the next generation being identified as the need to read more deeply 'in between the lines' when reflecting on the damage of structural racism in Britain. This remains true to a great extent. However, upon reflection, this has always been the case during every era in which Black people have lived in the post slavery context and world. We have always had to wrestle with such injustices that were treated as the 'norm' or were deemed acceptable. Namely, that structural

---

[21] Ibid
[22] See 'the Introduction' to this text.

racism is nothing new. In many respects, this age is no different, and Black people need to continue embracing that struggle.

So simply put, my question, for this essay was: 'what is the passion of the next generation; where next in the struggle for justice?' My response is: to not let the passion for justice die out. For African Caribbean people, we should draw comparison with the injustices faced by our grandparents who came during the Windrush era. We must not be bullied into believing that we are not fighting for a cause as strong as they did in the past. I will continue to point to a map in my room and follow the journey I made across the North Atlantic from Jamaica back to England. I must never forget the courage that migrating communities showed in taking that leap into the unknown.

The 'Apology' vowed to promote racial justice. The 'Journey' aims to build a multicultural union and we, as the next generation of young, Black British people, must be committed to seeing this through, in ways that are real to the society in which we live out our faith. We must seek to make a difference for future generations.

Mrs Ferguson
Tim Judson

Lyrics to a song written in November 2015

Mrs Ferguson, how do you do?
Here's a letter I had meant to send your way
Mrs Ferguson, it's taken time
For I've been struggling to find what words to say
But that's the problem, my words get heard whilst yours are gone
And the white man gets to speak when it was you who lost your son
In this world, the TV hides your cries away
And they tell the likes of me, that everything's ok

In these white walls
Built with bright gold
Stained with red blood
Poured from black souls' veins
Brought on brown ships
'Cross the blue sea
Under grey skies clouding my eyes
To make me colourblind

Mrs Ferguson, how did you feel
When I told you I'm not prejudiced at all
Mrs Ferguson, now I see it's not enough
To say we're both made in God's image as you fall
In my defence, I claim equality is won
And embrace distorted dreams with a chess board and a gun
While the strange fruit we are eating, familiar to taste
Was sold back here in Clifton or thrown out with the waste

In these white walls
Built with bright gold
Stained with red blood
Poured from black souls' veins
Brought on brown ships
'Cross the blue sea
Under grey skies clouding my eyes
To make me colourblind

Mrs Ferguson

Mrs Ferguson, how can I say
I am sorry for ignoring all your tears
Mrs Ferguson, shall we look
And maybe open up the very thing I fear
To lament a shameful story that sowed wounds upon the earth
And made the bells of time and justice ring
Please guide me to the one who bears the scars of all your pain
So we can offer him the worship of our sorrow when we sing

In these white walls
Built with bright gold
Stained with red blood
Poured from black souls' veins
Brought on brown ships
'Cross the blue sea
Under grey skies clouding my eyes
To make me colourblind

Rationale

When I first read about the shooting of Michael Brown in Ferguson, Missouri, on August 9th 2014, I was outraged. I thought to myself, 'How can people be so blind?' The subsequent deaths and videos I saw of people being abused because of their skin colour made me angry. I spoke to an American tutor at my college who told me to write a song about it. However, despite my best efforts, I did not feel that I was addressing the issue in the right way.

Later in term we had a day at college where Anthony Reddie and Wale Hudson-Roberts talked about the issue of racial justice, speaking particularly about their experiences of racial discrimination within the British Baptist church. I was horrified to hear that this went on recently, in my city, in my college! Yet, as they spoke, I realised the profoundly humbling reality that I was part of the problem.

I would never call myself racist. On the contrary I despise racism. Yet, as Anthony and Wale spoke, I saw for the first time that whilst my nature as a White, middle-class, educated male, is not wrong or sinful in and of itself, I unwittingly have an element of privilege and power, within which I sometimes operate. I feel confident expressing my opinion and can articulate my thoughts, expecting to be heard, and assume that I deserve to speak.

Reflecting on my experience of life, I came to understand that some people have never been given a voice, often been interrupted, rarely been acknowledged, only occasionally been valued. Even in trying to address this injustice myself, I could perpetuate the problem by the very nature of who I am.

In addition to all the aforementioned, whilst studying for an MTh in my third year of ministerial training at Bristol Baptist College, I became tangibly aware of the fact that the building I was in (most of Clifton in fact) was undoubtedly built on profits from slavery, whether directly or indirectly. Through the blood of enslaved Africans, I am able to study theology in this building. This story, however, is never told. Stories of those who suffered are never told. In 1996, Bristol celebrated its maritime history and the prosperity of the city through its shipping trade. However, the BBC, HTV and the Evening Post failed to mention anything about the Trans-Atlantic Slave trade. The narrative of those who suffered was silenced.

At that time I went to see my wife's gospel choir perform and there was a tangible sense in the majority Black hall that things are not alright, that people are hurting. This was confirmed when a man called Miles Chambers, who is a Bristol-based, Black, spoken word artist, shared some pieces. He was erudite and profound; deeply challenging with regards to his perceptions of Bristol, the city in which we both reside.

I cried many tears that evening, realising the way in which I have unintentionally contributed to the disempowerment and silencing of those who have suffered racial injustice. I wept, confessed, repented and was humbled, in realising that I must learn something of the Christ experienced by my Black brothers and sisters back then, and indeed, today. The song I wrote is a harrowing acknowledgment that I must allow the story of those who suffered to be told, sometimes by me, but mostly by them, and to confess on behalf of all White people that we are responsible for a corporate sin.

Reconciliation will only ever truly be embedded in our society when we stop justifying our individual innocence and fail to fully embody the crucified Christ on this earth. This song is a flawed attempt to confess some of these things to those whose pain has been trivialised, overlooked, silenced or explained away. I pray that those who are willing to be disturbed will indeed be disturbed, and that those who are not willing, will experience something of the Christ who I have heard of from my Black brothers and sisters.

Leadership Perspectives within Baptists Together
Lynn Green

Introduction
I believe that the 'Apology' of 2007 was a 'Karios moment' and one that has propelled us into what I feel is a 'Karios era'. The changes in our wider social context that have already been explored, together with the specific events, that led up to the 'Apology' and our commitment to embark upon the 'Journey', are having a significant impact on our society and our churches. In response to all this, what is needed is for us to proactively seize the opportunity and be faithful in seeking God's Kingdom in all its fullness, richness and diversity. It is vital for us to continue to keep our focus on God's heart for God's creation which longs for the time when, '...every nation, tribe, people and language...'[1] will worship Jesus. As the Psalmist writes, 'All the nations you have made will come and worship before you, O Lord; they will bring glory to your name.'[2]

The World Baptist Congress of 2015 gave me the opportunity to glimpse a foretaste of heaven as Baptists from all around the world worshipped, shared experiences, prayed, listened and laughed together. Multi-cultural church is not just some idea we cooked up ourselves, this is a vision from God's heart and we must never forget that!

However, being together at the Congress for five days is relatively straightforward; earthing that 'all nations, Kingdom vision' in our own locality though, is a huge challenge, but one we must rise to if we want to keep in step with God's Holy Spirit in this 'Karios era'. For me, leadership is the key, in enabling us to become all that God is calling us to be at this time. So, in the next few pages, I want to explore the leadership issues that we face as Baptists Together on the 'Journey' together with the challenges and opportunities that lie before us.

Racial Justice and Leadership – where are we now?
If you know anything about British Baptists you will be aware of the centrality of the local church in our discernment and governance. We do covenant together regionally in Associations, and nationally through the Baptist Union of Great Britain (also known as 'Baptists Together'), but all leadership exercised in this way is offered and willingly received (or not!), in the context of our covenant relationships. The important factor here is to note that without a centralised authority structure, our ability to address issues of justice and

---

[1] Revelation 7:9 & 10
[2] Psalm 86:9

bring about change is achieved primarily through modelling different approaches and influencing others, to embrace a Kingdom vision.

For some this is a frustrating and inefficient model of being church! For myself, I am passionate about the strengths our model brings; we need to discern together and discover ownership in order to move forward. This may make us slow at times, but when we do hear God's call, our networked mode of being can mean that we can respond quickly and effectively!

BUGB Five Core Values, which were adopted in 1996, are one good example of this commitment to articulate a Kingdom vision and influence churches and leaders in their ministry. Since the 'Apology' these have been revisited and a renewed expression of the culture that we want to intentionally embed within Baptists Together has been embraced. In brief we seek to be a movement of Spirit-led communities, to inspire others, to feel like one team, to embrace adventure and to share a hunger for God's coming Kingdom[3].

Of particular relevance to us as we are thinking about multi-cultural leadership and our commitment to racial justice are the aspects of our culture where we are seeking to:

- *Feel like one team*: celebrating diversity; valuing, respecting and trusting each other as we work together in partnerships – making sure everyone feels included and listened to (I Cor. 12:24b-27)
- *Share a hunger for God's coming Kingdom*: nurturing a 'holy discontent' that arises from our desire to give practical expression to our vision of God's purposes for creation – confronting evil, injustice and hypocrisy and challenging worldly attitudes to power, wealth, status and security both within and beyond our Union (Matthew 6:9-10).

For me it was significant that this latter aspect of our culture should arise from the positive desire for God's Kingdom to come. Racial justice, or any kind of justice for that matter, is not helpfully reduced to simply a critique of all that is wrong; we are engaged in the positive purpose of seeing God's Kingdom come, on earth as it is in heaven. One of the key areas where we have been able to intentionally broaden our participation and address issues of justice in our national life together has been through our Baptist Union Council and its representatives.

Up until 2012 Council comprised of c.200 members who represented Associations, our Colleges, the Committee structure of the Union, our partners, our President and past Presidents and co-opted members. The largest bulk of membership came from the thirteen regional Associations, each having 9 places on Council, although the London Baptist Association had 12. Regional Associations were urged to take diversity into account (in terms of ethnicity, gender, lay, disability and under 40) when selecting their

---

[3] A fuller expression of this culture can be found here http://www.baptist.org.uk/Groups/258896/The_story_behind.aspx, together with an account of the story of how our culture and values have developed over recent years.

representatives to serve on Council, but no mutual accountability was exercised with regard to those serving. Through the work of the Council's 'Nominations Committee', the provision of co-options allowed for marginalised groups to be intentionally strengthened, but this was also used to gain places for people for other purposes, e.g. enabling the Moderators of working Groups to sit on Council that had not found a place through their Association.

During 2012 we engaged with an extended period of prayer, listening and reflection that became known as the 'Futures' process. This involved a large scale re-imagining of what our life together should look like. The role and composition of Council was significantly reviewed and proposals for this were adopted at Council, in November 2012, with amendments accepted at a subsequent Council in March 2013. Three key changes took place with regard to multi-cultural leadership. Firstly, the overall size of Council was reduced from about 200 to about 90. Secondly we adopted an intentional commitment to increase diversity together with a concrete definition by which this might be measured. Thirdly, it was recognised and affirmed that minority voices needed to be statistically overrepresented in order for them to be truly heard and have impact. The Governance Report sets out this commitment unequivocally:

> We recognise that, for a minority voice to be heard, it needs a representation greater than the strict percentages in the constituency. We therefore recommend that the BME presence in Council, Trustees and ultimately, Baptist Steering Group should be greater than the percentages of Baptist Union membership drawn from BME constituencies. Our recommendation is that Council and Trustees should follow the following ratios:
>
> - No fewer than 20% BME
> - No fewer than 40% women
> - No fewer than 40% men
> - No fewer than 30% lay
> - No fewer than 10% people with disabilities
> - No fewer than 10% people under 40 years of age.
>
> Although Baptist Steering Group is unlikely to meet the lay/ordained ratio, and may struggle to fulfil the ratios for age and for people with disabilities, those appointing members to it should seek to come as close as possible to fulfilling other ratios.[4]

The reality is, however, that the numbers of BME members of Council have not been raised significantly.[5] The average from 2007-2012 was 12.5 members, whilst the average for the 5 Councils in the new style has only

---

[4] Chris Ellis, David Goodbourn, Paul Hills, Rupert Lazar, Richard Nicholls and Jenny Royal *The Governance Report*, 2012.
[5] See Appendix 'Baptist Union of Great Britain Council Membership Statistics'

increased to 13.4 members. However, given the reduction in the size of Council, the percentage of BME members is now much higher and averaging at 17% against our goal of 20%. For comparison, the average from 2007 – 2012 was 6.5%.

This has impacted on the feel of Council. The voice of BME members is much stronger now enriching and impacting our work together. The challenge that remains is that we cannot achieve our intentional commitment using co-options alone. We need to see an increasing and intentional engagement and participation of BME people across Baptists Together as Deacons, Elders, Ministers, Regional Ministers, Association Moderators, Treasurers and more, if we are to create the truly diverse Council that we have envisaged. One of the concrete actions we need to take, as a response to this, is to strengthen our data collection so that we can easily and objectively measure our progress towards the future that we envisage for the Council and the Union as a whole.

This intentional approach of 'quotas' has many strengths, most importantly, it signals our clear intention to grow into a fuller expression of God's multi-cultural Kingdom. By identifying what needs to change, and suggesting a more representative and richer approach to leadership and governance, we are holding before people a clear vision of where we are going.

Furthermore, this makes us look further and think harder about who is gifted to serve in regional and national roles. Then, we either bring to the fore someone who may have been easily overlooked, or are made to be acutely aware of our limited networks and tendency to move within circles, of 'people like us'. I would also argue that the Baptist Union's intentional commitment to justice in recent history has modelled something for our churches, and enabled a wider range of ministries, to be both exercised and experienced. This has been a painfully slow process at times, but I believe that we are gathering pace, on the 'Journey'.

There are, of course, many weaknesses to this approach as well. Whilst I applaud the intentionality of percentage representation I am also uncomfortable about the risks of tokenism that may be embedded in such an approach.

In our earnest desire to express our diversity, we can risk being unhelpfully pre-occupied with race, gender and disability, rather than looking for the gifts a person brings. Furthermore, as I mentioned earlier, our tendency to draw leaders and representatives from a small pool means that those who do bring diversity often end up being asked to undertake a disproportionately high burden of representative type work. This runs the risk of burnout for such individuals, which becomes the inevitable outcome, of this well intentioned form of working.

An additional weakness of this approach, for us as British Baptists, is that our 'flat' structures, coupled with our local church focus, means that there are a relatively small number of regional and national 'institutional' leadership opportunities. Add to this the almost non-existent 'pipeline' of roles that have existed in the past to enable people to gain experience, and we can see all too clearly, the challenges that face us on this journey towards multi-cultural leadership.

I am encouraged that I am seeing wider opportunities emerging. The rise of Regional Ministry teams has created roles for a greater diversity of leaders. The London Baptist Association's model of District Ministers is also another example of how trans-local leadership opportunities are growing, which can serve as development roles as well as providing a valuable ministry, in their own right. Other Associations have also implemented similar initiatives.

So, whilst our current Regional Minister Team Leader cohort does not represent the Biblical diversity that we are striving for, I am hopeful that we are beginning to nurture the conditions that will lead to greater change. One thing that I have discovered recently, however, is that we have no records of the ethnicity of our accredited ministers as a Union. If we are serious about the 'Journey' we need to ensure that we are capturing the data that we need in order to objectively measure our progress.

As I have reflected on our percentage representation approach, however, and also reflected upon my own journey as a woman leader within Baptists Together; I am aware that there are deeper and more profound issues we need to address if we are to make real 'this many nations, Kingdom vision'.

Thinking more deeply about leadership
I have sat in many meetings and appointments groups over the years where the lament has been, 'We are really open to appointing women / BME / disabled, but none have applied, so what can we do?' In fairness, there has been a genuine disappointment about this, but there has also been a lack of organisational will to take a critical gaze upon the deeper issues that lie beneath these conversations.

Speaking personally, I have come to reflect that the first and most foundational issue we need to own relates to the fundamental shape of our life together, and the leaders that we call to perpetuate that life. The *way* that we relate and organise ourselves excludes people; we do not intend this to be so, indeed many are shocked when this is suggested, but it is nevertheless true.

Let me give you a simple, but related, illustration from my own experience. Our local ecumenical minister's cluster experienced a renewed desire to seek God together in prayer for our churches and community. I was excited about this along with everyone else. A plan was soon formulated that we would gather to pray once each week and the time agreed was 8am on a Wednesday morning for an hour. There was much enthusiasm for this and the commitment to this time every week felt like it was a mark of true dedication to prayer and discipleship. When I shared that I would not be able to come at that time, because I had to care for my children and take them to school, I felt like my discipleship and leadership was pretty flaky!

My contribution was considered briefly by my male colleagues and it was declared a shame that I would not be able to take part. The cluster met for prayer at 8am every Wednesday morning most often without me. These were good people, fellow leaders, with whom I got on well. I am sure that no one intentionally wanted to leave me out, but nevertheless, the *way* that the time for prayer was organised, excluded me.

A completely different experience for me, however, has been that I have been able to serve as a regional minister and as General Secretary because others have been willing to think differently and create a space for me to serve. This creative way of thinking has enabled me to fulfil these roles because they perceived God's call on my life. The alternative could have been very different. Others could simply have said 'This is the shape of the role - what a shame that only White British men have applied for these roles.'

Alternatively, I felt able to offer my gifts, passions and sense of call, for wider discernment, and that there was a recognition that I would fulfil those roles in a different way to those who had gone before me. I have been not only deeply humbled by the privilege of being able to imagine different ways of being a regional Minister and a General Secretary, but also, greatly encouraged by the possibilities that this offers others.

I feel excited and proud to be part of a movement that is willing to think outside the box, and I want to continue to challenge the patterns and expectations of leadership in the local church, as well embracing this thinking more consistently. I have tremendous hope that as new patterns and shapes of leadership are blessed we will release the dynamic potential that God has entrusted in us.

So you will not be surprised, then, to hear that one of my passions as a leader is to create a culture of leadership where everyone's gifts are discerned and then we find or create roles to release and enable people to serve. Let us stop trying to shoe-horn leaders into 'male, White British boxes,' unless that is who they are! So one of my dreams, here, is that we will develop a leadership discernment approach that is about getting together with small groups of leaders to get to know each other better, to hear their passions and discern together, their unique gifting and 'shape'. What better place to start that than with our BME leaders.

My prayer would be that through this intentional relationship building and discernment, we would be much better equipped to release gifts into existing roles, and perceive new ones that we could create. Our pool and pipeline would be improved, but more importantly, the Lord would have greater opportunity to shape us as Baptists Together for God's mission.

So my point is that this is not simply about just getting leaders from our BME communities into key roles, we need to think much more carefully about the way that we do things, and the sort of roles that are available. It is about being open to exploring how we need to change the way we do things, so that everyone can feel valued and included, and able to exercise their gifts. So our challenge is to ask ourselves deeper questions about leadership. What is it about the way that we operate the BUGB Trustee Board, for example, that seems to make the opportunities for serving as part of this team unappealing or difficult for some? What is it about our gathering in Assembly that perpetuates this as a predominantly older generation, White British event?

I have been interested to observe how this sort of underlying issue is being addressed with relation to ministerial formation within the London Baptist Association. Recognising how established patterns of ministerial formation can unwittingly exclude BME leaders, the London Baptist Association, in partnership with Spurgeon's College, have pioneered a portfolio route into accredited ministry.

Rather than simply lamenting the lack of BME applicants for ministry, the Association and College have proactively considered what it was about 'the way formation was offered' that excluded people. This route is now being actively explored as a model for Baptists Together, as a whole, and serves as an object lesson for us to think more deeply about leadership and to be willing to think outside the box.

Genuine multi-cultural church and leadership

It is not just the *way* that we do things that can exclude, however, it is also about the nature of the leadership roles that we have and what we value about leadership. I referred earlier to our 'flat structures' of leadership; this means that there are relatively few trans-local leadership opportunities within Baptists Together. It would also be true to say that the leadership opportunities that exist are largely what we might term, 'institutional'. In other words our current trans-local leader roles need to have the skills and passion for leading and running an organisation. Each Regional Association is a separately constituted charity, for example, and that lends itself to a certain approach to leadership.

I would offer two observations in relation to this. Firstly, that with leadership roles that offer more predominantly spiritual oversight we seem to achieve multicultural leadership more successfully than in other areas. To be clear, this is not to suggest that BME individuals are unable or unwilling to provide strategic and administrative oversight in all areas of our life together. We have been more successful, however, in positioning BME leaders in the role of the President and the Accompanying Group to the Baptist Steering Group than in other areas of our common life together. How might this observation assist us in developing and articulating the roles of Regional and Specialist Team Leaders and Moderators of Associations for example? If BME can lead in one area of BUGBs life, then they can serve in other areas, also.

My second observation would be that many (not all) BME leaders who have actively participated in Baptists Together in the past have been married to White British spouses. Once again, like my previous point, this is not to suggest that BME leaders whose partners are not White cannot or indeed do not participate fully within the life of Baptists Together. This observation may have no substantive weight to it other than being an interesting sociological observation.

So whilst we rejoice and are deeply appreciative of the contribution of these pioneer BME leaders we must not be complacent. We have to look critically at the structure and the institutional culture that is prevalent in Baptists Together. We may be on the way, but we certainly have got to press on, and do some much deeper reflection about the way we shape our life together and the nature of leadership that we value.

I perceive, also, that we have real challenges ahead as we have to recognise that the blessing of migration has and will change and challenge the White British approach to being Baptist that has shaped us thus far. Our current culture as Baptists Together is largely shaped by our following of Christ and our reading of the Bible in the midst of our unique historical context. Distinctives that British Baptists have traditionally defended, passionately, like the liberty of the local church, tolerance of difference within our community, as well as those with other faith convictions, and discerning the mind of Christ through the local Church Meeting, for example, are now in the crucible of contemporary history.

I do not believe that we should be defensively trying to protect our distinctives at all costs by resisting the perceived threat of 'the other' as we encounter different approaches to being Baptist from around the world. It is imperative that for the White British Baptists amongst us, we own our history and realise that our cultures and perspectives have shaped the way in which we have been Baptists Together. This admission will assist us as we engage in the Kingdom work, affirming all the creative gifts that make us unified in our diversity.

So we need to listen to one another and be willing to embrace the gifts and opportunities God is giving us through our older and more recent BME communities in Britain. Listening to one another, praying together, discerning our strengths and gifts, and reflecting together on how our cultures have shaped our church leadership practices, will allow God to forge something genuinely new amongst us that encompasses all of our strengths and limitations as we draw closer to God's Kingdom vision.

History has always been thus. There is no static notion of being Baptist that was imparted from on high at a particular moment in history. In fact, our history specifically highlights that we are to walk together '...in ways known and to be made known.' We are on a journey into the unknown, with each era following hard on the heels of Jesus, as best as it can, continually open to the work of God's Holy Spirit; gently, persuasively, compellingly leading us on to enter into God's Kingdom life and purposes.

We must all be prepared to let go of aspects of the past in order to have our hands free to embrace the promise of God's future. This is, particularly, the case for White British Baptists who have traditionally been used to exercising control and leadership in our common life together. It will feel like loss for a time and we will grieve, particularly, White British Baptists, but we journey on in faith, trusting that God is moving us towards something that will be better than we have ever experienced before.

In terms of local church leadership I am encouraged to see multicultural teams developing. A longstanding and developed approach is being modelled creatively by Greenford Baptist Church; a church which has a White British heritage. I am pleased to report that new multicultural teams are being established in Shoeburyness and Thorpe Bay Baptist Churches. I see this as an exciting part of the new things that the Lord is doing amongst us. This is another significant step on our journey towards that many-nations-Kingdom vision we see in Scripture. I believe that this is key, because our true and deepest challenge as a movement, is to reach the millions in our population who do not yet follow Jesus, the vast majority of whom are still of White British heritage.

In all truth, we cannot rest on our laurels and assume that a specific or particular model of being church has got it absolutely right. There is much our different traditions can learn from each other, whether they are BME in complexion, predominantly White British or somewhere in between. As Baptists Together, I believe that God is calling us to respond to this challenge. This means that the journey we are on is not simply an issue of justice in leadership, although one must not minimise the importance of this, as Baptists Together. Our Journey is also an issue of missional leadership.

If majority White churches cannot embrace the blessing of migration that God is bringing us, and welcome and make space for the life, discipleship, faith, prayerfulness and vitality that is being added to its own, are they refusing a move of God? If we as Baptists Together cannot embrace the blessing of BME leaders (as well as women leaders, those with disabilities and younger leaders) that God is bringing us and welcome and make space for the life, discipleship, faith, prayerfulness and vitality that is being added to our existing cohort of leaders, are we refusing a move of God?

Conclusion
I believe that we are in a 'Karios era' and are making progress on the 'Journey' we embarked upon following the 'Apology' in 2007. There is clearer intentionality about making room for the voice of less represented groups to be heard in Council and our BUGB Trustees. We celebrate and appreciate the impact and richness that this diversity is bringing to Baptists Together. At the same time, however, we also recognise that we need to think much more deeply about leadership. We need to deliberately widen our networks and positively nurture trans-local leadership from BME leaders. We need to ask some hard questions about what excludes multicultural participation in the way that we do things and the roles that we invite people to consider. More than anything, we need to actively embrace and move towards genuinely multicultural leadership and church; not a sticking together of lots of different approaches, but the forging of a genuinely new stage of Baptist identity for our Union that weaves together our strengths and realises God's Kingdom vision.

I do not believe this is an issue of whether Baptists Together will nurture multicultural leadership or not. The future *is* multicultural leadership and it *will* come because that is what is in God's heart and is an essential part of the vision of God's Kingdom. Our challenge as a White majority movement at present is whether we will resist and fight this move of God, defending our past, our privilege and our power, or whether we will embrace the 'Journey' and choose to live in the beauty, the blessing and the richness, that the Lord wants us to experience.

Reflections on the Bicentenary of the relationship between BUGB, BMS and the JBU and on the reaction to the delivery of the 'Apology' to the JBU from a Jamaican perspective

Karl B. Johnson and Merlyn Hyde-Riley

This essay will offer reflections on the over two-hundred year relationship between the Jamaica Baptist Union (JBU) and the Baptist Union of Great Britain (BUGB), with the historic apology for slavery and the slave trade made by BUGB at its 2007 November sitting of Council in Swanwick, England, receiving particular attention. There is a general consensus that the 23rd February, 1814 marked the formal commencement of our relationship when John Rowe, from South Penderton, and his wife, were met on the wharf in Montego Bay by the Hon. Samuel Vaughan, a magistrate of the town.

A point not to be overlooked, and which always bears repeating, is that British Baptists did not start the witness in Jamaica. By the time Rowe arrived, Baptists numbered in their thousands, most of them enslaved persons. Baptist work in Jamaica is credited to God's activity in taking one George Liele (an African American who knew firsthand the experience of slavery) here as a free man to proclaim the gospel. It ought also to be noted that this Liele undertook his work a full decade before the launching of the modern missionary movement.

When John Rowe came from the Baptist Missionary Society (BMS) in 1814 he did so to help Baker and Liele in their work. The Baptist movement needed organization, coordination and leadership and history has proven that Liele, et al, were right in reaching out their hands to seek partnership and accompaniment, on their missional journey. God, in God's providence, led the British Baptists to labour alongside us and, as has been said, the rest is history!

Like any longstanding partnership there were, and will be, moments of disagreement, misunderstanding and even tension. True relationships, however, are usually robust enough to withstand those threats and today we have much more to celebrate than commiserate about how God has led us over these two centuries. Indeed, the BUGB/BMS relationship is interwoven in much of our story as a faith community, and we are grateful that in recent years this friendship has enjoyed a kind of 'revival', primarily linked to the journey they have been on arising out of the 'Apology'. We thank God for the opportunity to accompany you on that journey in search of wholeness and harmony in racial and multi-cultural relationships and pledge to be 'as Christ to you' in pursuit of that goal.

The Bicentenary celebrations of 2014 gave us time to pause and recall some of the ways our relationship has brought glory to God and upliftment of a people and country. Understandably, space does not allow for a full treatise on this but we could not but reflect on how, in tandem with our British partners, by the end of the 18th century Baptist witness was in every parish. We recall how many of the pastors were Jamaicans trained at Calabar Theological College. How, by the middle of the 19th century, through the Jamaica Baptist Missionary Society (JBMS) and BMS, Jamaican and British Baptists had spread the Good News to other Caribbean islands and Central America.

Our relationship gave voice and opposition to the monstrosity of chattel slavery. As Baptists we were at the forefront of the fight to abolish slavery and to affirm the dignity and development of the African through the establishment of communities of empowerment. Little wonder, then, that three Baptists are numbered among our National Heroes. While there were those who obeyed the caution from Britain not to involve themselves in 'domestic matters', we celebrate the ones who could not quench the fire of justice that burned within them, and played their part in confronting the forces of evil.

The Bicentenary led us to recall, with appreciation, the church planting and church plants of the nineteenth century. We also recall the governance/organizational framework that was established, elements of which are still with us today. We remember the crucial focus on education, especially theological study, alongside early childhood and secondary schooling, which was emphasized over the years of the partnership.

This focus was evident from very early in the relationship as the Calabar Theological College and Normal School was established in 1843 in Rio Bueno, Trelawny to train men for ministry and for missionary work in Africa and the Caribbean. Calabar Theological College existed until 1965/1966 when it joined in an ecumenical venture now known as the United Theological College of the West Indies.

It was under the ambit of theological education that our British friends bequeathed one who was to become one of the legends of the relationship, the Rev. David William Forrester Jelleyman, a British National born to William Charles Jelleyman and his wife Marguarite Mary Forrester. Arriving in Jamaica on the 4th June, 1948 to become Tutor at the Calabar Theological College, Mr. Jelleyman brought with him a passion for, and commitment to, the Gospel and the cause of Christ. He had a keen, alert and scholarly mind and a love for sports, among other things.

The Rev. David Jelleyman's contribution to the Mission of Jesus Christ was not the erection of monuments on the pathway of life but the formation of men and women for the task of leadership in the Caribbean Church. His contribution to the Church in the Caribbean in that regard was seminal and to date unsurpassed. He had a profound impact on Theological Education and Ministerial Formation in the Caribbean; that for over thirty-six years he remained an unwavering fixture in the process.

From his substantive position as Tutor at the Theological College the Rev. David Jelleyman made himself available to serve the Jamaica Baptist Union in many and varied ways. He was a well-respected voice on the consultative and decision making committees and assemblies of the Union, and his influence is still felt to this day in some of the policies and practices of the

Union, especially in the selection and training of Ministers. For many Ministers who knew him he was more than just a tutor because he took an interest in their total welfare and became a trusted and loyal friend.

Another lasting positive outcome of our partnership was the establishment of the Calabar High School for Boys, which opened its doors on the 12th September 1912, with the Revds Ernest Price and David Davis at the helm. It was born out of a felt need, at the time, to provide sound secondary education for the sons of Baptist Ministers. It was akin to what was already available for girls at Westwood in Trelawny, through the instrumentality of the Revd Menzie Webb, then pastor of the Stewart Town Baptist church.

Since that time, Calabar High School has produced and provided for Jamaica and beyond, outstanding leaders in all spheres of endeavour. Be it the sciences, arts, law, music, politics, sports, religion, Calabar graduates have been at the top of the field at some time or another. The longest serving Prime Minister, to date, was a Calabar Boy, the Most Honourable, Percival James Patterson. Jamaica's first medalists (Arthur Wint and Herb McKenly) at the Olympics in 1948 in Wembley Stadium (2 gold and 2 silver medalists) were from Calabar High School and in the 2012 Olympics in London, it was a Calabar student who received the bronze medal in the 200 metres final.

In fact allow us a moment of sports trivia, as in that same 200 metres final, the first three past the finishing line all had some links with Baptist work and witness in Jamaica: Usain Bolt attended a Baptist school, William Knibb Memorial High; Yohan Blake spent his early formative years in a Baptist Church, Bogue Hill Baptist and Warren Weir in addition to having attended Calabar High, also has strong ties to a Baptist Church, namely Mona Baptist.

There is the unchallenged view that Calabar High School has produced more people in the full-time ministry than any other High School in Jamaica. Certainly for us, as Baptists, no single school has provided more Presidents of the JBU (Devon Dick, Stephen Jennings and Karl Henlin) and a General Secretary (Karl Johnson), in recent memory.

Lest one gets the impression that our relationship was only 'one way', we celebrated the role we played in assisting British Baptists to interpret the Jamaica way of life on the heels of the 1950s wave of migration. Many of these Jamaicans would be searching for a church home and in need of spiritual guidance, hence the decision to have JBU ministers assist our British counterparts, in understanding Jamaican culture. To this end, JBU Ministers Menzie Sawyers and Clement Gayle spent time in England as part of this venture, while Clarence Reid was asked to remain in England after his studies at Regents Park to minister to Caribbean people in Manchester.

The 'Apology'
It goes without saying that the relationship between Jamaican Baptists, BUGB and BMS traversed one of the most iniquitous period in human history, the Transatlantic Trade in enslaved people. For many years dealing with this important matter in a direct and Christian manner has been an issue clogging up the communication lines of our relationship. The fact is we were walking

together without any formal acknowledgement and expression of regret on the part of the British Baptists for their part in the trade in Africans (TIA) and slavery.

A welcome, historic and significant step was, therefore, taken when BUGB demonstrated through the delivery of an apology that they were cognizant of their role in the awful human and societal tragedy that was slavery. We witnessed their sorrow for the sins of the past committed against generations of human beings robbed of their dignity and humanity.

The history of the TIA and slavery, as practiced in the British West Indies, is one that cannot be described without evoking painful emotions among those who were impacted as descendants of slaves. According to Beckles:

> ...slavery as practiced by the Spanish and Portuguese and perfected by the English in the 17th century constituted the most dehumanizing, violent, socially regressive form of human exploitation known to humankind.[1]

In speaking specifically of Jamaica, Patterson makes the point that the island developed into what it would remain for the rest of the period of slavery: a monstrous distortion of human society.[2] It was not just the physical cruelty of the system that made it so perverse but the astonishing neglect and distortion of almost every one of the basic prerequisites of normal human living.[3] Noted historian Green in his classic work *British Slave Emancipation* states that 'West Indian society was erected on the principles of inequality and subordination, with race being the main determinant of status.'[4]

In light, then, of the horrors and atrocities of slavery, the necessity for an apology cannot be underestimated. Many make the mistake in thinking that because the TIA and slavery took place many years ago, the present generation cannot be held accountable for the evils committed by their forebears, and that meaningful relationships can develop outside of an acknowledgement and apology for these wrongs. This perhaps accounts, in part, for the fact that despite the call for many years by Jamaican Baptists, an apology has been a long time in coming. Sam Reid, from as far back as the 1950s, then the Rev. Trevor Edwards in 1997, acting on behalf of the JBU Executive, and the Rev. Karl Henlin, President of the JBU in 2007, all called for an apology that was not forthcoming.

---

[1] Hilary Beckles, *Britain's Black Debt: Reparations from Caribbean Slavery and Native Genocide*, (Kingston, Jamaica: University of the West Indies Press, 2013), p.19
[2] See Orlando Patterson *The Sociology of Slavery*, (Fairleigh Dickinson University Press, 1967)
[3] Ibid, pp.9-10
[4] William Green *British Slave Emancipation The Sugar Colonies and the Great Experiment 1830-1865*, (Oxford: Clarendon Press, 1976), pp.33

Former Prime Minister of Jamaica the Honourable Percival James Patterson makes the point that

> ...the attempt to trivialize and diminish the significance of 300 years of British enslavement of Africans and the trade in their bodies reflect the continued ethnic targeting of our ancestors and their progeny for discriminatory treatment in both the annals of history and in the present.[5]

The 'Apology' arose through the inclusive work of the Racial Justice Working Group in Britain and from Jamaican Baptists. Despite the length of the time it took for the 'Apology' to emerge, nevertheless, it was received with openness, grace and a spirit of forgiveness. The significance of the decision of the Baptist Union of Great Britain at The Hayes Conference Centre, Swanwick from the 12-14th November, 2007 was a true Kairos moment. Subsequent to this decision representatives of the Baptist Union of Great Britain travelled to Jamaica and issued the apology as stated below:

> As a Council we have listened to one another, we have heard the pain of hurting sisters and brothers, and we have heard God speaking to us. In a spirit of weakness, humility and vulnerability, we acknowledge that we are only at the start of a journey, but we are agreed that this must not prevent us speaking and acting at a kairos moment. Therefore, we acknowledge our share in and benefit from our nation's participation in the transatlantic slave trade. We acknowledge that we speak as those who have shared in and suffered from the legacy of slavery, and its appalling consequences for God's world. We offer our apology to God and to our brothers and sisters for all that has created and still perpetuates the hurt which originated from the horror of slavery. We repent of the hurt we have caused the divisions we have created, our reluctance to face up to the sin of the past, our unwillingness to listen to the pain of our black sisters and brothers, and our silence in the face of racism and injustice today. We commit ourselves, in a true spirit of repentance, to take what we have learned from God in the Council and to share it widely in our Baptist community and beyond, looking for gospel ways by which we can turn the words and feelings we have expressed today into concrete actions and contribute to the prophetic work of God's coming Kingdom.

Jamaican Baptists took note of the fact that a few months prior to the issue of the 'Apology,' at the Baptist World Alliance Service of Memory and Reconciliation held at the Slave Castle on the Cape Coast, in Accra, Ghana, July 2007, the British Baptists refused to join with others in apologizing for their role in the slave trade and slavery. A number of Jamaican Baptists were present and were deeply hurt by the experience, which impacted their initial reception of the apology, when it was finally given.

---

[5] See P.J. Patterson, *Open Letter to the Rt. Honourable David Cameron, MP. Prime Minister of the United Kingdom and Northern Ireland*, 2015

Reflections on the Bicentenary

Many openly wondered what had changed in so short a time and questioned the sincerity of the 'Apology'. Conversely, the 'Apology' helped to bring healing to a wound that had reopened in this refusal. The General Secretary of the Baptist World Alliance, Neville Callam, a Jamaican Baptist, in expressing disappointment for what happened at the service on the Cape Coast and in responding to the apology to the JBU stated:

> ...now that this has happened, some of us can bring closure to the experience of the service at the slave castle and are now better able to partner with our fellow Baptist Christians in the UK to deal with the issues of prejudice and racism which are our collective charge today.

Jamaican Baptists saw the 'Apology' as a necessary and critical step on the journey. There is a strong sentiment, however, that there are accompanying actions that must take place for the 'Apology' to withstand the test of time. Jamaican Baptists are deeply concerned with the institutional racism that exists in Britain and is experienced daily by Jamaican emigrants and other minority ethnic people living in your nation.

Black people are still marginalized and discriminated against, and excluded from positions of power in the education, justice, economic and social institutions, inclusive of the church. Patricia Hill Collins' notion of 'Intersecting systems of oppression'[6] continues to exist in the UK. Black people are discriminated against on the basis of race, class, gender, etc, in light of the continuous suppression, silencing, omission and the disregarding of the worth, work and concerns of minority ethnic people.

British Baptists must, therefore, continue to work consistently towards justice if the 'Apology' is to continue to make sense to those to whom it was delivered and the many others who advocated for its delivery. The expressions and intentions as conveyed in the 'Apology' should have implications for the place of our Black brothers and sisters in BUGB and for the kind of prophetic and advocacy role that the church will play in British society. Our oneness in Christ should make any discriminatory practice abhorrent and something we constantly work to eliminate. Even the very perception of complacency in the face of the indignities suffered by Black people, due to racism, is a challenge to our Christian witness.

There is a strong sentiment among Jamaican Baptists that BUGB should advocate and lobby the British government to also make an apology to the people of Jamaica for their role in the trade in Africans. This is in keeping with the call in the wider Jamaican society and indeed throughout CARICOM for an apology. This step would not be inconsistent with the commitment expressed by BUGB in the apology:

> We commit ourselves, in a true spirit of repentance, to take what we have learned from God in the Council and to share it widely in our Baptist community and

---

[6] See Patricia Hill Collins, *Black Feminist Thought* (Boston: Hyman, 1990)

beyond, looking for gospel ways by which we can turn the words and feelings we have expressed today into concrete actions and contribute to the prophetic work of God's coming Kingdom.

David Cameron, the then Prime Minister of Britain, made a historic visit to Jamaica and addressed the Jamaican parliament on Tuesday the 30th September, 2015. He admitted that slavery was and is abhorrent in all its forms and had no place whatsoever in any civilised society. He acknowledged that the wounds ran very deep, but without making an apology or signalling any kind of tangible action to correct the wrongs of the past, he expressed the hope that 'as friends who have gone through so much together since those darkest of times, we can move on from this painful legacy and continue to build for the future.'[7]

To believe that because an action took place in the distant past, due to the passage of time one can just move on and develop friendships and relationships without addressing the issues that created the hurt, pain and unprecedented suffering is either ignorance or denial. Reconciliation is absolutely necessary but it cannot simply come about by ignoring the past. Having taken the significant step of making an apology, BUGB should seriously consider that one way to 'engage in concrete action and the prophetic work of God's coming' would certainly be to engage the British government in conversation towards the issuance of an apology for its participation in the TIA and slavery.

In addition to advocating for an apology by the British government BUGB could also lobby them to address issues such as immigration laws that are discriminatory in light of the fact that slavery and later emigrants contributed substantially to the economic development of Britain and to the society on a whole. The creation of more favourable economic policies with respect to former colonies, such as Jamaica, as well as greater access to housing, education and health care for Black British people, many of whom are of Jamaican descent and have been 'ghettoized' in Britain, are areas that require serious attention.

What BUGB has done through the 'Apology' is a good starting place and the JBU would not want to make light of, or indeed, attempt to diminish its importance. This was a significant event of great import. The 'Apology' could assume greater depth, however, if it was complemented by the ongoing advocacy to address the anomalies to which mentioned has just been made. Too many Jamaican migrants to Britain still experience oppressive and debilitating conditions in the midst of what appears to be deafening silence.

---

[7] See the following link for a transcript of David Cameron's speech to the Jamaican Parliament in 2015. https://www.gov.uk/government/speeches/pms-speech-to-the-jamaican-parliament

Reparation

Increasingly there has been a call in Jamaica for the British government to make reparations for slavery. Jamaican Baptists are also of the view that this is in fact a legitimate issue that should be given the highest priority. The call for reparations is often interpreted to mean monetary payment but is in fact only one possible outworking of reparation. In fact, no amount of monetary payment could ever compensate for the indignity, inhumanity and the destruction of the lives of the over fifteen to one hundred million Africans who died, as well as the destruction of the societies of which they were a part. So for many, to speak of compensation is almost to attempt to put a monetary value on the lives of people, which serves only to further the indignity experienced by the ancestors.

In a column in Jamaica's *Sunday Observer* Bishop Howard Gregory expressed the view that while reparation involves a monetary transaction, 'it is about much more than that. It has to do with the acknowledgement of wrong, the healing of the one who has been wronged.' Reparations are concerned with the restoration of the fractured and distorted relationship that has developed, since monetary compensation alone cannot restore that which was broken.

Reparation also requires addressing social infrastructural problems (in education, health, the justice system) and the inequitable distribution of wealth. In terms of the latter, this includes the eradication of cumulative debt, the elimination of racism, which is rooted in the experience of enslavement, and generally, the placement of former colonised countries in a position where they can survive as partners in a so-called 'global village.'[8]

On the other hand there is also a strong argument for monetary compensation. Whereas money can never truly compensate for the atrocities of slavery it is a gesture on the way to offering some amount of compensation for what has been taken from the Africans and their descendants. In speaking on the issue Beckles makes the case that Britain took the lion's share of the profits from selling enchained Africans and continued to build its fortunes and power from the sweat and blood of millions of the enslaved on Caribbean plantations.[9] He also notes that Britain has persistently refused to apologise for its crimes and has generally ignored any call to engage officially in a formal discussion about reparations. Instead they have set out on a path of denial, refusal and confrontation. According to Beckles:

> ...the silence imposed by the West, by Britain especially has made the call for reparations seem confrontational rather than conciliatory. The concept of

---

[8] Verene Shepherd, *Jamaica and the Debate over Reparation for Slavery: A summary Overview (Article adapted from the lecture "Reparation: A route to World Peace and Understanding"* delivered to the Rotary Club of Spanish Town, Hilton Hotel, Jamaica 26 February 2008. www.ohchr.org

[9] Hilary Beckles, *Britain's Black Debt: Reparations from Caribbean Slavery and Native Genocide*, (Kingston, Jamaica: University of the West Indies Press, 2013), pp.10-12

criminal enrichment from slavery that applies to Britain's elite commercial families and institutions has not taken root in the public's imagination, through members of ruling class society are aware, at varying levels of clarity, of their own ancestral links to these crimes... in every conversation the reactions have been shame, guilt and awkwardness in confronting the legacy of slavery. These emotions have conspired to produce the deafening denial and solemn silence that define the responses of the British nation. Only constructive dialogue based on truth can break this cycle. It is a precondition for the actualization of the process called conciliatory reparations.[10]

The reparation discourse seeks to make possible this process of reconciliation. The arguments that countries such as Britain continue to use as an excuse for not facing up to the issue of reparation are indefensible. These arguments include:

- slavery being legal at the time it was imposed on the Caribbean
- African slavery in the Caribbean is too remotely rooted in the past to attract legal redress in the twenty-first century
- No identifiable victims nor defendants
- Africans also participated in the trade
- Current governments cannot be held responsible for the activities of governments of the slavery era.[11]

The aforementioned are all excuses. Not surprisingly, therefore, despite the appeal to the British government from various quarters in Jamaica and beyond there has been a refusal to even discuss the subject.

Shepherd cites the history of the appeals to the British for consideration to be given for the import of reparation. She cites the response of Queen Elizabeth II, which came in 2003, and while acknowledging the immoralities of the TIA, nevertheless, disconnected the history of Britain's grand participation from its present government.[12]

Understandably, Jamaican Baptists still struggle with the fact of the unwillingness of the British Government and Monarchy to apologise for slavery and disconnecting the current government from participation in slavery. It is heartening that BUGB was able to move beyond the justifications and excuses offered by the government. Thankfully, they have moved beyond the posture adopted by the government of Great Britain on the question of an apology. BUGB, however, should start a conversation on the reparation issue among themselves, and be prepared to take the discussion further, raising the consciousness of its constituents with a view to exploring the issue at the highest levels. Critically, as British subjects, British Baptists through the auspices of BUGB can put pressure on her Majesty's government to think

---

[10] Ibid, p.5
[11] See Verene Shepherd, *Jamaica and the Debate over Reparation for Slavery.*
[12] Ibid.

again on the efficacy of offering an apology and engaging constructively in honest discussions about the reparations issue.

There is also theological justification for reparation. The concept of making restoration by giving back what has been unjustly taken has precedence in scripture. In making restoration 'Zaccheus stopped and said to them Lord, half of my possessions I will give to the poor, and if I have defrauded anyone of anything, I will give back four times as much. And Jesus said to him today salvation has come to thine house' (Luke 19: 8). So too, in light of the TIA in Africans and the profits made, there is need for giving back in order to offer some kind of compensation

Reconciliation
Notwithstanding the issues still to be resolved, the journey of the relationship between BUGB and the JBU continues with tremendous possibilities, because reconciliation is possible. Reconciliation refers to the restoration of relationships, the end of hostility and enmity, and the overcoming of alienation. This is made possible because reconciliation is an act of God. God was in the world reconciling the world to God self through Jesus Christ (2 Corth 5:19).

> What God has done for the world in Jesus Christ, therefore is the pivotal moment to which each act of healing must return, and from which it draws its potential for achievement. The doctrine of the incarnation inaugurates that reconciling process. The suffering and death of Jesus goes into the very wound of each transgression, and that resurrection both transforms the wound and confirms God's reconciling work.[13]

Paul's writings make it clear that equally important is the reconciling of people to each other in Christ. Christians must affirm and celebrate their reconciliation to God, by sharing it with others, for God has given to us the ministry of reconciliation. Reconciliation becomes a necessity as long as we are in Christ, and as such, if anyone is in Christ he is a new creature: old things are passed away; behold all things are become new (2 Corth 5:17-20).

When Christians speak of reconciliation it is not restricted to reconciliation of individuals, but of whole communities and nations, and justice is an important element of any reconciliation process. Justice is not served when the necessary measures to address structural wrongs are shunned. In as much as sin has separated us from God (Romans 14:15; 1Cor 8:9; Eph 2:11-22; Phip 2:1-5). 2 Corinthians 5:17-20... (Romans 1:18-3:20) let us be reconciled to God but also to each other. The process has begun and we can build on it through careful listening and a willingness to make amends as the Spirit of God directs.

---

[13] Robert Schreiter, *The Distinctive Characteristics of Christian Reconciliation*, 2016 cpn.nd.edu

Conclusion
Our generation of Jamaican Baptists has recommitted to leaving for those coming behind a strong legacy of partnership and accompaniment with our British friends. It is a legacy that is being informed by God's gift of mutuality and acceptance, given to us in the Gospel, and its concrete expression in the Body of Christ, the Church (cf Romans 12:1-8). We hold firmly to the conviction that the church in any authentic expression of its life, is an integrated, non-discriminatory community of believers with a shared commitment to Christ Jesus and is empowered by the Spirit to serve a common cause. This common cause goes beyond its own self-nurturing but embraces a definitive missional purpose.

The common missional cause is to be pursued within, beyond and across boundaries and frontiers of a varied nature, be they geographical, ethnic, racial, socio-economic, cultural and ideological. At this juncture on our missional journey, as partners, we are determined to eschew any pretence that we have arrived at where we need to be. We speak, understandably so, as people whose experience has been shaped by an historical context of the underside or otherside of mission history, as some would say; namely that we represent the 'mission-field' with all that this implies.

Thankfully, our age is benefiting from a growing awareness that serious shifts, movements and changes are taking place in the ongoing missional dynamics. Clearly, one of the opportunities that have become more manifest is the emergence of fresh possibilities for missional causes to be pursued on the aforementioned basis, namely, one that is located within a community of integrated non-discriminatory wholeness. It is a moment for the re-appraisal of the essential but varied gifts that are available for the shared commitment and the experience of giving and receiving and of the reciprocity of dependence and inter-dependence. There is clear indication of the need for radical overhaul and renewal of relational strategies, respect, acknowledgement and appreciation.

Our two-hundred year relationship can grow stronger and in so doing offer to the global Baptist and wider church family the gift of a partnership model built on mutuality and reciprocity. For this to happen we must face with openness and honesty the lessons learnt over the past two hundred years. Some of these lessons will remind us that there are 'matters arising', which we may have to allow ourselves to even be vulnerable in resolving. This ought not to scare us or make us defensive, instead we should trust our God, who has been with us for two centuries, to enable us, as God's people, to show what is possible to the church, indeed the whole world.

Appendices

Baptist Union Council Membership Statistics

Year	Numbers of members	White British	Other	% (20%)
2007	199	169	12	6
2008	201	168	15	7
2009	193	169	14	7
2010	194	177	14	7
2011	179	167	11	6
2012	171	161	9	5
New Council				
Nov 2013	87	73	14	16
March 2014	87	74	13	15
November 2014	88	76	12	14
March 2015	85	71	14	16.5
October 2015	79	65	14	21.5

The Apology for Slavery

Council Resolution
November 2007

As a Council we have listened to one another, we have heard the pain of hurting sisters and brothers, and we have heard God speaking to us.

In a spirit of weakness, humility and vulnerability, we acknowledge that we are only at the start of a journey, but we are agreed that this must not prevent us speaking and acting at a Kairos moment.

Therefore, we acknowledge our share in and benefit from our nation's participation in the transatlantic slave trade.

We acknowledge that we speak as those who have shared in and suffered from the legacy of slavery and its appalling consequences for God's world.

We offer our apology to God and to our brothers and sisters for all that has created and still perpetuates the hurt which originated from the horror of slavery.

We repent of the hurt we have caused, the divisions we have created, our reluctance to face up to the sin of the past, our unwillingness to listen to the pain of our black sisters and brothers, and our silence in the face of racism and injustice today.

We commit ourselves, in a true spirit of repentance, to take what we have learned from God in the Council and to share it widely in our Baptist community and beyond, looking for gospel ways by which we can turn the words and feelings we have expressed today into concrete actions and contribute to the prophetic work of God's coming Kingdom.

The Resolution was agreed unanimously, and each member of Council bowed in silent prayer and personal commitment.

It was then proposed:

In the light of our discussions concerning the transatlantic slave trade and the statement that arises from the discussions, Council asks the Mission Executive, Trustee Board and other appropriate bodies to continue to develop ways of promoting racial justice within BUGB and wherever possible in the world beyond.

The amended Resolution was approved unanimously.

Appendices

Faith and Society Team, Baptist Union of Great Britain, Baptist House, PO Box 44, 129 Broadway, Didcot OX11 8RT

Tel: 01235 517700 Fax: 01235 517715 Email: faithandsociety@baptist.org.uk
Website: www.baptist.org.uk
Registered Charity Number: 1125912

The Baptist Union of Great Britain Faith and Unity Department

THE JOURNEY

This document was sent to Council in March 2011 and unanimously approved.

INTRODUCTION

Diversity is the Lord's mark of creative ingenuity. It should bring us joy, vitality, excitement and rewarding challenges. Sadly, through sin, humanity has misused and abused this wonderful God given diversity. Humanity is united by its propensity to divide.

Thankfully through Christ we witness God reversing the effects of our sinfulness. As Christians we are called to work with God to see the kingdom come and God's will be done in a manner that reflects the heavenly picture of every nation, tribe, people and language living and worshipping together, on earth as in heaven.

To achieve this goal we must address and overcome the sin of racism, which the Baptist Union of Great Britain fully recognizes to be present among individual Baptists, our churches, associations, colleges, central offices and structures. This will be painful. Yet, as we do so and embrace the riches that each brings, not only will the Baptist family be enriched, but we will also be empowered to proclaim the gospel of reconciliation and renewal to a divided and broken world with credibility, because we will be seen to practice what we preach.

Recommendation: *The Baptist Union of Great Britain wholeheartedly endorses the report's recommendations as ones that will lead us to become the people that God wants us to be for God's honour and glory.*

DEFINITION

The word 'multicultural' is used throughout the recommendations that follow. It is a word that has been under intense scrutiny, with some in public life openly questioning whether it is appropriate to pursue the goal of a multicultural society. Thus it is important to be clear what is meant by the use of this term.

The basic premise is that there is only one race – the human race. This is true both biologically and biblically. The human race is expressed in various 'ethnicities' that are in turn expressed through various 'cultures'. A 'culture' is the whole way of life of a people, and therefore it has many different dimensions. Language, gender, class, age, and religious practice, all play a part in shaping culture.

The word 'multicultural' is being used as a way of talking about diverse and distinct cultures living together and learning to interact with one another. It is not about each culture living separately, so creating self-contained ghettos. It is about valuing diversity, and recognising and respecting the contributions that can be made by different cultures to each other. It is not about each culture claiming a right to be accepted uncritically. It is about all cultures engaging in critical dialogue with each other, so that all can contribute to the building of community and a cohesive society.

Our conviction is that cultural diversity is a gift of God. Our churches need to strive to be multicultural so as to reflect the rich, grace-filled patterns that are part of our world and our society. And all our different cultural norms and practices need to be examined and challenged in the light of the gospel lived out in the life of Jesus.

RECOMMENDATIONS

1. Building Multicultural Congregations

Council calls upon the Faith and Unity Executive to listen and work with churches that desire to become multicultural and to gain an understanding of, and engagement with, the 'world church'. This will involve:

- a) The commissioning of research that will guide the planting and development of effective multicultural congregations.
- b) The development of resources to encourage culturally diverse worship.
- c) The development of resources that encourage congregations to welcome the stranger (Lev 19:33-34), including asylum seekers and refugees.
- d) The development of resources to assist understanding of, and engagement with, the diversity of Christian churches throughout the world.
- e) The development of multicultural theological resources to equip churches in their journey

In many multicultural inner-city communities the dominant expressions of church are struggling white and elderly congregations, declining in numbers and energy and often burdened by trying to maintain premises that are no longer fit for purpose, and vibrant young black-led congregations, often growing in numbers and sometimes struggling to find anywhere suitable to meet. There are encouraging examples of sharing facilities and of mixed congregations, but to a significant degree the churches reflect and reinforce ethnic division. Most of the growing congregations are unable to reach out effectively beyond their own ethnic constituency. Various strategies are required to address this situation. One of these may be the formation of multicultural church planting teams, commissioned to plant multicultural churches and modelling from the outset the multicultural communities they are planting. This strategy is under discussion within Urban Expression and with BMS World Mission.

These recommendations will take these plans forward. They will identify Baptists able to carry out the necessary research, pilot multicultural approaches to congregational planting, develop practical strategies and resources based on new and alternative approaches, work closely with the Mission Department, Associations, Colleges and churches, and develop and encourage partnerships with other appropriate organisations. Work already done on the sharing of buildings (see BUC Guidelines C5) will provide background guidance.

2. Training

Council calls upon the Faith and Unity Executive to listen and work with Colleges, Associations, and churches in developing effective multicultural training patterns to include:

a) Programmes that are consistent with the needs of the particular Associations and the churches within them, the different Colleges, and Baptist House.
b) A programme for ministerial formation and training in cross cultural understanding and communication.
c) A programme for leaders of churches attempting to become more fully multicultural.

There is already significant experience of providing racial justice training within BUGB. Opportunity to participate in the 'We Belong' programme has been offered to all ministers over recent years, and the Colleges seek to provide students with the necessary training during their years of formation. Yet it is clear that this has been of limited value due to the very different and complex situations that Associations and churches find themselves in. A much greater responsiveness to particular agendas is needed.

The recommendations will be carried through by the Racial Justice Coordinator and the Racial Justice Group, working in close collaboration with Regional Teams, Colleges and church leaders, to ensure that all training is

Appendices

adaptable and meets the needs of their target audience. The 'We Belong' programme will continue to be revised, developed and extended as required. One particular way forward will be to resource and encourage the development of BME leadership within churches.

3. Multicultural Events

Council calls upon the Faith and Unity Executive to listen and work with Association teams and Baptist House in organising, shaping and participating in events that will reinforce the importance of cultural diversity. These will include:

- a) The Gathering event to happen regionally as well as nationally.
- b) A diverse range of celebratory multicultural events in Associations, Colleges and churches.

Different events have proved an effective way of enabling people to experience the value of being in a multicultural environment. As well as national events, there have been individual Associations and Colleges that have held events of significance, often with a particular focus, that provide models of best practice.

These recommendations aim to build on what continues to take place at present. They recognise that The Gathering has been predominantly London-focussed, and steps need to be taken to replicate this in other parts of the country, working in close collaboration with Associations. The planned events would aim to address such identified needs as lack of awareness, the presence of different ethnic communities, identification and encouragement of BME leaders around the country, the telling of stories, and the importance of empowerment issues.

4. Establishing Culturally Inclusive Structures

Council calls upon the Faith and Unity Executive to listen and work intentionally with all those involved in Baptist life to develop structures that are owned by representatives from both minority and majority cultures. This will include:

- a) Encouraging the presence and implementation of Equal Opportunity Policies throughout BUGB, particularly as they affect race and culture.
- b) Ensuring appropriate BME representation and involvement in BUGB Council, all committees, and other meetings and

gatherings. Co-option policies should be used to provide an ethnic balance.

c) Identify the challenges and address the issues that prevent full participation in BUGB Council and committee meetings.

The audit of Colleges, Association and Baptist House uncovered many examples of good practice. These included, not only the presence of policy statements on equal opportunities and genuine attempts to ensure diversity of representation, but also imaginative ways of making sure these proved effective ways of building multicultural awareness and engagement. However, there is still a significant way to go if structures are to be fully inclusive.

These recommendations will involve research as to the reasons why inclusion is achieved or why it is lacking, including identifying and disseminating models of good practice. Work will take place with Colleges and Associations to identify where a BME presence is lacking and how this can be addressed. Council co-options will be looked at, as well as the ways in which business takes place within the committees and executives of BUGB. Creative relationship building at all levels will be vital. Throughout the structures, the modelling of inclusive leadership has been seen as a key concern, and so exploring patterns of multicultural leadership must be a priority.

5. Youth Leadership

Council calls upon the Faith and Unity Executive to work with Associations and churches in facilitating the development of the leadership skills of BME young people. This will include:

a) Ensuring appropriate BME representation in any task group or working group set up to look at issues regarding children and young people.
b) Developing new initiatives with an emphasis on equipping churches, youth workers and ministers to identify and nurture leadership skills in BME young people.

The Mission Department is already doing important work on issues around children's and youth work development. Similarly the Racial Justice Committee have taken significant initiatives, particularly in working with the Ascension Trust on issues around gang culture.

These recommendations will look to work with the Mission Department to ensure outcomes of work with young people include a BME dimension. Connections will be made in order to seek to bring various pieces of work together, and to identify and respond to the particular issues and concerns faced by BME young people.

Appendices

6. Baptist House

Council calls upon the Faith and Unity Executive to work with the staff at Baptist House to:

a) Examine all BUGB structures and relationships to ensure they reflect a full commitment to being a multicultural Union.
b) Ensure that all staff working for BUGB receive appropriate training in issues of racial equality.
c) Ensure that publicity, communications and resources prepared by Baptist House on behalf of BUGB continue to reflect a commitment to racial equality.

The location of Baptist House offers limited opportunities to employ staff from diverse ethnic backgrounds, and this is a weakness that cannot easily be addressed. This highlights the need for an increased awareness of this lack, and the steps required to address it.

The recommendations require that a careful audit takes place of Baptist House, to identify the steps needed to ensure all aspects of the work reflect a commitment to an inclusive agenda. Regular race equality training must be a priority for all who work at Baptist House, and others who occupy key positions within the structures. Intentional opportunities need to be created for multicultural encounters for staff.

CONCLUSION

It will take time to follow through on the various recommendations outlined above. It will be the responsibility of the Racial Justice Group, supported and guided by the Faith and Unity Executive, to determine priorities, timeline and budget, and to ensure the delivery of the various pieces of work agreed by Council.

The implementation and adoption of each of the six recommendations will lead to a radical shift in attitude, behaviour and culture, and give the tools to Associations, Colleges and churches to take crucial steps forward in building of a multicultural Union.

Faith and Unity Department
February 2011

JAMAICA DATELINE

1494: Christopher Columbus lands in Jamaica.

1655: Jamaica captured from the Spanish by the British.

1740-1800: By the end of the eighteenth century, the principal product of the island was sugar, generated by slave labour forcibly imported from Africa.

1783: Arrival in Jamaica of emancipated slave-preacher, George Liele, as an outcome of the American War of Independence. Liele establishes Baptist work in Kingston and writes to John Rippon, minister of the Carter Lane Church in London, 1790, who publicises his work in the *Baptist Annual Register*. Thus Baptist work in Jamaica precedes the foundation of the BMS, and aspects of the work exist beyond the cautious superintendence of the committee in London. Those in this tradition are sometimes referred to as 'Native Baptists'.

1784: Moses Baker, another American freed slave, established the church at Crooked Springs in Western Jamaica and wrote to John Ryland seeking the help of the BMS in sending missionaries to Jamaica in the context of mounting antipathy and inhibiting legislation by the planters and the House of Assembly to Christian work among the enslaved population.

1807 Abolition of the Slave Trade within the British Empire.

1813: BMS responds by appointing John Rowe, a Bristol student, to work in Jamaica where Rowe began work in 1814. Although he was dead within two years he pioneered a significant partnership

1814ff Rowe was followed by other distinguished missionaries who were not prepared to follow a 'no politics' rule in their missionary endeavours. Significant leaders were James Coultart, Lee Compere, James Phillippo, Thomas Burchall and William Knibb, though their work has to be set alongside the testimony and costly witness of Jamaican leaders like Sam Swiney, Sam Sharpe and later Paul Bogle and G.W. Gordon. The last three named are three of the seven declared Jamaican national heroes.

1827-31: Short lived General Baptist Missionary Society work in Black River, Lucea, Green Island and St Ann's Bay', became insolvent after the death of John Allsop in 1829 when the work was transferred to the BMS

1831: Large-scale slave revolt provoked by a suspicion that the planters were holding back on an act of emancipation already passed in the British Parliament. Initially planned as a peaceful, passive resistance movement led by Sam Sharpe of the Montego Bay Church and often called 'the Baptist War', the rising was savagely put down by the plantation authorities. 312 slaves, including Sharpe, were convicted and executed and 144 Baptists chapels destroyed by white mobs.

1833 The British Parliament passes the Slavery Abolition Act but this was followed by the implementation of the apprenticeship system which delayed full emancipation until 1838. To the embarrassment of the London leadership missionaries on-the-spot became increasingly critical of the penal ways in which the apprenticeship system was implemented, and so the famous Emancipation Service In Knibb's Falmouth church when shackles were buried and the announcement made : 'The monster is dead, the negro is free'.

1838ff: There was still work to be done - Baptists were instrumental in establishing "free villages" for the newly emancipated people, buying large parcels of lands and dividing these into small holdings, which were sold to families. These villages also included a school and a Baptist Church

1840s: Economic depression followed by major cholera and smallpox epidemics leading to thousands of deaths

1842: Jamaica Baptist Association becomes financially independent of the BMS

1842: Establishment of the Jamaica Baptist Missionary Society to engage in mission in other parts of the Caribbean and in Africa: the Jamaican Baptists had become a missional church, no longer simply a mission field.

1843: The founding of "Calabar Theological College" for the training of ministers for the local ministry and also as missionaries to Africa and other parts of the Caribbean. Baptist work in the Cameroons, West Africa, was started by the Baptists of Jamaica in 1846.

1849: Some of the Baptist Churches in Jamaica came together to form the Jamaica Baptist Union seven years after becoming independent of the BMS.

1860s: Increasing failure of sugar production in a world of free trade –leads to much unemployment/impoverishment, compounded by two years of drought in 1863/4. BMS Secretary, E.B. Underhill writes to the Secretary of State for the Colonies commending the encouragement of economic diversification away from the over-concentration on sugar production. Underhill's letter leaked to the press leading to antagonism between planters and their labour force who organised so-called subversive 'Underhill' meetings in favour of his suggestions.

1865: The Morant Bay uprising takes place in reaction to an intransigent and oppressive regime with Baptists taking a leading role amongst the protestors. G.W. Gordon, Baptist member of the Jamaican House of Assembly, and three native Baptist ministers, executed for sedition, 439 negroes shot or executed, and over a thousand homes destroyed. But this was a pyrrhic victory – Governor Eyre was eventually dismissed, the House of Assembly was abolished and planter supremacy brought to an end. Jamaica became a crown colony, the church disestablished and grants made for a nation-wide system of elementary education.

1872: The capital was moved to Kingston, as the port city had far outstripped the inland Spanish Town in size and importance

1880s: A measure of self-government was restored, when islanders gained the right to elect nine members of a legislative council.

1907: Great Kingston earthquake: 1,400 lives lost and all the city's Baptist churches destroyed.

1912: opening of Calabar High School, a boarding school for boys, in the first place principally for the sons of ministers. Until 1942, the school shared staff and site with the College, but came to be highly regarded as offering excellence in secondary education.

1929ff: Further problems for the Jamaican economy in the wake of the world depression and associated slump in the sugar market.

1938: In the spring, sugar and dock workers around the island rose in revolt over wages and working conditions. Although the revolt was suppressed, it led to significant changes, including the emergence of an organized labour movement and a competitive party system.

1940s: Jamaica gained a degree of local political control in the mid-1940s. The People's National Party (PNP) was founded in 1938 and its main rival, the Jamaica Labour Party (JLP) in 1943. The first elections under universal adult suffrage were held in 1944.

1941-4ff: In the context of a lamentable lack of pastoral oversight in many of the island's churches, the BMS agrees to re-engage with the Jamaican situation as one of its fields of mission

1952: movement of Calabar High School and College to a new more attractive site enhances their usefulness and Baptist influence in the island.

Appendices

1958: Jamaica joined nine other British territories as a province of the Federation of the West Indies. After a 1961 referendum in which voters chose independence, the nation withdrew from the federation.

1962: Jamaica achieves full independence from the UK, remaining as a sovereign state within the Commonwealth with Queen Elizabeth II as monarch

1966: After many years of co-operative activity, the United Theological College of the West Indies, on a site adjacent to the new University of the West Indies at Mona, comes into being. The Revd Dr Horace Russell served from 1972-6 as its third president.

1969: The Jamaica Baptist Union becomes an incorporated body and all BMS property on the island was transferred to it.

1970: The Jamaica Baptist Union plays a leading role in establishing the Caribbean Baptist Fellowship, a constituent body of the Baptist World Alliance.

2007: Jamaican Baptist pastor, the Revd Dr Neville Callam, was appointed General Secretary of the Baptist World Alliance

2014: Jamaica has a population just short of 3 million but there is a diaspora of Jamaicans and those of Jamaican descent living abroad of an estimated 2.5 million

2014: The Jamaica Baptist Union now has 330 Churches, 122 ministers and approximately 40,000 communicant members across the island.

www.ingramcontent.com/pod-product-compliance
Lightning Source LLC
Chambersburg PA
CBHW050440240426
43661CB00055B/2456